Spirit of the Stones

A Retrieval of Earth Wisdom

Amalia Camateros

To Elizabeth

Blessings on your Spirit path, to your essential Self. May the Spirit of the stones reveal to you the brilliant diamond light that you are

Amalia

EarthSpeak Publications.
Big Island, Hawaii

In delivering the truest account of this story, all names in this book are non-fictitious, except for the few, whose permission could not be granted. The retrievals presented herein are unedited in order to preserve the true and specific information in which they were received.

ISBN-10 0-9774097-0-8
ISBN-13 978-0-9774097-0-9

Library of Congress Cataloging-in-publication Data: 2005936283

Spirit of the Stones 1st Edition

Printed in the USA

Cover design: Amalia Camateros
Book design: Lise Mardon Smith
Editing: Joan Parisi Wilcox
Front cover photo: Manjari Graphics
Front cover emerald spiral design: Dylan Clissold
Bio photo: Yolanda Pelayo

EarthSpeak Publications.
78-6697A Mamalahoa Hwy, Holualoa, Hawaii 96725
Phone: 1-808-895-1984
info@earthspiritwisdom.com ∎ www.earthspiritwisdom.com

Tributes

To all who have supported this project with encouragement and loving kindness, I graciously thank you.

I sincerely thank Lucky Bennett and Anita Emerson for their generous patronage and unconditional love, and for unerringly holding me in their highest regard. I am in deep gratitude. Also, a special tribute goes to Krish David for assuring the life of the project.

To my close friend and ally Lane Badger, I express my heartfelt appreciation for her multifaceted support both personally and professionally and for her prayers and candle lighting at times of need. Also thank you to Merrill Badger for his trust and support.

To all my beloved spirit sisters who truly "see me" and who have encouraged me throughout the years: Enocha Ranjita Ryan, Kamala Taroni, Salena Valentini, Jura Doucette, Tara Grace and Ginna Carruthers. I love you all.

I thank once again Lucky Bennett and Anita Emerson, Rebbecca Tzigany and James Bertrand, Maria Mitchell and Andre Nogez, Shankari, Tara Grace and my dear friend Yolanda Pelayo for unconditionally welcoming me into their homes and allowing me to nestle into their family life.

To Nassim Haramein, Amber Hartnell and the Resonance Project, who continue to provide a resonant field in which to evolve, I am grateful. Also a deep felt thank you to Martin Karagounis for his multidimensional soul work.

For the outlet of pure fun, I once again thank Yolanda Pelayo; and for the exceptional music that has inspired me greatly throughout the years, I thank Hareesh Onmars and Ed Benoit.

In addition, I'd like to thank all those who assisted in the lengthy process of reading this manuscript and for offering suggestions and corrections: Tara Grace, Mark Courtman, Leslie Safavi, Susanne Sims, Skywalker, Jael La Femina, Jura Doucette and Ginna Carruthers. Special appreciation goes to Rebbecca Tzigany for her allegiance in this process. Thankfulness also goes to Rick Smith for his guidance and support; and I offer great acknowledgement to Joan Parisi Wilcox for her helping me navigate the territory of this story and for editing the book, which has made all the difference.

I deeply acknowledge and offer thanks to my dear mother, Georgia, for her unconditional love and support.

Finally, I bow in great reverence to Earth and Nature as my mentors and guides of wisdom, and I offer a grand salute to the Rocks, those silent sages of the Earth, who have ushered me into the silence and stillness to listen, feel and know.

"In Right Remembrance of Earth,
~ Our Living Home."

Contents

Chapter 1:

Messages and Meanings.

I was in crisis, wedged between two worlds that were closing in like two rock walls that were about to crush me. With nowhere to turn, I was face to face with my fear of giving up all I had worked so hard to achieve and unsure if I could continue in my marriage of almost fifteen years. Why was I being called to leave all that I knew and everything that felt safe: my relationship and home, my work as a Naturopathic doctor, my family and friends, and even my country? I wasn't really sure, except that I knew at some primordial level of my spirit that I was being asked to live my beliefs that we are all spiritual beings with a sacred mission to fulfill. Still, my trust in even this belief was being tested. While everything that had happened to me in the past ten years seemed to be leading me to this point of transformation, I didn't know if I had the courage or the stamina to follow the path that Spirit seemed to have mapped out for me. The messages had come slowly at first, and then they had come with more urgency through a series of unmistakable synchronicities. I was to be a retriever of Earth's wisdom, a messenger for the spirits of the stones, recovering the ancient wisdom of Earth Mother so that we can access a deeper and more authentic connection to her and I was to start on the other side of the ocean from Australia, at Sedona, Arizona, a place I had not even known existed until only months ago.

But I still wasn't certain what any of this meant. Was I deluding myself about this most unusual of callings? Had I finally gone too far in my passion for things of the spirit? Could this have been what my sister, Nola, had meant when she picked me up in her arms in my early childhood years, proclaiming through her tears that I was here on Earth to do something special? I simply did not know. Although I was paralyzed with uncertainty and bound by fear of the unknown and lack of faith in myself, I knew that if I didn't find out, I might be missing the most important work of my life.

I had always been a free spirit and connected at a visceral level with my natural surroundings. My exuberance of spirit and the care freeness in my soul had caused the unending disapproval from my father. Even though I was a "good girl," my father also saw something in me that he deemed different and unusual. It was this side of me that he could not understand. My parents are of Greek heritage, although they were born in Egypt and lived there most of their lives. I was raised in a patriarchal household, my father's personality as strong as the Greek sun, which could shine so harshly, even mercilessly at times. I remember how when I tried his patience he would bristle at my willfulness, staring into my eyes, pointing his finger at me, and shouting, "I'll kill you!" He was not being literal, as that is an expression in Greek that means something more like, "Don't push me!" or "Stop it, now!" But somewhere deep inside I had taken those words to heart in quite a literal way; and each time I heard them, they further wilted my sense of self and scorched my confidence. Little by little over the years I had learned to keep my spirit in check.

If my father was the sun, my mother was the moon who emanated a quality of light that I caught occasional glimpses of and that bonded us at a heart level. In fact, it was she who introduced me to the moon. I remember one night in particular when we had been standing at the kitchen window, the Australian night looming large, the sky black and dotted with stars. The moon was a brilliant disk of hard light, and for a moment in time it captured us in its radiance and bound us together. We were captivated by and in awe of the beauty of this other world, a world we remembered in our souls, and we sighed a breath of hope for a new day and a new way for all that is mysterious and malleable in life. Neither of us spoke; we simply leaned our heads together, our cheeks touching as we rested in the silence of the moon's enticing glow.

Although I dearly loved my parents, by the time I was eighteen I knew I was in danger of losing all sense of myself, and that I had to leave. I didn't know who I was, but I knew that I would not discover my true self, if I stayed in suburbia. So one day, after rather haphazard planning, I wrote a letter expressing my appreciation to my parents for their love and all they had done for me, and I left, with only a backpack and a tenuous feeling of anticipation. I literally hitchhiked into my future.

That's when my journey began in earnest—a journey that would lead me into the mystery of myself, of my connection with the Earth, and of my kinship with the spirits of the stones. It was a circuitous journey often led by the inner voice of my own spirit. The first leg took me to the northwest coast of Australia, to a little pearl mining town called Broome. Nestled like a pearl itself and set at the end of an isthmus, Broome glistened in its natural charm and rugged beauty. It was an interesting town of historical bearing filled with a hodgepodge of people: Malaysians, Chinese, Thursday Islanders, and Aborigines. I stayed with one of those Aboriginal families, which is how I met Uncle Cassy, who was half aboriginal, and half Malaysian. He was a small, friendly man, black as the Australian night, with a smile as bright as the morning star. Before long, he became a friend and mentor to me, teaching me many useful skills, such as how to make a fishing net or cook a good curry. He introduced me in new and deeper ways to Nature, as we spent a lot of time outdoors together. We hunted dinosaur prints in the ancient rocks that verged the sea and as we studied them in fascination, he unselfishly shared his culture with me, telling me the stories of his tribal ancestry and his people's plight. I understood how close our bond had become when one day he invited me to share a meal of his people's sacred spirit animal, the sea turtle. He taught me how to carve a heart from the turtle's shell, then string the shell on a cord and wear it around my neck. That shell carries power. I could feel it then and can still feel it today as can many of the clients in my healing practice I have worked with. As with my mother, Uncle Cassy connected me with the feminine energy of the moon. He nick-named me "Moony," and when I finally asked him why, he simply said, "Because you remind me of the silvery moon." Many nights he would hold me captivated with his stories, and other times we would simply sit swathed in the mantle of kinship, listening to the silence of the night.

Broome was an initiatory arena for heralding the fusion of sun and moon energy in my life. They had become important symbols to me: of duality in general, of the dark and light, and of the twin sides of ourselves of the masculine and feminine. One night in particular brought this metaphor home to me in a beautifully visceral, and oddly mysterious way. I was sitting by the ocean at dusk—the hour of power, at the magical moment of transition. I knew it was to be a full moon that night, a moon of the king-tide, and I watched for it in the growing darkness. As the ocean waters receded into the horizon, a lustrous golden sun bid its farewell in the west while the pearlescent moon began its ascent in the east. The last rays of sunlight reflected off the undulating sand formations along the shoreline mudflats and suddenly and magically coalesced into a golden shimmering stairway that led to the sinking orb of the sun itself. I was transfixed, held spellbound, and at some level of my being I felt my spirit ascend that stairway to heaven. I accepted this solar vision as a blessing for the next leg of my wandering journey. Although I later learned this atmospheric phenomenon is known as the "Golden Staircase to the Sun" and that it occurs about every twelve years, at that moment I took it as a personal message that it was time for me to leave Broome.

I left the very next day and traveled across the hot, dusty desert to the other side of Australia, to the lush tropical terrain of the Atherton Tablelands on the northeast coast. To an area that in the mid-1970s was known as the hippie area, where the people were reputed to be loving and carefree. I noted to myself as I arrived that I was entering the "love zone." I worked a series of odd jobs over the next several months, and lived for a while as a nanny in the cramped quarters of a trailer with a couple and their two children.

Although I enjoyed my work with the children, in only a few months I was feeling ready to move. That's when I had heard about a man, Don Ananda, who lived in the mountains and made dulcimers, a stringed instrument with a curvaceous body that creates a sweet melodic sound. It is the only instrument indigenous to the white Americans of the Appalachian Mountain area. Don Ananda was taking on apprentices, and I was interested. I had heard the celestial voice of the dulcimer back home in Melbourne at a festival a year or so before, and I had been deeply moved. I thought now that I should take this opportunity not only to learn more about this instrument, but also to learn how to play one, or even make one myself. So, off to the mountains I went, backpack over my shoulder and luck my only guide.

Hitchhiking was still a relatively safe mode of travel back then, in 1970s Australia, but I still wasn't used to doing it, and I was rather nervous as I stood there by the side of the deserted road. It wasn't long however before I heard the hum of a car engine and saw a light blue station wagon coming toward me. As it stopped at the side of the road, I was delighted to see that it was occupied by two elderly people, apparently husband and wife, appearing to be in their seventies. Their faces showed concern and warmth as the woman, who was in the passenger seat, rolled down the window and in a few words agreed to take me a stretch down the road. I jumped in, curious about these two. Although I had been staying in the "hippie area," I'd never seen people with quite the same demeanor or look of these two. They both sat upright, with excellent posture, and seemed quite quiet and centered within themselves. They gave off a sort of energy that I hadn't felt before, one of surety, of calm and steadfastness. They did not say much although the woman did tell me her name was Laurie and then considerately introduced me to her husband Tom. I quietly and as unobtrusively as possible leaned over from the back seat to get a better view of them. On the front seat between them was some weird-looking food that I had never seen before. One item resembled a block of white pudding floating in a small tub of water. Next to it sat a small bottle of black juice and a small, plastic bag filled with some hairy springs of weeds. I was fascinated and even wondered which planet they may have come from. It wasn't until many days later that I learned what these foods were: a block of bean curd (tofu), a bottle of tamari (a type of soy sauce), and a bag of alfalfa sprouts. As I continued my survey of the strangely silent man and woman, Laurie turned to me and smiled. Her eyes were warm and wise. She asked me two questions, the second of which took me by surprise: "Where are you going?" she asked, quickly followed by, "And what do you want from life?" I was taken aback. We hadn't talked much and now here she was peering into my soul. I took a moment to answer, as I decided how personal I wanted to get. I explained my fascination with dulcimers and that I was headed to the mountains to learn more about them. But I wasn't finished. Without even realizing it, I blurted out more: " I want to go somewhere where I can be by myself, live peacefully and do some simple gardening." I hadn't realized until those words spilled out of me of their own volition how much I was craving solitude, and I found myself near tears.

Laurie leaned toward me and flatly stated, "We have just the place for you." She then described some property she and her husband lived on, in community with seven other elders, and a small, adobe dwelling with stained glass windows that I could stay at in exchange for working in the community gardens for a few hours a day. I didn't think twice before saying yes to her offer. I loved the warm openness and sincerity I was feeling from these mild mannered people. I decided the dulcimer adventure would have to wait. Laurie looked deeply into my eyes as she received my answer, then she smiled and said, "You know, this must have been meant to be! This is the first time in twenty years that Tom and I have taken this route home—and the first time we've ever picked up a hitchhiker." Well, it certainly was a new experience for me, too.

We soon arrived at their property, called simply and descriptively The Farm. As the car slowed and pulled through an enormous, though rickety, wooden arched gateway, I was startled to attention by the sight of a skinny old woman of petite stature, hoeing a row of greens. She wore baggy pants and no shirt, and her sagging breasts swung with every stroke of the hoe, flinging glistening droplets of sweat onto the earth. Her milky skin, with surprisingly toned muscles flexing with her every move, showed no sign of exposure to the sun, no doubt because her face and upper body were cast in shadow by a conical Chinese straw hat. To make the scene even more peculiar, a handsome man who looked to be in his early twenties swung a hoe in the row next to her. He, too, was shirtless, his upper body bare except for a massive, eight-inch metal cross that dangled from a thick chain around his neck. Where was I? What had I gotten myself into? Even for the freewheeling late 1970s, this was an unfamiliar and unexpected scene.

When she saw the car, the old woman walked over to us, her stride sure and steady. Laurie introduced her as Tiny. Tiny didn't say anything, just nodded her hello and held my gaze. Her eyes fascinated me: they were sharp, broadcasting in no uncertain terms that she was a woman who brooked no nonsense, and yet they glistened with the light of gentleness that made me think of fairies. Peering into the window of the car, and ultimately into the windows of my soul, she finally spoke, stating matter-of-factly, "We've been waiting for you." My first reaction was to wonder if I had been lured into some kind of set-up, perhaps for some strange cult. But almost as quickly, I dismissed that thought. Although I was a bit thrown off balance by the strangeness of the day, I had to admit that I felt nothing but sincerity and steadfastness from these people. They felt harmless, and even loving.

My emotional assessment of the people of The Farm turned out to be accurate. I spent several wonderful months there, blossoming in ways I could not have elsewhere. Once I got settled into the quaint adobe house, I quickly developed a routine. Most mornings I practiced yoga on the flat, sun-warmed rocks by the river. Later in the day, I'd garden, learning organic and environmentally friendly ways to cultivate the earth, and being introduced by Tiny and some of the others who lived on The Farm to the Devic (elemental) spirits of nature and to the fairies that they so intimately worked with. Sometimes I spent hours in the pastures, watching or patting the horses. In the evenings, I wrote, painted, or read.

Tiny, especially, became my mentor. Like Uncle Cassy, she was one of a kind—a free spirit who from long experience and many adventures held a deep well of knowledge and who gently tended to my spiritual, and natural, self. With Uncle Cassy I had experienced an intense connection with Nature, especially with the sun and moon. I had witnessed the Golden Staircase to the Sun on my last night in Broome and now, here at The Farm, I bonded more deeply with Mother Earth and with Nature. And, the celestial connections continued. One night while walking back to my little adobe home from Tiny's house, I witnessed quite a spectacular showing from the moon. It was a cloudless night of a clear crescent moon, and the moon's light naturally caught my attention as I walked home. But this was no ordinary light. As I looked up, the moon appeared to be ablaze, radiating streams of light every bit as fierce and fiery as a midday sun. At first I thought I had something in my eyes that was refracting the light, creating this light show, but after vigorously rubbing my eyes, nothing changed. I stopped walking and simply stared, allowing myself to be bathed in this lunar light show. I couldn't explain it. Usually the moonlight was subdued, almost velvety in quality, but now its light was streaming forth in distinctly angular rays that reached all the way to the ground, as solid as swords piercing the earth. I had never seen anything like it, and as I stood there transfixed, I thought of my experience of the Golden Staircase to the Sun, and thought that surely this experience was counterpart to that one. "The Sun and the Moon are initiating me," I thought, although I had no idea what I meant by that. I finally continued on home and fell asleep that night wondering what these light shows were trying to communicate to me, for they felt like messages that I could not yet decipher.

It was not long after this lunar light show that I had another distinctive experience with a force of nature—this time with Mother Earth. It was a sunny day, and I was happily digging a hole in the soil to plant a small shrub. Suddenly, I heard a voice coming out of the ground. I was startled, and looked around to see if someone had come up behind me. But no one had. I was alone. As I turned back and looked down at the rich, dark soil under my feet, I heard the "voice" again. It was not a voice that came from without, but one that seemed to be speaking to me from within myself, although in some inexplicable way I also knew that it had come up from out of the earth. The voice, sounding ancient and primordial, spoke my name, "Amalia." The sound reverberated through me and shocked me somewhat, for I had not been called Amalia since childhood, which was my given name—after my maternal grandmother—but since I started school I had been called Amelia. My teachers had made the change, declaring with authority that Amelia was a name "more befitting an English-based culture." My almost instantaneous reaction to this primordial voice from the earth, after my astonishment, was to feel that my primary identity, my birthright, had just been given back to me. Amalia variously translates to "Worker of God," "Light Energy," or "Soul Mother of the Garden." At the moment I heard that name spoken by the earth, I felt as if all the disparate pieces of my life fell into place, that I was somehow restored to a natural state, reborn even.

I suddenly understood how having been called Amelia had limited the experience of myself, constraining my passionate spirit and prodding me to conform to what others expected of me as a "good girl." I realized it was a name attached not to my inherent spirit but to that part of me that learned to survive emotionally in a culture that did not take kindly to upstarts and freethinkers. Upon hearing what I thought to be the voice of Earth speak my real name, Amalia, I felt renewed to my original nature. I was now able to reclaim what I had lost—the connection of my spirit to my body. In a flash I knew that my time here at The Farm was at an end, and that, strange as it might seem, it was time for me to return home. I felt a sudden and powerful urge to see my namesake, my Grandmother Amalia, whom I had never met. I knew from my most recent phone contact with my parents that she was due to arrive any day from Egypt for her first family visit to Australia. I wondered if the voice I had heard might in fact have been hers.

Perhaps that was so, but the voice nevertheless arose from out of the depths of Earth. I recognized a call on two fronts: an immediate call home to meet my namesake and a more ambiguous call to continue connecting in deeper and more nurturing ways with Mother Earth. While I was very hesitant to leave my little haven by the river with the elderly wise ones of The Farm who had taught me so much about nature, and about myself, I also could not deny myself the opportunity to meet my grandmother.

So, nearly a year after I had left home, I reluctantly returned to the place I was raised in, Springvale, a suburb in Melbourne, Victoria. I had always called Springvale a "quarantine area," as there was very little life-force energy there, hardly any trees, and even less spontaneity or gaiety of spirit. The nearer I got to my childhood home, the more my body and soul seemed to protest, cautioning me in whispers, "Stop! Go back to nature." But it was too late. I felt obligated to carry out my inclination to reconnect with my family and my heritage.

My reunion with family was joyous. My parents, although they had separated during my time away, and sister were happy to have me home safe and sound. My father particularly surprised me. Our reunion was especially warm, as he showed none of his usual disinterest in me. In fact, since my parents were now living apart, I stayed with my father, and we got to know each other in a new, more mature and nurturing way. My Grandmother Amalia lived up to all the family stories I had heard about her. She was of small stature, but regal bearing. She was outspoken, but kind. We connected almost immediately, and became fast friends, and even confidantes.

Even though my reunion with my family had gone much better than I expected, it took an enormous amount of focus and inner strength, and a huge leap of faith, for me to stay in the city environs. And stay I did—my homecoming back to Melbourne was to last eighteen years! I decided to study to become a Naturopathic doctor, to try to marry my love of things natural with the necessity of earning my keep. I remember talking with my Auntie Felia, telling her of my longing to escape from the concrete jungle of the city and return to a more natural way of living. Her response helped me stay the course of my new endeavor. "Amalia," she counseled, "by going back you will be with those people who are already on the path of natural living. Here is where you are needed, in the city!" I didn't like that answer, but I couldn't argue with the truth of her logic.

School and study were difficult, for after living with the Aborigines in Broome and the spiritual elders in the magical northern tropical zone, I had grown accustomed to the free life. It had been a way of life in which electric-blue butterflies meandered by, reminding me of my own freedom, where smelling the frangipani flowers reminded me of how the petals of my own inner flower were opening to the sweetness of nature. Instead, here in the city, I was spending four days a week in a ghastly blue-walled classroom, sitting under the glare of fluorescent lights with the traffic droning in the background, while I learned about health and the nature of the body. The paradox and hypocrisy were self-evident. As I sat all day, struggling to remember the horde of information required for the next examination, I found my mind continually drifting back to my year of freedom. I remembered the "real" feeling of health, the fresh air that I breathed, the birdsong that had been my backdrop, and the exquisite coolness of the earth against my bare feet. The first two years of my degree study seemed like an eternity. I could not have made it through them had I not loved the study of naturopathy and escaped occasionally to the countryside during school breaks.

The difficulty of city living, however, finally triggered in me the desire to take a year off my school program to reconnect with the true nature study from Mother Earth herself. So, I went to stay at Bodhi Farm, a Buddhist spiritual community in the tropically lush zone of Northern New South Wales. I was back in nature and living with like-minded people, and I was continuing my study of natural health by learning Foot Reflexology. I also participated in meditation retreats, which nourished my spiritual self. I learned to sit in silence, becoming aware of every breath as it moved in and every breath as it moved out of my body. I experienced my body with conscious awareness, even down to the cellular level, and it was an ecstatic experience. Although I could hardly believe it, I progressed from sitting in meditation for minutes to sitting quietly for hours, and finally for days.

Watching the slow evolution of my inner process was fascinating. Sometimes I experienced absolute stillness and at other times I was overcome by emotional tidal waves that would come crashing down over me. At those times, I felt like a sailing ship at sea, being tossed on the tide of emotion, and having to maneuver myself to stay afloat. "Quick raise the sail, turn the wheel, pull in the jib!" Instead of observing my process and not getting attached to the feelings, I would be seized with anxiety. With time I learned to let the waves pass, allowing them to flow through me so that I was unaffected by the storm and returned, emptied, to a place of equilibrium and inner quiet. While these inner storms were some of the most challenging emotional experiences I have ever faced, they were also some of the most rewarding, for by learning to allow them to blow through me, I also learned not to be blown over by them. This was a lesson that was to stand me in good stead later in my life.

When I returned to the city for my studies a year later, I was reinvigorated by a more mature sense of self, a deeper commitment to my studies, and a renewed passion for inspiring others to improve their health and style of living. I also took up the art of dance, which I discovered bonded my body to my spirit in surprisingly powerful ways. Through dance I experienced the emotion of the body in a kinetic way. By allowing the music to move through me, and by feeling its rhythms, the music and my movements became one. By freely moving my body and stretching my fingers and toes to their fullest extension, I could fling any heaviness from myself. Stress, worry, doubt—they were all banished in the joy of freeform movement. I could extend my spirit and emotions outward beyond myself to reconnect to the free flow of living energy. For me, dance became an expression of pure joy, a sacred undertaking, and a prayer of the body.

It was also during this time that I connected with Marcus. He seemed to keep appearing in my life. I had met him briefly at several of the ten-day meditation retreats I attended. He showed up one day at the dance school and had also enrolled at the same naturopathic college course. As the classic tall, dark, and handsome type, he had definitely caught my eye. His green eyes flashed with brilliance, his teeth were perfect and white and his tall frame was lean and muscular. He was self-confident and emitted an enticing warmth of heart. It seemed inevitable that we would become a couple. Our relationship formed quickly—and intensely. We thought of ourselves as a "conscious couple," able to be open and honest in our emotional life, committed to work that was of service to the greater good, and dedicated to our spiritual growth as individuals and as a couple. We dated for two years before we finally married, and within three years we opened a Natural Therapy clinic together. Over the next few years, for all intents and purposes, we were living our vision, yet deep inside, I knew all was not well with us. Marcus would invariably lash out at me with his emotions, which caused me to close up and feel unsafe, so I could not really relax into the relationship. The more Marcus would scream and yell, the more I would close down. This pattern became the bane of our relationship. It didn't take me long to see that in our relationship, Marcus was the prosecutor and I was the accused.

Deep inside I felt the ever-stronger stirrings of discomfort and denial, and I squashed any admissions about our problems under the weight of daily responsibilities—our clients, the clinic upkeep, rental commitments and car maintenance. I slipped back into old patterns. As I had with my father, I began, almost without realizing it, to let Marcus take control in order to keep the peace, and in the process I allowed my spirit to be squelched and bent to another's will. It's not surprising that during these many years, I gradually lost my connection to the earth, as I rarely had time alone in nature to unravel the complexities that bound me. As a result, I became confused and trapped between wanting to stay in the relationship and wanting to leave it. When my emotions seemed to press upward out of the shadows of myself, I simply danced myself into feeling better. Or, I worked harder.

When after many years of marriage, our problems finally became too obvious for either of us to ignore, we became determined to actively work to heal our union. After all, we were healers weren't we? But even our sincere attempts to heal the relationship couldn't blind me to the reality that we were acting more out of the fear of losing each other than from our love for each other. At one point, we enrolled in a course called "The Loving Relationship Training," with Sondra Ray, the author of a well-known book, *Loving Relationships*. The insights we gained under Sondra's tutelage helped, and Marcus and I began to consciously engage in a more considerate, dynamic relationship. Seeing such good results, we participated in a few more workshops and thought we had everything under control, that our healing as a couple was real and lasting. It was not to be, and we had not realized the inevitable yet.

As our relationship began a temporary ascent, our working lives, which had always been bountiful, became even more so. Our clinic, one of the first of its kind in Australia, was a huge success. We had an attractive and inviting building, which was situated next to a health food store and across the road from a beach where dolphins made regular appearances. We had more than a dozen practitioners offering various healing modalities, including yoga and dance. We owned an upscale home, two cars, and a motorbike and enjoyed an eclectic group of close friends. We were even contracted to serve as massage therapists and consultants for the famous Australian rock band INXS. Over six years, we frequently traveled with the band and ministered to them after each of their physically demanding shows. We were twenty-six years old, considered by those in our part of the world as pioneers in our field, and secure in our professional and social life. But because of my marital troubles, my entire life was really a house of cards, one tottering on the verge of collapse.

Although the marriage counseling and workshops seemed to be helping, when Sondra Ray and her colleagues invited us to go on a "Rebirthing" pilgrimage to Egypt, we decided to accept. We enjoyed working with Sondra and the rebirthing work was billed as helpful for uncovering repressed feelings and releasing emotional tethers to inner wounds, which helped one be reborn to one's integrated and more balanced self. Plus, I was eager to visit Egypt, the land where both my parents had been born and raised. It was, of course, also a desirable destination for us because of its spiritual significance as the land of the gods and goddesses, of the pharaohs and queens, as the land of the desert sun that brings light into the darkness and thus illuminates spiritual consciousness. I had a strong intuitive feeling that although this trip could further the healing in our marriage, it would also open new pathways along my personal journey, perhaps reorienting me to directions I had turned away from or had been detoured from exploring.

Everything about Egypt was intense, even the air was extraordinary; so suffused with ancient history that you could cut through it with a knife. I remember walking through the streets of Aswan, and marveling at the kaleidoscope of colors in the marketplace, which teemed with carts filled with goods from exotic fruits to textiles. At one point, as I was walking along the narrow street, I turned my head around and my eyes exactly met those of a black-veiled woman staring at me from a window. Her eyes pierced through me in a look of disbelief as if I was an apparition from a world she had only dreamt of. The energy she exuded felt to me like that of a caged black panther, and her projected feeling was of a longing for escape from the confines of her world and culture. That feeling followed me down the bustling street.

Standing transfixed before the mighty Sphinx, I saw how its smile was enigmatic yet just as expressive as the eyes of the veiled woman. John Anthony West, the Egyptologist guiding our journey, explained that the Sphinx, which is half-woman and half-lion, commemorates through its feminine side the constellation of Virgo and through its masculine side the constellation of Leo. I thought of my connection to the sun and moon, for like them the feminine and masculine principles of Virgo and Leo unite to form something larger and more meaningful than the sum of the parts.

The mournful sound of the chants and prayers wafted along on an afternoon breeze that was thick with dust and warmth. Those sounds pulled me backward into history, into prehistory even, to a time and place of first beginnings. They also lulled me outward and upward, into the unfathomable beyond that this ancient land stands testament to. The chanting seemed a harbinger of something sacred, although I didn't know what. I felt on the verge of remembering something important and new, yet ancient and familiar as well. It was with the lingering recall of these sounds and with the tentative and ambiguous feelings of something opening in me that I prepared to enter the Great Pyramid of Cheops the next day.

Morning broke and the piercing sun seemed to melt the desert sands into a lake of fluid fire. Everything about Egypt seemed piercing—the sun, the black-veiled woman's eyes, the prayers of the faithful, and now the pinnacle of this stupendous pyramid. The Great Pyramid dwarfed Marcus, Sondra and I, and the group of other journeyers who were with us. As I prepared to enter the dark confines of this temple of stone, I seemed to awaken to a part of myself that I could only describe as the inner priestess. Just as

I was about to enter, an Egyptian man who was standing silently to the side of the entrance bowed to me, both his arms outstretched, and said in heavily accented English, "The Moon Goddess has finally arrived." I stopped in my tracks, astounded. My thoughts flew back to my mother and the time we had spent gazing out the window at the moon, and to Uncle Cassy, who called me Moony because I reminded him of the silvery moon. I was propelled back to the night I left Tiny's house and was stopped on the trail by the radiance of strange angular beams streaming earthward from the moon. I was stirred from my momentary reverie by the person behind me, gently urging me forward, and so I shook myself back to reality, entered the pyramid, and left the strange man behind.

The passageway into the pyramid was so low and narrow that we had to walk hunched over and I thought how this posture physically displayed the humility and reverence one must feel in the presence of a king or queen, or a god or goddess. When we finally reached the King's Chamber, we arranged ourselves on the stone floor in a circle, and Sondra, our group facilitator, nodded to the guards to switch off the lights. Marcus had brought along his didgeridoo, an indigenous Australian instrument made from a hollow tree branch that one blows through to make deep, droning sounds. He began to play the didgeridoo now, in King Cheops' empty sarcophagus. Deeply resounding tones pulsed forth and echoed back toward us from the empty tomb. The sound was otherworldly, penetrating deeply into my physical body and stirring my emotions. Sitting in the darkness with the waves of sound flowing over me, I felt as if the base of my spine were extending itself, penetrating into the base of the pyramid. At the same time, I felt the crown of my head begin to vibrate faster and faster, until suddenly it felt as if it opened and a cord within me reached up to connect with the pinnacle of the pyramid. Then it stretched even further, reaching toward and connecting to the stars above. The deep droning and vibrating sound from the didgeridoo intensified, and we all began to hum and tone along with it. The resonance built in power until it felt as if some kind of energetic barrier had been breached. It felt as if a primordial force that had been still for eons was once again set in motion, whirling and turning the wheel of Earth and the spiral galaxies through the great expanse of the heavens. Everything felt connected, and moving.

I had my eyes open, the chamber was in absolute darkness and I could see nothing in the dense blackness. There was no reference point outside of myself, and I felt as if I might dissolve into everything and nothingness at the same time. I felt untethered from everything—there was no center point outside my own thoughts and nothing by which to orient my mind. "This is the void," I thought, in a state of ever-increasing awe. "The unfathomable place, where the known and the unknown meet, where love and fear dance together in perfect step and counterstep, where light and dark converge, and where integration emerges out of the resolution of duality." At that moment, in the absolute darkness, with the energy having reached a pitch, and with no absolute frame of reference, I suddenly felt birthed into a new state of awareness, as if my eyes opened wide to the blind eye of creation. Just as suddenly, a massive circular disk of translucent white-violet light appeared before me. It hung in the blackness just above eye level and seemed so natural that I wasn't startled. It was if I had been waiting all my life for this moment, this unveiling. From a central point within the luminescent disk, a vertical line, like the hand of a clock, extended outward toward the edge and began to rotate clockwise around the circumference of the disk. The drone of the didgeridoo was like an acoustical radar blip, seeming to facilitate the rotation of the "hand" on this cosmic timepiece. The bright white hand was positioned at twelve o'clock, and as it moved around the circle of light, it slowly changed color to a fluorescent violet, deepening in color and then lightening until it was bright white again as it once again reached its starting point of twelve o'clock.

I watched this rotation many times, unbelieving. I leaned toward it, rubbed my face, and widened my eyes in an effort to make sure it was real. It never wavered. I could do nothing but marvel at this light show—and wondered if anyone else was witnessing it. Just as I was coming to terms with this visionary display, the disk disappeared and in its place and to the left arose the image of an immense emerald crystal city of light. This image, too, was suspended in the darkness before me, shimmering in its intensity. The colossal crystal shafts were of the most gorgeous, deep emerald color I had ever seen, and I could see the whole spread of the city without knowing how close it was to me, or how far away. My perception of dimension and proportion was unfamiliar and strange, and as I was staring mystified and awed at the sight of this glowing crystal cityscape, it suddenly exploded before me in silent unison with a massive emotional eruption in my heart. Millions of brilliant emerald-green stars showered over me in slow motion as my heart overflowed with ecstatic joy. I heard myself sigh deeply, trying to accommodate this inner explosion of love. It dawned on me that two of my chakras, (energy centers of the body) had just been activated; the third eye area, which is of the violet ray had been unveiled and my heart chakra of the green ray, had been opened. I knew with certainty that somehow, sitting here in the dark of the King's Chamber of the Great Pyramid, I had been initiated.

I never cried as much as I did in Egypt. After that initiation, it was as if a current of emotion had found its way free of some confining banks within me and began to flow wildly. I found myself spontaneously breaking into sobs at various ruins and temples, unable to explain why to my companions, and even to Marcus. The energy of certain of these ancient sites seemed to connect me to dualities that expressed themselves emotively. For instance, at one ruin I felt accosted by a sense of smallness of self and unworthiness that was almost immediately countered with a sense of personal magnitude and self-love, and I would break out into tears. To maintain my composure I had to dig deep into my bag of self-help tools. I tried a technique I learned through Vipassana meditation that involved observing my body's sensations without judging them along with the rebirthing technique of taking deep breaths to release any limiting thoughts I had about myself. They each helped to one degree or another, but the bottom line was that here in the desert, the floodgates to the river of my soul broke open, as did my connection to my ancestry. In one suspended moment in the hot daze of a lazy afternoon, I heard the laughter of my parents playing in the streets as innocent children. I found myself weeping at the connection, for I felt for the first time in my life that I truly understood my mother and father. In a way, I too had now "grown up" in Egypt. I had no idea what the vision in the pyramid meant, but I understood that it had caused an opening in me that I had no desire to try to close.

While I experienced magic in Egypt, I had to return to a less than alluring home life. The return was made more difficult because I was changed. I could no longer deny that my life lacked the magic I wanted for it, that my relationship with Marcus could not fill the part of me that yearned for the enthrallment I had encountered. I loved Marcus, but I suspected that I just didn't love him enough. I was torn between staying in the relationship where I was fundamentally unhappy yet safe and leaving and plunging into the unknown in an effort to rediscover my true heart's desire. I couldn't make a decision because I really didn't know what that desire was. This tug of war at the core of my being created a lot of friction between Marcus and I, setting us back from the progress we had made as a couple.

I found ways to avoid having to come to resolution with the state of my marriage and with my own uncertainty in what I should be doing with my life. Mostly I threw myself into my work. At other times, I headed out into nature. At one point, desperate for some clarity, I decided to undertake a vision quest and spent four days alone in nature, fasting, praying, sitting in meditation, observing nature and my own thought processes, and just gave myself over to Spirit. On the final, fourth day of the quest, I felt emptied and clean. At one point, late in the afternoon, I found myself standing tall before the small meditation hut that I had been staying in. The sky was filled with clouds, which drifted freely across the blue expanse. My thoughts drifted to the bats that I had seen flying at night and to the gargantuan spiders that were living in the hut. I had at first been rather frightened by both, but now I seemed to be listening to the whisperings of their teachings, which revealed that what I had judged in these creatures was what I most judged and feared in myself. I heard a voice inside my head state explicitly, "What you judge has nothing to do with anything outside yourself and everything to do with yourself." I realized that I, like many people walking the spiritual path, had feared and denied the darker aspects of myself, those parts of myself that I considered "less than" and weak or unspiritual. I tended to focus only on what I deemed positive and good, only on what I felt was connected to light and love. I now understood the value of acknowledging my own shadows, and I knew that creating such a duality required that I judge one aspect of myself divine and the other not. Such a split was neither real nor fair. I marveled at how far I had gone off course and how easily I had forgotten what was so self-evident. I heard that inner voice again, saying, "Love brings up everything unlike itself for the purpose of release and healing." I was astonished at that truth. How could I have missed it all these years? Of course, I had known these truths on an intellectual level, but I had let the "stuff" of my life take control—the emotional pain and then the denial of it, the confusion and even fear of leaving behind all I had worked so hard to acquire and achieve, the anger I felt at not being able to make my relationship with Marcus work, and the frustration and animosity I felt he projected toward me.

All of these emotions had blinded me to my own power and I had lost my balance.

And yet, believe it or not, I also, at that moment, chose to recommit myself to the relationship. I felt that now that I had a clear sense of my own disequilibrium, I could work to repair our relationship. After all, wasn't this my most ardent wish—to heal what was wounded in myself as reflected in my relationship with Marcus? As I stood there under the twilight sky, I asked as fervently as I could of Spirit that I be given guidance to facilitate my healing and to assist in my comprehension about my mission here on Earth and my future. I did not receive an immediate answer, and when the answer did come, only a few hours later, it was not the answer I expected.

Feeling my quest complete, I packed up and headed home. Marcus was there to greet me, but he did not ask much about my experience, as he honored the privacy of the process I had undertaken. I felt renewed and ready for us to work again at rediscovering our love for each other. No sooner than I got home, I received a phone call from some people I had spoken to six months earlier. They were just around the corner and wanted to meet me. Even though I had never met them before, I was eager to, so I invited them over. I was curious about the timing of this visit, believing that there are no coincidences.

Soon Dana, Georgia, and her daughter Cassandra, showed up. They were involved in study with the "Ascended Masters," a group of highly evolved beings in Spirit who once walked the earth plane. Marcus and I had explored this course of study and were eager to hear more about it. We talked for a while, and then my new friends asked if they could perform an energy healing on me. I agreed, and as they worked on me, I had wonderful memory recall of my maidenhood. I remembered occasions when I would look up toward the starry sky and plead, "I want to go home, take me home," for I had felt trapped on Earth, as if it were a penal colony or a labor camp. That was a time when I felt especially limited in my self-expression by the constraints of strict parents and authoritative schoolteachers. I felt that Earth couldn't be my real home. My real family was somewhere "out there," in the stars. One evening, in particular, came to mind. I had stepped out under the night sky, my bare feet planted firmly upon the earth, looked up to the stars, and pleaded, "I want to go home! I want to go home!" as I had so many times before. Then I remember solemnly asking a question, "Why am I here on Earth?" A zinging sensation of electrical energy had risen from the earth, sizzled into my feet and upward through my body, sparking my heart with the answer: "To love the planet Earth." I had been bowled over by that answer. What did that mean? I had been filled with disdain, for I wanted out! Or better yet, off! I liked being out in nature, but I didn't want to be here on Earth, never mind to love being here.

These thoughts floated through my mind as the three of them worked on me. I thought how much my attitude had changed. I had learned to truly love Mother Earth. I recalled the time at The Farm when I had heard the earth call my name. Yes, Earth energy appealed to me now, and I spontaneously made another connection between it and my name. My last name, Camateros, when broken down sounded like "Karma-Terra-Eros." Perhaps my karma that was linked to the terra firma, the earth, was to love (Eros) the earth." Of course I am here to love Earth!" I now thought. "It is evident in my name itself." Amalia Camateros, "Soul mother of the garden whose karma is to love Earth." I somehow knew that my destiny was tied to Earth, but I still didn't know how.

Over the next several weeks these extraordinary and decidedly "out there" people then gave me a "grounding" session to connect me with the core of the earth. Energetically, they explained, they were going to drive an etheric black-and-white double helix grounding rod through my eighth chakra, which they explained is in the thymus area above the heart, and send it down through my body and into the core of the earth. The Ascended Masters would then transmute and clear any blocked energies that were interfering with the progression of my personal mission. I marveled at the synchronicity of their words, the memories I had just been having, and my plea to be sent some guidance to help me better know my heart's purpose. Georgia and Cassandra stood on either end of the massage table, moving their hands and arms in what appeared to be Egyptian-like mudras, movements that symbolize specific meanings. Dana explained that as the energy flowed through me, it would "trigger the remembrance of who you truly are, and open the gateway in acceleration of your passage home." This appealed to me as I still reserved a special place within for my stellar origins.

As the process neared completion, Dana continued to talk to me, describing the place he saw in the cosmos from which I had come to Earth. "Amalia, you are the priestess of the Sacred Wind," he said. "On your planet, there are huge, emerald-green crystal pyramids, lots of them everywhere. The emerald crystal blocks that make up these pyramids contain a recorded history of the ancient pasts of many different seeded cultures throughout the universe and a recorded history of the futures waiting to come. The pyramids themselves are like a library or the Akashic Records."

As he spoke, I felt an "opening" sensation in my head, as if the correct combination of a lock had just been found and the safe door had swung wide open. What he was describing was strikingly similar to the emerald crystal city I had seen while in the Great Pyramid. As my friend spoke, it felt as if another piece of the puzzle of my life was falling into place, and with that feeling, another correspondence flew to mind. The name of the road I lived on for the first eighteen years of my life was called Emerald Drive! What was it with the color emerald green in my life? It did not seem haphazard or coincidence. It had some significance, but I wasn't sure what.

Then, to make matters even more interesting, Dana began drawing on a sheet of paper what he explained was my "emblem" and "gateway shield." Using colored markers, he drew an emerald-green triangle surrounded by a violet disk. Without knowing it, he was illustrating my vision from the Great Pyramid. Then he drew the golden wings of an eagle spread wide from the sides of the violet disk and an olive branch flowing from the eagles' mouth, which, he explained, represented the gift of peace that I had bought with me to this planet. I wasn't sure about the peace part, but I did laugh to myself as I thought of how Marcus always called me his "little black olive," because I loved olives and ate so many of them.

When this group of healers left, I was spinning with energy and with questions. What was my life all about? Was I doing the right thing by giving my marriage another try? Did the emerald-green and violet disk that had showed up again in my life mean anything? Was I being sent synchronistic messages that I was unable to decipher? I knew my Earth connection was strong, and I felt that Mother Earth below and Spirit above were sending me messages, but I still didn't know how to read them.

A few weeks later, just when I had convinced myself that I was being a bit flighty to think that Mother Earth or the universe were trying to send me messages, I got another one. These messages were getting more and more in my face, and I could no longer deny that they seemed specifically directed at me. This message came through a girlfriend, Jan. She offered to perform a visualization journey for me, leading me through a meditation during which she would retrieve a helping guide for me. She explained that such guides usually take the form of animals. When she was complete, she leaned over and whispered in my ear, "Amalia, your spirit animal totem is an emerald-green snake." Needless to say, I was taken aback, not at the snake totem but at the fact that it was emerald colored. This jeweled hue was becoming a constant theme in my life. Jan didn't know of any of my experiences involving this color, so she could not have been influenced in any way. It was as if I were being given individual pieces of a puzzle whose larger picture I just couldn't fathom.

A few months later still another message was delivered. I was giving a massage to a close friend, Greer, who came regularly for massages, and there was nothing out of the ordinary about this visit. But then, for no apparent reason, Greer began crying, in a soft whimpering and weeping. Before I could even express my surprise, she lifted her head and shoulders from the massage table and cried out, "Oh! There's a beautiful woman standing there." I didn't quite know where "there" was, even as I tried to follow Greer's eyes. "She's an empress! No . . . she's a queen . . . no, a . . . a. . . ." Greer struggled to interpret what she was seeing, but I knew who this woman was. "Is she a priestess?" I asked Greer, not wanting to lead her too much. "Yes! Yes, she's a priestess." Greer seemed relieved to have correctly identified the spectral woman. "And, she's telling me something."

I remained silent, trying to energetically "hold the space" of the moment.

Greer whispered now. "She's saying, 'Rise up off your knees, and stand tall and strong within yourself.' Oh! Her face is constantly changing." Greer was still mostly reclined on the massage table, her head lifted and her expression one of awe. I too, was stunned, for I had the uncanny sense that in some inexplicable way, that priestess was either myself, or she was here for me! I knew because the words Greer quoted the priestess as saying were the very words I often spoke to clients of mine who needed encouragement or support. "Rise up off your knees, stand tall and strong within yourself." That was my mantra to selected clients, and a few had reported to me that as I spoke them they felt as if my face transformed into someone else's face. This phrase was very special to me, for it integrated a duality we often get caught in. It asks that we use the strength of our inner male to rise up and meet our inner female to reach a place of balance.

Greer now seemed to be in a trance-like state. She continued stammering as she sought to correctly interpret what she was witnessing in her vision. "We are in a room—a castle . . . no, it's a cathedral . . . no, it's a—."

I complete her sentence for her. "It's a temple."

"Yes, that's it!" she said. "It is a temple. But it has no windows or doors, although there is a lot of bright light filling it. Oh! She's. . . ." She paused for a while, and I thought she had lost the connection to her vision until finally, with a cry of surprise, she continued her narration. "Oh! She's carrying me over an emerald-green threshold!"

I felt as if a bush fire burned right through me, consuming any doubts I had that these "emerald happenings" were coincidence. I was alight with a new openness toward them, and afire with questions. The tears that streamed down my cheeks sunk silently into the towel that hung over Greer's body.

Greer's vision seemed to be over. She laid her head back on the cushion and remained silent. Unsure of whether I should question her, I struggled for a moment before I reined in my curiosity. I finished the massage, and neither Greer nor I talked about the vision during the rest of the session. When we did discuss it later, it remained a mystery to Greer, and because of the personal nature of the messages I seemed to be receiving about my life, I didn't say much to her. I put it down to just another anomalous, and delightful, "emerald event."

Chapter 2:

Heeding the Call.

I have to admit that I was a slow learner. Perhaps I should say more accurately, that I was a reluctant student, for the universe appeared to be sending me messages that I preferred not to hear. It was easy to distract myself with the clinic and business responsibilities, with traveling with INXS, with caring for our house and cars, and with the dance classes that I was now giving. I had all the excuses I needed not to delve deeper into my own spiritual process. Except that my marriage, now going on thirteen years, was not getting any better. In fact, as the years flew by, I became more and more emotionally subordinate to Marcus' emotional reactivity and backlashes. In this area of my life, I felt like a soldier negotiating a minefield, wondering where the next explosion might come from, how badly I might be wounded, and how I might survive it. As a result of the pace of my life over these years, I had little inclination to reflect deeply or to heed the enigmatic messages offered to me from Spirit, from Mother Earth, and from my inner self. I was aware that an "Emerald Realm" was somehow inserting itself into my reality through the vision in the great pyramid, the emerald-colored snake, the emerald crystal pyramids, the emerald threshold, and even the name of the road I had grown up on, Emerald Drive. I have to admit that it was getting more and more difficult to ignore these odd events, visions, and coincidences.

It was a book that changed my attitude from one of being merely intrigued but inattentive to bringing a more direct intro-spection to these messages. I, of course, knew that my connection to Nature and Earth was somehow connected with all of this and that my "mission" was somehow connected to Earth wisdom, although it was still unclear how. But when I came across the book *Conclave Meeting* by Tuieta, this metaphor was extended for me in a way that shed new light on my situation. It is a very "new age" book, about a council meeting of the Ascended Masters of Light, who each offer their unique and specialized expertise on how we can better approach life here on planet Earth. The Masters address such issues as better methods of childrearing and of improving our educational and political systems as well as warnings about the misuse of drugs and sex and potential Earth shifts and upheavals. Their intent is to show us how we can best overcome our limitations and fears in order to enhance the healing and ascension of Earth and of humanity. Each Ascended Master of this council was described as he or she offered a message.

As I read the descriptions of three of the Masters, I felt over-come with what I can only describe as a "remembering." Those three Masters—there are a total of at least eight described in the book—were said to wear magnificent emerald rings. Plus, each of the members of this council referred to Earth as the "Emerauld-Jewel of the Universe," as a planet that is observed and cherished by other intelligences in the universe. Upon reading this description, I felt an influx of information coming through me like a wind. It was as if I had retrieved some long-forgotten memories about the "Emerald Records." I "remembered" that these records were encoded in different places and by different means on the Earth—in the Egyptian pyramids of Giza, or the Temple of the Sun and the Moon at Teotihuacán in Mexico for instance. I heard my inner voice declare, "I know the Emerald Records! They were sealed in the star system of Sirius long before they were finally reopened and brought to Earth. As the key information descended into physical manifestation on this planet, it was coded and recorded in the rocks of the Earth and in the Emerald Tablets, (said to be the oldest records of spiritual wisdom recorded in history) as templates for the matrix of energy it held. Hence it was seeded in the soil of humanity's consciousness, germinating and sprouting, slowly releasing its energy until the time when human consciousness can fully receive it."

Even before I had purchased this book, I seemed to have intuitively tapped into its message. During my meditations and when I found time to get out into nature to sit quietly and go within, I had often found myself communing with the intelligence found on one particular star (which I intuited to be Sirius). I received "communications" about Earth changes, Christ's purpose for visiting Earth, and stellar energy and how we would tap into it in the future as a source of new energy-power for planet Earth. The information I had received was almost the same as that recorded in the book, which further spurred my interest in the book.

Another "coincidence" occurred in relation to this book that also caught my attention. One evening Marcus and I were in bed, lying quietly and holding hands as we drifted off to sleep. Marcus' eyes were closed and his breathing was deep and regular, but I was unable to sleep. I was looking up at the ceiling in the dark, my eyes focused on nothing in particular at the upper corner of the room, when suddenly I saw of flash of light. The afterglow of the light hung there, and then slowly took more solid form. A cloudy white light coalesced into an opaque ball with a radial arm of rainbow light projecting from it. This arm rotated slowly clockwise, reminding me of the vision of the violet disk I had seen in the Great Pyramid. Here it was again—this time a rainbow arm of light rotating around a cloudy ball of light. As I stared at the glowing ball, I felt an immense wave of peace and love wash over me. I felt no awe, no fear and no excitement—just an intense sense of all-pervading love, of eternal compassion. I had never experienced this depth of love in such a visceral way. It was not just a perception, but had an actual tactile quality to it. Then I heard a deep, resonant voice say, with reverence and sovereignty, "Amalia, I love you and will never leave you." It seemed as if these words were coming directly from Marcus. That spooked me a bit, and I looked over at Marcus, sure he had just spoken. But he was still asleep and his breathing deep. The voice had not been his in tenor or temper, but somehow the words seemed to have come from him. I looked back to the corner of the room near the ceiling and watched as the milky disk with its rainbow arm dissolved into nothingness. I was charged with energy, sure that I had just been visited by an entity of some kind that had "spoken" through Marcus. For that moment I felt truly loved—loved with a freedom that bore no burden of personal fear or psychological overlay. It contained within it no fear of separation, for that depth of unconditionality could contain no separateness within it. I felt fully acknowledged for who I was, and accepted with no reservations. I felt a deep sense of peace and relaxation flow through me.

One week later, while I was reading the final paragraph of Conclave Meeting, I came across a passage about how we need to live our lives through the eyes of our hearts. It was information attributed to the Master called Sananda, who is considered to have incarnated on Earth as Christ, He closed his discourse wih, "I am Sananda and how you will come to know me is by a rainbow anchored by a cloud." At first, I envisioned in my mind's eye a cute, puffy, white cloud in the sky with a curved rainbow streaming over it, such as you might see in a children's book. But then I was flooded with the memory of the vision I had had the week before: the cloudy white ball with the rainbow arm moving clockwise around it, and the voice that seemed to come from Marcus that expressed its love for me. I now pondered the possibility that I had indeed been visited by the energy of Lord Sananda and I wondered if I should take all these strange messages as real.

My inner conflict centered on two main issues. First, although I loved my work, I was as yet not doing what I felt I was meant to do. Second, I was staying in a marriage that did not really fulfill me because, as much as I hesitated to admit it, it was safe and secure. What were my alternatives? To give up all I had worked so hard to achieve in my business and to strike out on a path that wasn't even clear to me? I simply did not have enough information about what I was "meant" to do, to trust that I should actually go out and do it. In the meantime I was content to settle for what was safe. The "good girl" part of me still did not want to upset the apple cart of her tidy and prosperous life. I thought about these issues a lot over the next several months.

For the more than fifteen years that I had been receiving these intriguing messages, I had felt the pull of a calling I didn't understand and couldn't claim. I had also rationalized my relationship with Marcus, riding a roller coaster of emotions about whether or not we could heal our marriage. Finally, I decided I had had enough. I knew that in truth there was no "right" thing to do. All I could do was take responsibility for making a decision that felt true to my heart and to my spiritual self. I also simply got sick of struggling with the question of my marriage: stay or go? stay or go? stay or go? I knew I had to finally provide myself an answer, once and for all.

Although I pondered all these issues, it was not until days later—just another ordinary day—when I finally reached my limit with myself. In utter frustration, I threw myself on the mercy of the Creator, asking from the depths of my being, "Please help me! Please give me a sign that will help me see clearly. For the love of God, please help me!" I was at end of my emotional tether as I pleaded with Spirit, and I remembered the Buddha's decision to sit under the Bodhi Tree until he reached enlightenment, no matter how long it took. I decided I would do something similar. I felt compelled to grab a sheaf of paper and a packet of crayons and then I simply sat down, waiting to see what would happen. I sat, and I sat, and I sat. And then, in a flash of inspiration, I began drawing. I grabbed a crayon and let my hands fly, not intending anything. I saw myself draw two overlapping circles, creating the Vesica Pisces, an ancient Celtic symbol of the masculine merging with the feminine, of the merging of opposites. In the left circle, I drew one of the realities in question: my life as it was at its potential best. I sketched out the beautiful house that we had built, then added in the children we hadn't yet had. It was a picture of a beautiful and happy, secure family life in which I was the adored and appreciated wife and mother. In the right circle, I drew the opposing reality, which for me was leaving the marriage and heading out into the unknown. I was surprised by the images that appeared on the page. I drew palm trees, birds flying toward the sun, a man and a woman connected by a heart, symbols of music, and spirals. The sense of the picture was of pure potential, and that potential felt magical and adventurous. I then connected and merged the two opposing realities by drawing portions of each picture in the central overlapping circle. I wanted wholeness no matter what, to embrace both possibilities as equally valid and divine.

So, there I was, sitting in front of my life's artwork, in deep contemplation, and deep in my aloneness. I felt wonder at what I had just drawn, but I also could not control my mood as it sank like a ship into the unconscious depths of the dark seas. Suddenly, I was overcome with emotion, a pattern that I recognized as indicating I was getting close to a truth I did not want to fully acknowledge.

This descent into the darkness of my inner emotions was accompanied by a wave of heat, as if a fever were rising in my body. I felt a stinging, hot sensation deep inside and yet, strangely, it was accompanied by a simultaneous coldness, an inner chilliness. I felt my emotional life flash before my inner eyes, as a melange of thoughts flooded me. I was certain I was facing my madness, and the fear kept rising, higher and higher. I felt headed for oblivion, and I struggled to maintain my equilibrium. Just as I managed to subdue this riptide of emotion, an image filled my inner vision. I saw two white, stone pillars rising a short distance in front of me, flanking me on either side. It was a vision, not a hallucination, but it seemed very real. In the vision, I saw myself walking between the pillars into a garden, and instantaneously I was cloaked with a sense of peace, as if someone had covered me with a soft blanket. I felt stilled inside. Quiet. The storm had passed almost as quickly as it had come. And, then a knowing arose. I understood, with a certainty I had never felt before, that there was no rush, no need even, to make a decision. I felt so complete, so sure that every-thing was unfolding in my life as it should, that any need I had to control events vanished. I felt as if a guardian were watching over me, and I need not worry so much because the plan for me was all laid out and I would walk it when I was ready.

After that day, my emotional life became much calmer. I was somehow less attached to my emotions although I was in no way anesthetized to them. It was not that I denied or repressed my feelings; I just was not fixated on them. I appreciated the simple beauty of life, the extraordinary in the ordinary. I felt no need to analyze my situation or myself and I now felt no compulsion to make a decision about the future. I was able to accept what I was feeling without needing to ferret out a storyline to explain my emotions. I could simply, in a very Buddhist way, observe myself feeling them, observe the sensations of energy move through my body. I did not need to defend or protect myself because I could acknowledge that whatever I was feeling was true to that moment. Each feeling was a valid and even a divine expression of the "me" of that moment.

It was in this frame of mind that I found myself out on our land one day, sitting in my circle of stones in meditation. Calmness was in the air, accompanied with silence, and from this silence arose a word, a single word: "Sedona." I had never heard that word before. As the sound of the word reverberated through me, I wondered, "Is this a place? Is it a name? Where did this unfamiliar word come from?" I couldn't answer any of those questions. But as soon as I heard the word, I felt an odd kind of energy inside and my body snapped into alignment. I heard three inner clicks, and with each click my spine became more erect. On the final click, both hands sprung up to either side of my head with palms spread wide opened and facing outward, as if they were a sounding board that was about to receive something into them. I was transfixed. I couldn't move from that posture. My hands began to vibrate slightly, and I sensed that they were receiving some kind of energy or information. I knew that I had to keep still until the "download" was complete. There were no words or even internal understandings, just a slight vibration of energy entering into my open palms. It was at this point that I realized I somehow knew that Sedona was a place. I guessed it to be in Italy or Spain, because it sounded to me like the word "Madonna." I don't remember any other thoughts as I sat there for perhaps fifteen to twenty minutes more, my hands raised with palms turned outward, receiving this flow of energy. Finally, I felt I could move again. As I slowly got up and went back into the house, I had no idea what to make of this latest weirdness. I was curious about what or where Sedona was, but, strange as it may seem now, I made no attempt to find out. Just as I was allowing my emotions to come without comment, I also allowed this experience to just be. The next night I had a dream that provided more information.

In the dream I was climbing a wooden staircase that zigzagged upwards, with a landing at each turn of the stairway. On each landing, a bowl of sweets was set on the broad, flat banister. I ate from each bowl to gain the energy to ascend the next flight. Toward the top of the staircase, I looked back over the staircase to my right and saw two huge megalithic reddish-hued rock formations soaring up toward the heavens. "Oh, my God," I said, staring out at the magnificent vistas, "this is Sedona, I am in Sedona." Then I snapped awake.

I was intrigued with the dream, but, again, I did not pursue meaning. I just let it be. I also was caught up in the busyness of my life again, so I neatly filed the dream away with all the other interesting things that had been happening to me. Two days later however, as I was working at the clinic, a new patient arrived for her appointment. Maxine was a large, fair-skinned woman with frizzy red hair and a pleasant demeanor. She looked like a medicine woman because of the strings of beads hanging around her neck and the flowing, long dress she wore. I welcomed her into my consul- tation room as we chatted, and then I asked her, as I do all my new clients, how I could best assist her. Her reply caught me off guard. She leaned toward me, her eyes flashing, pointed a chubby finger at me, and declared, "You are an amazing woman, Amalia. Do you know how amazing you are?" She repeated this a couple of times but needless to say, I was too caught off guard to reply. Her finger jabbed the air toward my chest and her eyes pierced into mine. "Amalia, you have to go to this place where I've just come from," she declared. "Amalia, you have to go!" Then pushing her finger into my upper chest with each word she added, "You would love it!" When she gave me no further clue as to what or where this place was, I tentatively asked.

"Sedona," she replied.

My jaw dropped. The disembodied word I had heard in the stone circle during my meditation was one thing, and the red rock vista I associated with Sedona in my dream was quite another—

but this was just too much. In disbelief, I collapsed onto the massage table. I rolled onto my back, covered my eyes with my hands, and proceeded to have an emotional melt down. I cried and cried. "Just give me a minute," I managed to stammer to Maxine, who didn't seem the least bit fazed that her therapist was an entire mess. Never in my more than fifteen years of practice had I released my feelings in such a manner in front of a client. But I was too overcome with the power of this meeting, of this in-my-face message, to really care. As I finally composed myself, I told her about the meditation during which I had received the word "Sedona." I also told her of my dream. "So, tell me, where exactly is it?" I cautiously asked, not sure I really wanted to know.

"In Arizona," she replied. "In America. It's the most awesome place you'll ever see, and I just got back a couple of days ago."

My thoughts raced. America! Arizona! A new connection formed. One of my quirks is that I'd always been attracted to names beginning and ending with the letter A—and with a Z in the middle. When I was young, I used to spend hours writing all the names I could think of with that spelling, and then make up new ones: Azalea, Amazonia, Anastazia, Australazia, Azteca, Auztria, Azia. Now here was a new one, I'd never thought of: Arizona. Plus, I knew the Hopi Indians lived in this general area of the United States. I was already very much connected to the American Native ways. In fact, at one time I had made dream catchers and worked with the ways of the Medicine Wheel. "Of course it's in Arizona, and not in Italy or Spain!" I said to myself. That fact suddenly seemed self-evident. And yet I couldn't get over marveling at it. Arizona! In the midst of my wonder, I gained a clear perspective of the big picture of my life to date. I felt like a huge eagle had picked me up with its talons and raised me high into the sky to gain the larger view of the events that had led me to this point.

As my thoughts quieted, my curiosity heightened. "Do you have any photos?" I asked.

"As a matter of fact, I do," Maxine replied, then went out to her car to retrieve them. As I looked over the snapshots, to my astonishment—although I should have been well past the point of surprise by now—I saw the same huge red rocks I'd seen in my dream. I was temporarily thrown into anxiety. "What's happening here? What's going on?" Something—some inevitability—seemed very close, and it scared me. I snapped the photo album shut and quickly squelched my growing sense of panic by switching to my professional persona. I urged Maxine to get up on the table and I proceeded to give one of the most attentive massages of my career.

Over the next few weeks, I made time to go out to the stone circle and just sit. I received no revelations, thankfully. I couldn't deal with much more. Instead, I sought grounding. I sought ways to keep myself from *going over the deep end* that something super-natural seemed to be happening in my life. The best thing I could think to do was to go out and simply sit on the earth.

Marcus had a general sense of what was going on in my life, but he didn't know the intensity of it. Still, it did not come as a huge surprise when one day I walked into the house from one of my "sit-ins" and declared, "Marcus, I have to go to Sedona. I have to go there to find out what this is all about. I think I have to go to Sedona to get something from the earth and give it back to the people."

His reply was pure Marcus—the Marcus who truly knew and understood me. This was the Marcus who totally trusted me and shared my beliefs and values. "Is it archeological?" he asked, matter-of-factly.

"No, it's not something you can see."

"Is it, like, a spaceship lying under the earth waiting to be found?" he teased.

"No, it's not something physical," I said. "It's not something you can see." Even I was surprised how emphatic I sounded. I somehow seemed to know what it was I was going to Sedona to retrieve without really knowing what it was at all. "I think I'm supposed to be a secretary for the rocks or something like that." I found myself saying. "I think I am to gather information from Earth—from the rocks. To record information and return it to the people."

I laughed as I mimicked typing and speaking to the rocks: "What did you say, rock? Could you please repeat that? Not so fast!"

We both laughed at my joke, and we left the question of what I was really supposed to do in Sedona hanging in the air unanswered. Although I had started this conversation by declaring my intention to go to Sedona, I didn't actually get around to going. My outburst had come almost despite myself, and it was easy to let it dissipate into the air with the sound of our laughter.

A few weeks passed, but the "Sedona thing" didn't go away. One afternoon, Marcus' friend Leeroy came to visit. He was from Tasmania, a large island off the southeastern tip of Australia, and he was making a spur-of-the-moment detour to see Marcus on the way to visit his parents. He had dark hair that hung halfway down his back, crystalline blue eyes, and a bushy beard. He was definitely a man of the land. We sat around the table chatting, and over time our conversation grew more serious. We began relating thoughts and experiences that had profoundly moved us or changed us. I shared some of the strange occurrences that had transpired around the color emerald in my life and this mysterious place called Sedona. With a smirk on his face and without taking his eyes from mine, Leeroy leaned over and reached for something in his rucksack. He retrieved a book and slid it across the table toward me; it spun to a standstill before me: *Sedona: A UFO Connection* by Richard Danelly. Silence descended and all eyes were on the book. Finally, Leeroy said, simply and very seriously, "You just hang onto this book for as long as you need Amalia."

I read the book, but I still made no plans to leave Australia for Sedona. The universe, however, seemed to be working overtime to prod me into taking that giant step. At that time, I was very interested in a set of divination cards called The Mayan Oracle, by Ariel

Spilsbury and Michael Bryner. I was daily consulting these cards and personally loved the essence and guidance they offered. They are based on the Mayan glyphs, and also have connections to the Hopi and other American Native traditions. Ariel was visiting Australia to share her teachings and knowledge, and I was excited to finally get to meet her. I attended her workshop, and hung on her every word. She began her talk by saying, "Some of you have now been called to a sacred place on this Earth." The hairs on my arms prickled. "You will know when you hear of this place that you will have to go to it. Some of you won't know where it is, why you have to go there, or just how you'll get there. But you eventually will have to go, and you will go." I was transfixed; sure she was speaking only to me. "The reason you have been called to these ancient sacred places is to retrieve parts of yourself that you have left behind in a past life. Now is the time to reclaim those parts in order to continue your divine mission."

We were all sitting in a circle on the floor, and I was suddenly overcome—something was happening to me far too much for my liking. But I couldn't control the emotion that flooded me. I crumpled back onto the floor until I was lying on my back with my arms back over my head, and I began to cry softly through my breathing. While no one seemed overly concerned about me, probably used to this type of behavior in such a New Age atmosphere, I certainly wasn't used to feeling this way. "What is happening to me?" I wondered. "This is not a joke! This is really happening to me! I am a part of some great unfolding, something beyond my comprehension." Then, in the midst of my tears, I heard myself make a huge cosmic joke: "Hang on, Amalia!" I advised myself. "Wax your cosmic surfboard, because you're going to ride a huge wave."

Although I was confused about these emotional tides that seemed to wash over me, I also felt something inside myself surrender that day. From that moment on, I did not resist hearing the messages that seemed to be coming at me from all directions.

Instead, I finally began to actively ask questions about and investigate this new "assignment" with open ears, open eyes, and an open heart. I learned in my research that the ancient peoples of the Sedona area were the Anasazi. I felt an immediate identification with them, and one evening, at a dinner party with Ariel, who was still in Australia, I asked her about them. She seemed to ignore my question, talking about something completely different. I let it go and continued to participate in the multiple conversations that were going on around the table. A short time later, apropos of nothing, Ariel turned toward me and, as if in a trance, delivered a mini lecture. "The Anasazi were a people of the Mayan tribes who'd traveled up through South America to Mexico, and then up into Arizona, where they settled and merged with the Hopi tribes. They were the ancient kings and queens of the land, and they were small and strong." She paused and then added with a strange emphasis, "A bit like you, Amalia." Then she went back to talking with the women at her end of the table.

Some major pieces of the puzzle were now being given to me, and I was finally starting to truly relax into the whole picture. Of course, as all good stories go, it is just at this time that the dam finally broke loose in my marriage. After fifteen years of struggling to work out amicable dynamics, of trying to "heal the relationship" as we often termed it, it just all fell apart. Marcus and I had played our roles magnificently. I was the victim and he was the prosecutor. The guilt we created for each other was as slippery as an oil slick and we simply could no longer keep our balance. One day I suddenly understood why I had waited so long to leave—I had been waiting for the call of the red rocks of Sedona. The specific call to Sedona explained the more general call of the Earth that I had been hearing in various mysterious ways over the past nearly two decades. Now I had to admit that the strong, stable, secure, serene, and silent landscape of red rocks contained all the qualities of the male that I had longed for but hadn't been experiencing in my relationship. I also realized that they were the qualities lacking in me. I understood that the weakness, instability, and need to control I'd judged so harshly in Marcus, were actually the qualities within myself that I refused to acknowledge. All these years I had judged my weakness to truly love myself enough to honor my need for a more nurturing relationship. I had been unable to say, "No more." I had been unwilling to leave what was safe and familiar, no matter how much my soul suffered. I'd slumbered to my true self by dream-walking through a busy life. The truth was that I had not taken responsibility for my feelings and had found it convenient and easy to blame my discontent on my relationship with Marcus. I understood now that there was nothing else I could have done other than exactly what I did, for it had taken all this time for my true path to unfold. As odd as it was, I did have a mission here on Earth. It involved the Earth, and the rocks, and uncovering hidden wisdom. And, I was finally ready to take the first steps to truly undertaking that mission by going to the place that had called me—Sedona.

Chapter 3:

The Journey Begins.

Finally, after all my emotional crises, I understood more clearly the path I had to take, but I was hesitant to share that decision with Marcus. I realized that my anxiety about doing so was arising from emotional habits that had long served me. Somewhere in my subconscious, I had set Marcus up as the paternal authority figure, and now, although I knew what I had to do, I was wary of actually growing up and leaving "Daddy's" domain. I was, to be truthful, a bit frightened of realizing my own power, for as a little girl when I had willfully done so, my father had shaken his finger at me and put me in my place with his anger. At some level I had internalized the fear that the person I most wanted respect and love from threatened my very existence when I expressed my true nature. I wasn't going to heal that kind of wound overnight, and so even though at an intellectual level I understood my fear, I still couldn't overcome it enough to tell Marcus of my decision. I felt that I was about to betray him by doing the very thing that I believed most terrified him—leaving him, or, as I knew he would see it, abandoning him. The last thing I wanted to do was to hurt "my Marcus." But now I had no choice.

It was at crucial times like this that I would write out my feelings, and so by describing them release them. But this time was different. As I undertook this cleansing ritual, I found I wasn't writing to get through a situation in order to be able to carry on for another day. No, this time I was writing an ending. I let myself go, and what emerged from my pen was a beautifully loving and compassionate letter to Marcus. I told him that I needed to go to Sedona to do as I felt I had been instructed to do by the spirit of the Earth. I told him that doing so was the only way for me to find out who I really am. I told him that I loved him, but that I needed to go away for six months to see whether this new path was a true path. I asked him to support me in this decision and to make my going easy for me. It was a complete and soulful letter. Unlike past rituals, when I would write to release emotion and then burn the letter, this time I gave him the letter.

Marcus read the letter in silence, with no expression on his face, so I could not anticipate his reaction. After he finished reading, he turned to me and said, simply, "Go Amalia. There's nothing I can do. If you need to go, then go. I understand." This was the Marcus I had once known so well but who had to me disappeared over the years—the mature, compassionate, responsive Marcus. For so long I had experienced the other Marcus—the one who lashed out without thinking and presided with unbridled reactivity. I was ecstatic that Marcus had responded to me this way, but I was also a bit dumfounded to actually see it happening—now that I had chosen to go.

So, the decision was made. But that did not make my leaving expeditious. I still had to attend to the reality of our business. We had to sort out clinic responsibilities, and bills and other financial matters. And even though Marcus and I had had a meeting of the minds and hearts, that didn't mean our emotional dynamics suddenly changed. I naively thought that once I'd finally made the decision to leave and Marcus had agreed, life was going to get a whole lot easier. I was gravely mistaken, for the most difficult passage was yet to be undertaken. Over the months that I prepared to leave, life at home with Marcus actually became disastrous. We found ourselves in a quagmire of resentments and bitterness. I often felt that he was interrogating me like a prisoner of war he had taken. One afternoon, during one of these episodes, my body literally gave way. I ran from the house, not being able to take one more second of this ferociousness, and I fell to the ground, my face buried into the grass, my legs and arms spread-eagled, and my hands clenching the grass. I cried and cried, feeling sorry for myself and for Marcus. In the midst of my release, however, I suddenly heard that inner voice I was becoming so familiar with, or perhaps it was once again the voice of Mother Earth. "Take your clothes off, take your clothes off," it commanded. I quickly disrobed and resumed the same position. It felt like there was a car crash going on in my head, so I pushed my face into the grass and screamed long and hard into the Earth. As my tears streamed into the ground, my menstrual blood also trickled and seeped into the Earth. And, as that scream unloosed my pain, my blood linked with Mother Earth, and I felt her receive it unconditionally and lovingly, the way she always does. I also offered my soul and body to God in that moment. I remembered Christ's journey, the indictment and prosecution he underwent until finally he was nailed to the cross. I felt like I had just been emotionally crucified, and as I released my pent up pain into Mother Earth, I suddenly understood what was meant by "the return of Christ." It wasn't that the savior, or even a new messiah, would one-day return to redeem us; it was, instead, that we had to redeem ourselves. We had to nail our illusions, stories, and pain up for clear viewing and then take them down, tenderly, and embrace them so that we can incorporate from them what is real and meaningful. In a word, the return of Christ is the act of forgiveness, of others and of ourselves. I spent a long afternoon just lying in the grass, letting the energy of Earth flow through me, releasing, for what I hoped would be the last time, the pain I held about my relationship with Marcus. I worked to truly feel forgiveness for how we had hurt each other even as we loved each other. I had felt my crucifixion and was now awaiting my resurrection!

The next day, still spent emotionally and physically, I went to one of my favorite massage therapists, Sheila. The massage was very healing, and when she was done, Sheila left me alone for a while so I could integrate the healing. I laid on the table, eyes closed, thinking about the day before, about my afternoon in the lap of Mother Earth and the healing I had received there. I thought I was drifting off to sleep because I felt woozy, like my body was becoming lighter and full of air. As this feeling increased, I felt that I was actually lifting off of the massage table. As I felt myself floating higher and higher, I heard a squeaking sound, as if some ancient rusty wheel had started rolling again after eons of remaining still. I felt the peace of Mother Earth and of the "resurrection of forgiveness." I had no doubt at all that if Sheila had walked in the room at that moment, she would have seen me floating two inches from the ceiling. The floating feeling lasted for several more minutes, and then I, or my spirit, descended slowly to the table. Later, when I finally prepared to leave the office, Sheila came over and hugged me goodbye. "Amalia," she said, staring into my face and looking slightly perplexed, "you look different. Something has shifted in you. You seem to have the light of Christ within you." I sure hoped I was different. I hoped my emotional resurrection had finally come, but I wasn't certain that this latest "release" into peace and surety would last. Others hadn't, although on a cumulative level I seemed to be moving closer and closer to figuring out my self and my purpose.

Sure enough, within a month, as I continued clearing obligations and making preparations to leave Australia, I once again crashed emotionally. No matter what I tried, I couldn't maintain my equilibrium. I started wavering in my commitment again, doubting my clarity and purpose. I couldn't seem to change the channel to experience a different way of being. As always, I turned to Spirit once again. One thing we can all be grateful for is the patience of Spirit; it never abandons us, no matter how defiant we are. One night before laying myself to sleep, I was again feeling confused and doubtful about my plan to leave. I began to bargain defiantly with Spirit. I demanded to be given some sign that I was doing the right thing. "Great Spirit," I pleaded loudly and clearly, " Send me an omen in my dream *tonight*. Is it meant for me to go to Sedona? Or am I creating a grandiose delusion to escape my life here?" If I was going to leave a fifteen-year relationship and all the hard work I had put into it, I wanted to know that I was not running away from anything, but instead was heading toward something that was for my highest good and towards what could benefit others as well. If I was to go to Sedona, I wanted the passage from my old life to the new to begin unfolding in as easy and clean a way as possible.

That night I was indeed given an omen in my dream. I was standing alone, with nothing around me but a single, empty chair surrounded by a gauzy white light. I felt no reaction to the lone chair. It just was, and I simply perceived it. Then, far in the distance, through the fog of light, I spied a small, black dot. I focused on it, and it began to grow bigger and move closer. My gaze grew more intent as it got larger and closer. Startled, I realized it was an eagle flying directly toward me. It zeroed in on me, flying a fast track toward me. As it neared, it swooped down and under the chair in front of me and cut sharply passed me to the right, soaring off behind me. But as the eagle had flown by, it took an aspect of me with it to a place of higher vision. I seemed to become lucid in the dream, aware that I was dreaming of this eagle totem, of the messenger bird of Great Spirit of the Native American Indians. On another level I was awake in the dream. My consciousness felt untethered from my physical body, and I seemed to be actually floating above my body. I felt as if I were looking down at my "smaller" self, which was still experiencing the dream. I don't remember what happened next, but I do remember acknowledging the passage of the eagle in my dream. "Thank you, Great Spirit. I receive this eagle as my omen," I said. As I gave thanks, I felt I was now as free in spirit as the eagle, able to soar anywhere I wanted.

When I woke up, I was acutely aware of the dream. I kept my eyes closed so as not to break the link to the world where the eagle had flown. I was disappointed. This was too metaphoric a message. "This just isn't enough! That was just a dream." I complained to myself and to Spirit. "I want more concrete and reliable proof that I am meant to go to Sedona." With all the might that I could muster, I evoked Great Spirit. "Great Spirit, if this dream eagle was my omen, then prove it. Send me an eagle outside my window *now!*" I turned in bed toward the sliding glass door that faced the open land. Part of me was aghast at my impertinent attitude toward Spirit, but most of me was defiant. I wanted a sign and I wanted it to be unmistakable and to appear now. As I gazed through the door, I could see the lawn beyond, and I really didn't expect to see anything but perhaps the little songbirds that usually flitted around hunting seeds. Maybe I would see a rabbit nibbling contentedly, or perhaps even the quick red streak of a fox. But as I stared out the slider, not two feet on the other side of the glass pane, an eagle flew past. Its head turned toward the glass door, and so it appeared that the magnificent creature was actually looking in at me! Of course, this "coincidence" was unbelievable. I was speechless. I actually slapped my cheeks to ensure that I still wasn't dreaming.

I turned to see if Marcus was awake, but he wasn't, he was fast asleep. I was entering this journey alone. I was scared and sad knowing that our relationship had come to the final close. Quietly,

I got out of bed and went to the sliding door. I was trembling, and talking to myself in my head. "Amalia, if that eagle is still flying out there, then it's real and you'll have to surrender to this sign. If it is there, you will know truly that heading to Sedona is the right thing to do." I opened the glass sliding door and scanned the yard and the hill beyond. There it was! A lone eagle flying over the nearby knoll. I watched spellbound for seconds, until I was overcome emotionally and physically with a wave of humility. Spontaneously, I assumed a posture of blessing and thanksgiving. I bent down on my knees and bowed down to the earth, my arms outstretched to acknowledge a power larger than myself. A sad, quiet knowing filled me, for I realized now, that the gap between Marcus and I could not be bridged, and I was about to walk into a new world without him. I spoke my truth with every fiber of my being: "I will go to Sedona to do my Earth work. I will go."

I knew now that I wasn't going to visit Sedona and then return to Australia, and to Marcus, in six months as I had planned or told Marcus. I was leaving Marcus for good. I knew it in every cell of my body. There was just no way to deny that I was being led by Spirit to follow a path, and I could no longer walk away from that calling. The process of my leaving began in earnest, and our separation became a reality when he moved out of our house. I was excited about the prospect of a new life, but I was deep in mourning about the ending of my life, as I had known it for nearly two decades. I remembered back to when I was eighteen and had left home—run away, really—and I had written a letter to my parents saying my good-byes and thanking them in gratitude for all they had done for me. I had expressed my thoughts that I knew they were staying together all these years in great unhappiness so that my sister and I would have the security of a home with parents. I had told them that now that I was leaving, they could unload themselves of the obligation they felt as parents and so begin to find the meaning of their own lives, as I was of mine. When I had left that day, I saw my father walking home from work and nearing the house. My heart sank from the heaviness of guilt as I imagined him entering the house to find my letter and railing with anger and hurt at the reality that his good little Greek daughter had betrayed him. These same guilty feelings were stalking me now, as I thought about my leaving Marcus. He said he supported me, but I knew he felt betrayed, just as my father had. Still, even in my anguish, I hung on to the small part of me that was firm in the resolve that I had to do what was best for me. I was to take the path of the eagle, and fly away to the east just as the Eagle had done outside my window that morning.

As I had so many times in the past, I again created an intentional ceremony to try to deal with the pain I was feeling and to make my leaving as emotionally clean as possible. A friend of mine, John, had suggested I break some plates as a "letting go" ceremony, especially of my marriage. That idea appealed to me, especially because in the Greek tradition smashing plates is part of certain celebrations and dances. I bought fifteen old plates, one for each year of my marriage, and on each one I wrote a negative or hurtful emotion or feeling I associated with my relationship with Marcus that I wanted to release. I started with trapped, then went on to obligation, fear, disappointed love, insecurity, constriction, financial pressure, emotional and verbal abuse, disapproval, sexual frustration, betrayal, heartbroken, victim, disillusionment, and ended with separation. One by one with a black marker pen I wrote out the word and then drew symbolic images of the emotion on the plates. Then I placed them around the circumference of the stone circle out on the land behind our house. It was the same meditation circle in which I had first heard the word "Sedona." I lit a fire in the center of the stone circle, and then I began the release ceremony.

Picking up the "trapped" plate, I raised it high over my head, symbolically reaching up to Spirit, and then I circled the fire, still holding the plate aloft. I breathed into the feeling of being trapped, and I then embodied that feeling, dancing its power out of every cell of my physical body and every nook of my mind. I owned the feeling, acknowledging it as a being, as a teacher, singing out, "Thank you for entering my experience, for without you I would not know how to use my wings and fly into freedom." Then, when I was certain I was free of the feelings of being trapped, I smashed the plate against the stones in the fire pit, breaking the illusion of being trapped and transmuting it through the alchemical flames into its opposite—freedom. I found the process exhilarating, and continued on to the next plate. With "obligation," I gave thanks for being taught how to take responsibility for my own feelings and for allowing others the responsibility for their own feelings. Thus, I was learning to speak my own truth and trust my own feelings. I next gave thanks to "fear" for being the greatest teacher of all and then acknowledged "love," as it's opposite. With "disappointed love" I embraced the lesson that I had to love myself before I could expect to love anyone else or to truly accept another's love of me. With "insecurity," I honored the gift of having been driven deep inside myself to listen to my heart and act accordingly. "Constriction" brought with it the transmutation to its opposite, expansiveness and the opening to the possibilities of my totality. "Financial pressure" revealed that my outer prosperity was a mirror for the inner richness I possessed. I expressed my gratitude to "emotional and verbal abuse" by dancing in the presence of my guides and angels, who helped me to see my own propensity for judgment and the depths of the well of unworthiness I had dug within myself. "Betrayal" brought insights about autonomy and sovereignty, and how my own actions had been inconsistent and self-defeating. As I danced "heartbroken, " I honored the gift of whole-heartedness, now feeling capable of applying it to this new phase of my life. On and on I danced, expressing each of the fifteen emotions and transfiguring them and myself into something more whole and integrated. My ceremony was a symbolic act of release that affected me in deeply cleansing ways, and within days of it I learned that Marcus had entered into a new relationship, which released me in an entirely different way. I was happy for him, for I knew and respected the woman he was seeing, although I have to admit that I also felt deeply hurt that I had been so quickly replaced.

I continued to read about Sedona, learning as much as I could. I knew I was to go to Sedona to work with the land and with the ancient knowledge encoded in Mother Earth, but I still did not know what exactly I was to do or what this information was all about. Then one evening while reading further about Sedona, I came across a description of Sedona that identified it as a land where the "Ancient Wise Ones," the shamans, used to reside. It was a place where many of these wise spirits, now incarnated back into the body, were being magnetically drawn to retrieve information from the rocks, where it had long ago been coded for safe keeping. I had a "eureka" moment. Yes, that's it! I had been correct when I had joked around with Marcus that I was going to be a secretary for the rocks. I remembered back to the day when I had been sitting in the stone circle and had first heard the word "Sedona." At that moment I had felt like something was clicking into place, almost as if inside of me a combination lock had spun, found the correct combination, and opened a locked box. I now felt certain that long ago I had been a record keeper, one of the ones who had encoded the ancient wisdom into the rocks. Now, I was to retrieve those records, the very information that I had keyed into rocks in ancient times. I was to return it to the people, who were now ready to receive it.

I was beginning to understand—and to accept—the enigmatic messages of the Emerald Kingdom I had been receiving over so many years. The records I was to retrieve were part of the Emerald

Records that have been long hidden from the human race. These Earth records were kept from us until such time that it was safe for us to receive such information. Mass consciousness was now ready to receive this information and our vibrational frequency and spiritual capability now able to integrate it. I realized it was time for us all to invite more light into the planet and into our lives. Mother Earth loves us, but we had lost our collective connection with her. I was to contribute to the remembering of the natural way and to the bridging of the separation between our own hearts and the Earth Mother's Emerald heart.

The messages continued to come. One day, during a massage with Sheila, I had a vision that took me by surprise. As Sheila pressed down onto two strategic points of the adrenal area of my back, I dropped into a vision. I saw my right hand reach out to shake hands with a huge talon. I thought it was the talon of an eagle, but as the bird coalesced into form in my vision, I was surprised to see an owl. It was huge—at least twelve feet tall, and its large eyes reflected the sun's light into mine. It seemed to bow toward me, in what I took to be acknowledgment and recognition, inviting me into the world of its own dreaming. My visionary self bowed reverently in response, and then the vision evaporated.

I didn't put too much credence in this experience and chalked it up as just another anomalous event in my life. I actually forgot about it until one evening when I was reading further about Sedona. It was with surprise, and even shock, that I read that the Ancient Wise Ones of Sedona were part of the Great Owl Clan.

During this period, my dream life was especially intense. Most nights I received dream revelations about ways that I could enter caves and work with the red rocks. I was shown how to place my hands in certain configurations on the belly of the cave wall in order to facilitate the energy flow and better attune to the rocks. I was shown how to "enter" into the rocks themselves. I was instructed to always keep my right hand moving, so that as I traveled into a dimensional doorway I could keep my awareness connected to my physical body, which would enable me to return to the physical plane when I was ready to return to it. I remember one dream that was particularly strange. It was as if I was observing myself in action in someone else's dream. I was having a conversation with the full moon, and she called out my name, "Amalia!" as if she were trying to awaken me from a deep sleep. Then I heard her suggest, "It's time to write your book, don't you think?"

"What shall I call it?" I asked.

"A Class Journey," she answered.

I awoke with a start, the name of the book reverberating through me. What an odd title, I thought. I turned in bed and stared out the window, and there was the full moon, willfully peeking through the tree branches. I remembered back to all the times the moon had captured my attention, drawing me with her light through a crack between this world and her own. I was indeed on a journey of some kind, in a classroom that seemed stranger to me than any I could have imagined.

During my last few weeks in Australia, I cleared up all the loose ends of my business and spent time with my family and friends. I said goodbye to the longtime clients I had had in my practice, and I negotiated still difficult territory with Marcus as we settled the final details of our financial life. I also visited my mother one last time. My visit was going to be short, only a few hours in which we could share a cup of tea and spend some quality time together, but while I was there I was abruptly overcome with a fever. For no apparent reason, my temperature skyrocketed, and my mother quickly put me to bed. It turned out that I had chicken pox! For days I sweated as my fever spiked, my mother ministering to me the whole time. Obviously, my inner child was expressing itself in the most direct and uncomfortable of ways. My body-mind was ingenious. The little girl in me needed nurturing, it needed to be home with her mother, and I came down with an illness that usually strikes children to get what was needed. I wish I had chosen another way, for the blisters were insanely itchy and my scratching only caused more stinging pain. I particularly remember my misery when on the fourth day I dragged myself to the bathroom very late one night, weak and miserable and in a lot of pain. My body felt dense, heavy, and toxic. On my way to the bathroom, I was bemoaning my state, feeling sorry for myself. My body was scabby with poxes and along with this unbearable discomfort I was suffering with menstrual cramps. I came to a stop, not able to move any further on the living room floor from the pain I felt physically in my body and emotionally in my still-broken heart, when I saw it—a silvery cord stretched outward from my navel. I followed the cord outwards with my eyes and was startled to see that there I was, another me at the other end of the cord. It was not a physical representation of me but a small ball of light. I knew it was me floating out there on the end of this ribbon of light, making my journey home. I energetically connected with this other me—with my light being—and instantly felt weightless and free, unencumbered by my sick body and my bemoaning state. I felt myself floating away, drifting off into nothingness, into freedom. Then suddenly I heard the voice of my higher self sternly admonish me, calling me back from wherever I was floating away to. "Amalia! Amalia, what are you doing? Come back! Come back now, Amalia!" Come on Amalia, you can do it." I didn't seem to have the strength or the will to return down that silver cord to my physical body, but as I heard my higher self command me to return, I somehow did. As I returned to normal awareness in my sweaty, throbbing physical body, I wondered if I had just come close to dying. (I was told later that chicken pox can be fatal to adults, and I certainly felt that to be true from how sick I was and how much I suffered.)

When I got myself back into bed, I knew I had to change my attitude. I could not allow myself to stew in my misery. I was a healer, and here I was indulging myself like the worst of patients. I had an advanced tool kit for healing, and I had better darn well start using it. If I wanted to serve others I had better start by serving myself, by returning myself to good health. Once I changed my frame of mind, it was easy to change my physical state, and I quickly recovered. In fact, I recovered not only my physical health, but gained a new zest for life. I found a deep reservoir of energy from which I drew to speed up my leaving, ready to take on the challenge of my calling.

Interestingly, just days before my departure from Australia, I attended a "Down to Earth Festival," which is a recurring event where thousands of people from all walks of life meet over four days to dance, hear music and come back to Earth to cut loose from their everyday routine. It was just what I needed and wanted, now that I felt whole and healthy again. So, I contacted some new friends, ones I had made after my separation from Marcus, and arranged to meet them there. As they saw me approaching, they began to shout, "Amalia is here! Hey, everybody, Amalia is here!" Then they broke out into an operatic version of the "Hallelujah Chorus," only they changed the words, singing at the top of their lungs, "Amalia, Amalia, Amalia Amalia Amaaaleeeya." Soon other people, strangers to me, joined in, all singing at different intervals, so the line was echoing throughout the crowd. I laughed with embarrassment and delight, feeling the love coming from my friends and the singing crowd. I felt that after my illness I had been reborn, and here was my choir of angels heralding my arrival back into the circuit of life. I knew at that moment that I had truly departed from my old life and accepted the call to embark upon the journey of a new life, one that waited for me halfway around the world, in Sedona, Arizona.

Chapter 4:

Aloha Hawai'i Dreaming.

I had imagined how I would feel on the plane that would take me from Australia into the unknown and now as I sat aboard the airliner, I felt exactly as I had imagined I would: a sad sweetness of surrender tinged with a joyful anticipation of adventure. I felt only a slight drag from the past, for I had worked hard to cleanse myself emotionally and materially. I also could not really project into the future, for I did not know what it might hold for me. This was a modern renunciation, from home to homelessness, with the detachment of blood ties toward an uncertain bonding with Earth and with my trust in Mother/Father God. I was like the eagle now; streaming on the current of fate and letting it direct my flight.

When I arrived on the beautiful shores of Maui, Hawai'i, the balmy breeze was welcoming, and I breathed it in, infusing myself with the promise of finding my own natural rhythm once again. I flashed back to the "Love Zone" I had experienced in the hippie-land of the northeastern coast of Australia, where the electric blue butterflies had so freely flashed their brilliance, allowing themselves to be carried on the wind from the nectar of one flower to another. If I was to journey to Sedona, I wanted to be as open and free as those butterflies. I wanted to be totally relaxed and clear in my sense of self, and healed of my pain and heartache, so that I could truly honor the information from the rocks that I was to retrieve. As I took my first steps on the ancient island of Maui, I reiterated my commitment to undertake whatever mission Spirit had designated for me, but first I needed to recharge my inner batteries—to rest, recuperate, and rediscover my playfulness. By doing so, I hoped to allow myself time away from the emotional intricacies of my relationships in Australia to recover my innocence and further heal my still aching heart. "Who am I without the struggle and pain?" I asked myself. "Who am I when I am at play in the Sacred Garden?"

I had friends in Maui, including Ariel Spilsbury, who lived on the island. I loved her sense of self, both outer and inner. Her silver-golden hair crowned her head like a unicorn's mane. Her blue eyes clear and true of which one could not help but trust for the wisdom they are windows to. Her every action and word was dedicated to the Goddess as she wielded her wit like a sword of truth with which she knighted those around her. She and her family greeted me warmly, and during my stay, they worked with me to help me find my inner child and embrace my own goddess within.

"Mother Maui," as the island is often called, was restorative to my spirit. The island is gorgeous in its profusion of greenery. I felt wrapped in the green mantle of love, accepted and expected to flourish in spirit just as profusely as the plants did in size and number and variety. This was literally the Emerald Green Realm. I felt my emerald vision reaching out toward me from all sides, interrupted only by the stunning white-break of waterfalls that cascaded down to feed secretive pools and the crystalline clarity of the green-blue ocean that graciously baptized me to my natural self every time I swam in it.

I soon fell in with a group of ocean-loving friends and we'd go to "Little Beach" every Sunday afternoon. When we weren't eating or playing in the surf, we would make music with abandon—playing guitars, didgeridoos, and drums—and dance until the sun had set. Then we would swim some more and howl as the moon rose. Whales and dolphins would sometimes swim by, perhaps drawn by our play. At such times I could hardly believe how radically my life had changed. I would look around to all my new friends and marvel at their freedom of spirit. They seemed at home here, at one with the tides and the sand, with the sun and the moon and the wildness of the landscape. I loved to simply observe them as they played like innocent children, their bodies natural, healthy, and toasted brown, or as they climbed a tree to scan the horizon searching for whales and dolphins. The call "Whale!" would bring all activity to a stop and silence would descend as we watched the mighty mammals of the sea breach the surface with grace and power. Then some of us would whoop and shout and crash into the surf to swim out toward the whales, wanting to get as close as possible.

The first time I swam out toward the whales, I was laughing so hard I could hardly swim. I wasn't a very strong swimmer then, so my laughter was directed not only at my awkward strokes but also at the pure joy of abandoning myself to the sea nonetheless and the awesome, almost magnetic, draw of the whales. I remember one such swim as particularly magical. It was early on Easter Sunday, and as I drew closer to the whales, I felt overcome with joy and touched with grace by the compassion that radiated from their magnanimous being. I felt cleansed, sanctified even, by the energy of these enormous and mysterious creatures of the deep.

That day held another gift for me. It was almost twilight, and we were dancing and drumming as the sun was descending toward the horizon. Its farewell always invoked a ceremonial dance in exchange for its solar blessing. The drums beat to the rhythm of the earth's heart, and the didgeridoos mimicked the low, deep droning of a whale's song, which brought back to me the distant dreamtime of Australia. I was amazed at the prevalence of didgeridoos in Hawai'i. This native Australian instrument was in vogue; while back home in Australia, the Native American drum was all the rage. I noted the irony of this musical exchange, for it seemed to me that ancient and sacred traditions were becoming the bridge that was helping connect all of us into a more global community.

As the pace of the music picked up, we pounded our feet into the sand in accompaniment to the drums, waving our hands in the air, swaying and swirling to the beat, our eyes closed and our spirits soaring. When the sun dipped into the ocean and the moon began to rise, our dancing transported us to those interior spaces where we were freed to our original natures and could easily slip the bounds of self to embody the ancient and primordial gods and goddesses. Then as the golden-orange sun was rolling under the horizon's brim, a lone, huge whale appeared. We watched transfixed as it mirrored the sun's motion, rolling on its side, disappearing under the surface except for one giant fin, which seemed to wave a greeting to us. We erupted in to song and praise; certain this was an Easter greeting or an omen of good fortune to come. The whale continued to roll, until just as the sun disappeared the whale too plunged back into the sea. As if that wasn't enough, it was a full moon that night and Haley's comet was riding the night sky leaving a blazing trail of light in the darkness. A day at the beach just didn't get any better than this Easter Sunday one.

In this magical land called Maui, I was able to release a lot of still unprocessed and pent-up pain. No matter how much I delved into myself psychologically, there seemed to be more blocks that needed to be recognized and released. As I continued to surrender to the flow of life, my emotions found their own natural flow as well, and I found myself shedding emotional pain along with my tears. At times like those, I often thought of Richard Bach's book Illusions. In the introduction, there is a story of a creature clutching a rocky bank in terror and fear that it will crash on to the rocks and die if it were to let go. Eventually, out of sheer exhaustion it lets go and when it does, its fear disappears as it enters a blissful free-fall into the flow of life's stream. I identified with that being, and allowed myself to unburden in a kind of emotional free-fall.

One day, during one of these weepy periods, I set off for Hāna, a more remote area on the eastern coast of Maui where I planned to stay for a short time. I wondered if this was a honeymooners' destination, since it was filled with couples walking hand in hand or arm in arm. I felt out of place, estranged even. "Could I be the only person visiting here who is alone?" I wondered. When the weather turned and it began to rain steadily over several days, I felt even more isolated. The weather seemed tied to my emotional state and it rained, and rained, and rained. After a few days of this down pouring, I thought I would go mad from the rain's incessant drum on the roof. Nature's relentless moisture provoked my own inner softening, and I cried and cried. The rain was cleansing and nourishing to the life of the island, and, alone and an island unto myself, my tears cleansed me. When the sun finally returned, so did my spirit and naturally enough, that's when I met Alejandro. My alone time was about to end.

Alejandro was a striking Argentinean, with big brown eyes, long dark hair, a dazzling smile, and healthy physique. Upon our first meeting, I recognized him as a "spiritual family member," one whom I felt akin to. I should have been wary of my attraction, for he looked astonishingly like my ex-husband, Marcus. I wondered if this wasn't Spirit's way of testing me, of providing me an opportunity to heal myself of Marcus once and for all. Of course, I had hoped this was not the case. I wanted Alejandro to be a fresh, new beloved, not an antidote to an old one.

Alejandro and I were like a match that strikes straw. We ignited quickly and flared brightly. Our rapport was instant, talking for hours on end, dancing naked on the starlit beach and laughing until our bellies hurt and our eyes teared up. We also spent time in sacred silence, or otherwise spoke soft healing words to each other. He was the most conscious person I had met in Maui so far and one who could match my energy and aliveness. Although I had made lots of wonderful friends, overall I found the people of the island quite "diluted" and a bit "floaty." I attributed this airiness to their being situated in the middle of the Pacific Ocean. They were a contrast to the pragmatic, grounded, and earthy types of Australia. Australians had the fire of the earth in them but the inhabitants of Maui seemed to waft through life like an ocean breeze or the swaying palm trees. I suppose that making such a judgment was unfair, but I couldn't deny it when I met Alejandro for he was grounded and concentrated, and I realized how much I missed those qualities. I emotionally dove into Alejandro as if he were the wild blue ocean. We became the best of friends and intimates. He reintroduced me to the silence that lies deep within us all. At times when I would get excited, Alejandro would hush me and urge me to go within, saying, "Amalia, remain still, be silent, it is in the silence that you will come to know yourself." This was challenging at first, as I felt chided, but I soon came to recognize the value of this silent place within my own inner sanctuary.

One weekend we camped on a beach where dolphins and whales often congregated and where we were energized by the constant rush of the ocean waves and freewheeling flight of sea birds. At night, we slept out in the open in sleeping bags under the glistening expanse of the star-filled sky and by day we thrummed along with the natural forces of life. It was here that I first began to actively listen to the wisdom from the records of time that lay deep inside me. At about four o'clock one morning, I was awakened by a brilliant flash of light. It was like God had taken a snapshot of us. I sat up with a jolt and scanned the still dark skies. I saw nothing unusual among the stars, so I simply sat in silence, with Alejandro asleep in a sleeping bag next to me. A tone then emerged from somewhere deep inside me, a sound both unfamiliar and familiar, for as a child I had often experimented with sounds my voice could make. This wasn't a beautiful and meditative tone, such as the mantra-like "Om" of Eastern traditions. It was a high-pitched clicking sound, even a little croaky, sort of what I imagined a dolphin might make if its click-like sounds were played in slow motion. It sounded like a coded language to me. Then just as suddenly as I had begun making the sounds, I stopped. I sat in the dark of silence for a while, and then I heard the inner voice of my Higher Self speak. It began to speak with what I can only characterize as some sort of frequency tutorial:

Whales, turtles, and elephants are all of the same soul kind. They are the keepers of the records of wisdom of the Ancient Wise Ones. They all have creased gray skin, and each carries its own brand of prehistoric similarities. They have traveled through the evolution of their souls with a "seeming suffering," and from this seeming suffering, the powerful posture of vulnerability, of innocent wisdom, is reached. Through the embracing of feelings, the pain of ignorance is transmuted into the ecstasy of knowingness, of "nowingness," of the innocence in the present moment that holds within it the wisdom and records of all time. This is an "Alchemy of the Soul." Dolphins have also reached an innocent wisdom, not through "seeming suffering" but through the joy of, and elation for life. They are the adolescents, whereas the whales, turtles, and elephants are the elders of the community. It is through the silence within and the embracing of feelings that one reaches this innocent wisdom. It is through this sonar sound, this cracking tone of the silence between the sound, that the gap between space and time opens, like the correct combination of a safe clicking open and giving access to the records of time found in stillness.

In the stance of stillness time stands still.

A few years before I had heard the words "Frequency Tutonics" in a dream that I had, and I now understood what it meant—it was the sound I had just made so spontaneously and that had opened me to recovering this "record" of the Ancient Ones. In a flood of insight I heard more:

It is through inner stillness and the simple awareness it brings that we connect to creation beyond time. Life-forms have actually become more complex over time, and the key to unraveling those complexities is the expansion into timelessness; this is achieved by accessing the stillness. It is in this stance of stillness, then, that actually unravels time, and in so doing there is a simultaneous unraveling of our spiral DNA and RNA, of our programming and conditioning, which releases locked memories. The feeling of accessing these deep memories is at first uncomfortable because tension is also released, similar to how kinetic energy is released when a tightly wound spring is allowed to unwind. This kind of "undoing" is also an entranceway into being and an opening to the freedom to live in the present. The "timeless now" is truly the only point when we can receive the gift of life and access the library of records that wait for us in the silence and stillness of the present moment.

I was startled at the information that flowed through me. I felt it was important, and that perhaps I had tapped into the wisdom of the ocean as a conscious being itself. I pondered about how whales move in the ocean; they move in slow motion, seeming to stretch time, which invokes the feeling of ecstasy, a feeling beyond time and space. Because of this, the whale's movement is forever remembered, and our memory like that of the whales becomes an infinite ocean that stands still in time. I was unraveling the complexity of time within myself, and many memories began to rise to the surface of my awareness. From that night on, I entered the realm of silence more frequently and became dedicated to the still-point within.

Not long after this tutorial, I experienced a different kind of still-point only this one was physical. One day, while I was frolicking at the edge of the waters, I felt so in tune with Nature and so at peace that I found myself not breathing. It wasn't that I was consciously holding my breath, but more that I simply felt no need to breathe. I felt wrapped in a blanket of profound stillness and safety, and felt elated and held in the midst of heaven on Earth. At that moment I did not need anything, desiring nothing, not even air. The world around me took on a tingling brightness. Everything looked acutely sparkly and new and I momentarily wondered if I had somehow entered another dimension. Then I remembered another experience like this that had occurred, just as strangely and out of the blue, several years before. Marcus and I had been dining at a seaside restaurant, celebrating our anniversary. Apropos of nothing that was happening then, I just calmly noticed that I had not taken a breath for a few minutes. As if this were a normal course of events, I looked at Marcus, and said, "I've noticed I haven't taken a breath for quite awhile, can you stay present with me and monitor me to see where this goes?" When I stopped talking, I once again did not feel the need to breathe. Marcus went along with me and observed, as I sat not breathing for several minutes. Then for several more minutes. I felt no pressure in my chest, no need to try to control my diaphragm muscles, or to take another breath. I simply felt serene and still rather, soft of spirit. When Marcus announced that five minutes had gone by, I hardly took notice. I felt safe and my body was not under any stress. Then, as Marcus marked the sixth minute, I felt myself take a gentle breath, and I returned to my normal breathing pattern again. About a year later, I read in a small Ascension booklet, that as we begin to raise our vibration, we will start to breathe from what is termed our "Morontia Body." This is explained as a crystalline matrix that is situated outside our body, and when we breathe through this matrix, we no longer need to take physical breaths through our lungs. By using this crystalline matrix, the book explained, we are breathing Spirit directly into our etheric body (our energetic body), which then feeds the physical body. This newest non-breathing episode seemed connected to the frequency tutorial about timelessness and I was beginning to experience stillness in ways that were different from my previous experiences in meditation. I was content to simply accept this information and these experiences at face value, feeling no compulsion to analyze or prove anything. I had finally caught up to the present living in the "now" with whatever was happening.

I had now spent six months in the magic of Maui. I felt rejuvenated and recharged. My immersion into the wildness of life with Alejandro finally ended, for he needed to return to Buenos Aires to take care of some family business and I knew it was time for me toá move on as well. We parted with the deep bonds of friendship, knowing we would see each other again some day.

I was now ready to continue my journey toward Sedona. That was where the voice of Mother Earth had commissioned me to go, but I felt I could not go there directly. My journey was a sort of zigzag, taking me from place to place, like stepping stones through the garden of the world. I would go first to Los Angeles, meeting up there for a few days with a friend, and then I would head south to Mexico, to the Yucatán Peninsula. From there I planned to take a northward skip to Sedona, Arizona, and the neighboring areas. The Yucatán was important for one main reason— it was the ancient home of the Maya, who traveled north to Arizona and together with the Hopi Indians, created the ancestry of the Anasazi, the original inhabitants of the Sedona region. I felt I needed to pay homage to the Maya and practice retrieving from the rocks there before I entered the heart of Sedona.

After wrapping things up in Maui, I made my travel arrangements, and prepared to leave. On the day of my departure however, I was once again waylaid by fate. At the last minute, I was invited to participate in a Native American ceremony—a vision quest followed by a Peyote Medicine ceremony, which would be led by a Native American teacher. I had already experienced my own personal vision quest on my five acres of land, but had never participated in a "real" one held under the guidance of a native elder. I was fascinated by what I had heard about visionary "plant medicines," such as peyote and had read a few books by Carlos Castaneda and had been intrigued by his descriptions of the spirit of this Earth medicine. Being a modern medicine woman myself, practicing herbal medicine and naturopathy, I was curious to explore this visionary plant in terms of its effects on both body and mind. I also had learned from experience not to dismiss lightly the workings of synchronicity, and felt that the opportunity for these experiences might be fate's way of preparing me for my work in Sedona. So, I changed my departure plans and headed for the ceremony.

I flew with five friends to the Big Island of Hawai'i, feeling a bit like I was off to see the Wizard of Oz. We were picked up at the airport by a couple of young and strong, handsome men who drove us in a battered pickup truck to the site of the ceremony, which was appropriately private. We met several others who would be joining us for the ceremony, and were then directed to a large teepee, where my friends and I would spend the night.

I slept well. In the morning, as I rummaged through my bag for a change of clothes, a small, gray mouse scurried out of it, ran up and over my hand, and out of the teepee. Mouse energy! In the Native American tradition, animals are associated with states of being, and mouse equates with adopting an attitude of innocence and watching for the details in life. So, I accepted this message from Spirit and noted that I should be like the mouse, alert to my immediate surroundings and in a place of trust and innocence during the ceremony. As we exited the teepee, a young man pointed to a tree whispering, "Look! There are two hawks mating!" Hawk, is the messenger of visions and acts as a guardian spirit. To catch a glimpse of hawks mating was rare indeed, casting a mantle of reverence over us, which set the tone for the quest. It seemed like animal messenger spirits were all around us, ready to witness our prayers during the ceremony and to deliver them to Great Spirit.

I thought we were going to go directly into ceremony, but the young men who had picked us up from the airport came over and asked if we would like to go for a swim with the dolphins. With great joy we accepted and piled in the back of the pickup truck for the ride to the beach. The drive was divine. The balmy, early-morning breeze rushed through our hair. Above, the emerald-green canopy of lush tropical trees was split here and there by brilliant blue sky, and on our left laid the vast ocean that was to receive us. We were told that this road was called the "Red Road" and was once the ancient trail for the Ali'i, (the ancient Hawaiian royalty.) I felt the stir of my ancient self. The Big Island seemed to me to be more primitive and raw than Maui and the fire in the belly of the earth—the volcano Goddess Pele—was located not far from here. I turned toward where Pele dwelled and thanked her for the opportunity to witness the magic she had laid down before us. When we reached the beach, we saw an elder man at the top of the ridge with a long, white beard. He was shouldering a large Macaw bird that was resplendently feathered in robust primary colors. We chatted with the man for a few moments, and the bird joined in with squawks and calls. This bird had a language all of its own that its owner William, understood and responded to. He told us the bird was offering us a blessing for our vision quest, a blessing we graciously welcomed.

We climbed down an embankment of ragged lava rocks to the shoreline, where the sand was pitch black. I had never seen a black-sand beach before, and it was so odd that I felt I was in a dream. We almost immediately spotted dolphins, about eight of them, and without thought we threw off our clothes and dove into the water. The dolphins accepted us, and we swam and frolicked with them as if we were all old friends.

I was the first to swim back to shore, and as I did, I passed a man bobbing up and down in the water, his arms up over his head so that his body was a like a spear poking up through the water's surface. We did not speak as I slowly swam past him toward shore, but our eyes met and we greeted each other without words.

Once back on shore, I dressed and decided to explore the area. Not far up the beach, at a section of cliff and rocks, I came across a small, shallow cave whose semicircular opening looked as though someone had cut it perfectly into the rock face. I decided to tune into the cave, so I crouched down and began to enter, but I had barely breached the opening when I was literally thrown out. I felt something, a strong energy; push me back and out of the cave. I instantly understood that the cave was not welcoming me, for whatever reason. I bowed down with my forehead to the ground and spoke to the spirit of the cave. "I'm so sorry. I don't know what I was thinking, please forgive me for entering without permission." When I looked up, I noticed a perfect spider's web at the top edge of its entrance. Dangling from a single web thread was a long elongated leaf, shaped like a feather. I was now captivated like an insect in the web itself, for this arrangement of web and leaf looked exactly like a Native American dream catcher. Originally, Native Americans made dream catchers by bending a thin, flexible branch, usually from a willow tree, into a hoop and scooping a spider's web into its circle. In modern dream catchers, the web is replaced with a manmade one, woven from sinew. Usually there is a small hole in the center of the web. The dream catcher's purpose is to snag negative energies, visions and bad dreams in the web as the feathers filter this negative energy back to the earth for cleansing. But good dreams and visions are able to pass through the small central portal and so come to the dreamer. To the upper left of the cave, a small but thriving beehive was buzzing with activity. I took note of it as another message from Spirit: to gather the sweetness of my experience and store it in the cells of my "bee-ing." I recognized this place as sacred and quietly left, knowing that I had just received another lesson in my education of attuning to the rock kingdom: to ask permission to enter their world before entering.

I walked back to the beach where my friends had returned from their swim. As I neared them, I heard a distant, melodic chanting, but couldn't determine from where it was coming. It was Hawaiian chanting, and the more I strained to listen, the more I felt memory rising within me. I knew this sound, although I was certain I had never heard it before in this lifetime. I had to find out who was chanting and why. Two of my friends, Stefan and Marnie, followed me as I tracked down the source of the beguiling sound. As we headed down the beach, drawing closer to a vegetated cove, I suddenly was stopped in my path by a purple light that seemed to be seeping up like vapor from the sand a short distance ahead. I pointed to it and called Stefan's attention to it. "Stefan, look at the purple light!" He looked toward where I was pointing but I could tell from the expression on his face that he couldn't see it. "Right there!" I insisted, continuing to point. The purple light was seeping up from the sand in several spots. "And there, and over there. Purple light. Don't you see it?" But Stefan shook his head and told me that he didn't. I turned to Marnie in hope that she may have caught sight of it, but she didn't see anything either. Onward we continued, my two friends looking at me a little strangely but comfortable enough with my "second sight" to not question my sanity.

We finally found the source of the chanting. It was the man I had seen bobbing in the water. We observed silently as he chanted while dancing on the sand, his long, dark hair falling down his back as he reached his arms up and turned his proud face heavenward. He was oblivious to us, in a world of his own, perhaps in the world of his ancestors. After a time, his dance ended, and he welcomed us as if he had been expecting us. He introduced himself as Manu Kiha Pai. He was quite eloquent in his speech and yet simple in manner, but during the course of time we spent talking with him, we learned that he is a kahuna-warrior. His name means "bird" and "supernatural lizard awakening." The Kāhuna, we learned, are experts in various fields who may function as shamans and preserve the ancient indigenous spiritual tradition of Hawai'i through their practice and teachings. Manu explained that his earlier bobbing swim in the ocean was actually a daily prayer ritual he performs. His chanting was for the healing and purification of Hawai'i and its people. As Manu told us ancestral stories and of his sacred commitment to the healing of his land, I felt myself traveling deeper and deeper into the timelessness of his dark eyes. At one point, Stefan asked him to say more about the chanting that had drawn us to him and told him how I especially had been pulled by it, as if I were a robot under someone else's command. Manu explained, "I was invoking the purple healing energy, the color of Queen Lili'uokalani, to help heal the peoples of Hawai'i and the Mother Earth herself." Stefan, Marnie, and I eyed each other as we silently acknowledged that the purple light I had seen seeping up from the sand had not been my imagination.

It was early afternoon before we returned to the teepee to prepare for the ceremony. Before we could begin the four-day vision quest, we had to cleanse ourselves with a sweat lodge cere-mony. This is a steam bath where water is thrown on to fired up rocks within the confines of a small domed structure that is specially built for the purpose of purification. Native Americans regard the sweat lodge as their church; a sacred place to cleanse and purify themselves and during which their prayers rise to Great Spirit on the steam from the heated rocks. Crawling into the small opening of the a sweat lodge on your knees is equated with humbling yourself on returning back to the womb of Mother Earth, and the rocks and water are seen as having their own living spirits that participate in the ceremony as our relations. This sweat lodge ceremony would prepare us to meet a vision during our four-day quest.

During the ceremony, the fiery lava rocks were aglow in the central pit of the lodge, and their heat and light rekindled my memory and strengthened my connection to the blood and tears of the earth as represented by the fiery volcano of Kīlauea, where Goddess Pele lives. As the water hit the rocks, sending clouds of hot steam upward, I felt the inner sizzling of my emotions, and I cleansed myself of buried pain with tears during the ceremony. When the lodge was over, I crawled out of the lodge feeling cleansed and refreshed inside. My body was another matter, feeling like an old weary elephant lumbering toward a graveyard to lay down its hulking body and surrender its life to Mother Earth. My body was telling me that although I had done a lot of clearing and divesting of my past and my emotional wounds, if I was going to be a clear vessel in service to the rocks and to Mother Earth, I still had more work to do toward cleansing my physical body.

Later that day, we were led into the jungle-like forest that surrounded us, to choose a private location where we would stay the four days and three nights of our quest. The area in which we were questing was a tropical site that featured an ancient volcanic crater-lake. It is one of the most beautiful sacred areas that I had visited so far in my travels, and I eagerly but solemnly introduced myself to the spirits of the land as I scouted out my spot for the quest. I settled upon an area where the ground provided a lush green carpet and one huge tree overspread its thickly leafed branches to create a safe haven for me. The area was heavily vegetated with jungle vines and evergreen trees and I felt as if I were in a living emerald cave. I marveled at the glorious landscape around me. I nestled into it as if I had always belonged there, and I drank in the alluring twilight as day dimmed to darkness. The stillness was intense and captivating. In the deepening darkness, I could just make out the glow of the ceremonial fire that had been made back by the sweat lodge. It was quite a distance from me, and all I could see was its slight orange glow in the dark. The fire keepers would tend that lodge fire for the four days we would be questing and Kingfisher, the Native American Elder and leader of the ceremonies, would "hold the space" for us to gain our strength and receive the vision we needed to align with our individual paths. The expanse of sky above was ablaze with stars and a crescent Shiva moon. I also saw my good and faithful star friends up there—the constellation of Orion, the Pleiades, and the Hyaides of the Taurus constellation. Legend has it that the gods put Taurus, the bull, between Orion and the Pleiades to prevent Orion from having his way with the Seven Sisters. I had thought to myself that Orion must have had a high opinion of himself to think he could seduce all seven sisters! The stars seemed especially bright that night, like diamonds studding the black velvet cape of night, and I felt content and satisfied to be me, there, in the dark, sandwiched between the lush green blanket of Earth and the dark cape of Sky. Two shooting stars shot across the sky, one after the other, bidding me a good night's sleep. I then tugged the blankets up around me as the night took me into its arms.

Morning, however, brought the work of the quest front and center. I was up at dawn, and since we were fasting during the quest, there was nothing to do but dress and get to the spiritual work that lay before me. I stood barefoot on the ground, sending my energy down into Mother Earth like a tree sends down roots, and raised my face toward the sky. I raised my arms and invoked the spirits of the land, my guides and guardian spirits, the angels of light and love, and the Christ within. "Great Spirit," I said aloud and firmly, "I am here to clear away anything in myself and in my genetic lineage that is impeding or stopping me from being a clear and direct conduit of your divine energy. I pray that the old cobwebs of pain and fear that hold me hostage to the past and prevent me from being here fully in the present moment be gently swept away. I am here to divine the energy of light and love and to anchor it here and now into my body, into the heart of matter itself, and to offer it to the earth for healing. Please assist me now, as I put this time aside to purify my body, mind and spirit." I spent most of my time silently observing Nature and alternately meditating and sleeping, but always, I offered similar prayers. With no one to speak with except the spirits and with no distractions like preparing food, I prayed and prayed and prayed.

On the second day, I was given a vision. As I sat meditating, a "knowing" arose within me and I felt a scenario unfold to my inner eyes that seemed as real as any landscape around me:

I am a gigantic, prehistoric dragon curled up, lying dormant in a colossal egg that looks like a huge extraterrestrial vessel or vehicle of some kind. My eyes have been shut for eons, and I am unknown to the outside world.

Then, in the same moment that my dragon eyes open, my own eyes opened and the vision ended. My heart was racing from the feeling of intense identification with the dragon. I had been the dragon, and I knew myself to be intimately connected to the earth, as an ancient guardian of Earth Wisdom. Aha! I had a sudden insight. The dragon is of the serpentine lineage, which is connected to the kundalini life-force energy known in the Hindu tradition. In that tradition, humans are seen as having multiple energy centers—wheels of energy called chakras that connect our physical being to the etheric realm. The kundalini is the energy that lies coiled like a serpent at the chakra center at the base of the spine, and it is said to rise up the spine to the base of the brain as one raises one's vibration and awakens spiritually and energetically. This serpentine energy also correlates to the helical DNA strands that provide the code for our humanness. The serpentine dragon also lies at the basement of the earth and once awakened, unwinds and releases the DNA codes—the wisdom of the earth back to the people. I understood the dragon vision, momentary as it was, to be a kundalini awakening: the wisdom lying dormant within me and in the earth awoke and sparked the force of new life into wakefulness, and into the waking "now." The dragon is also a symbol of illusion and magic, and with the opening of my dragon eyes, I felt that I saw through the illusion of my past and of my personal myths. My connection to myself as a wisdom keeper of the earth had now been further awakened.

However much I was awakened to live in the now, the third day of the quest seemed to drag out forever. Still, I kept myself centered and present until the urge came to dance, to honor the four directions and the elements of earth, fire, water and air. I had brought some swan feathers with me, which represent grace and transformation and took one up in each hand. I called upon Great Spirit to flow through my body and into my heart so that my dancing would become a blessing and a prayer to honor Mother Earth. As I began to move, I fanned the swan feathers through the air, intending that any cobwebs of the old be dusted from the innermost recesses of my body and being. I danced and danced, losing myself in the sway and swirl of my body and the elements around me. I had become connected to the "All of Nature." Eventually, I laid myself down on the earth, belly to belly to the Mother, and began to breathe in a pattern common to an energy technique called Rebirthing. I breathed strongly, with as little pause as possible between each inhale and exhale, so that my breath became a continuous motion, like a cyclic wave of air, rolling in and out, in and out. Within minutes, another vision came upon me:

I am combing Marcus's long, silky, dark hair. It is full of knots and I am gently combing them out. Then the strands of his hair morph into the spiraling strands of DNA and RNA, and as I comb his hair, I am clearing blockages created by my emotional entanglements with him. I am literally combing the knots out of my past! The word "emergence" rises to consciousness, and I somehow know there is a mountain nearby and the mountain cradles a huge egg deep within its recesses. I am in the egg. I can feel another me—a new me—curled up inside the womb of an egg and about to emerge.

What is this message? I played word games to decipher what the word "emergence" meant in this vision: energy, emerge, merge, urge—the emergency of the urge to merge with energy? I rolled over onto my back and on opening my eyes, I saw above me in the clear blue sky, the thrilling arc of a rainbow. What's more, two hawks were riding thermal currents high above, circling and soaring. I felt this to be a sign, an acknowledgment of my interpretation. (I discovered much later, that after years of intensive research, the owner of the land unearthed an ancient Hawaiian legend of *mo'o* (the dragon). Believed to be half woman and half reptile, the *mo'o* often resided in deep pools of water and guarded their eggs along with the land!)

It began to drizzle, and before long it rained down hard, so I quickly set up my tent and crawled into it. As I lay there with my eyes closed, listening to the drumming of raindrops, I saw with my inner eyes another egg, only this time it was small and cracked open. I was holding it in my left hand and with my right I held a green twig, which I tenderly dipped into the egg's yolk. I sat up to write in my journal. I let my mind wander, writing all the associations I could make about eggs and started with fertility, youth, potential, incubation, nesting, protection, hatching and ended with emerging into the next phase of life. Then I lay down again, closed my eyes, and almost at once the egg vision arose again. I was diving into the immensity of the egg's yolk, straight into the golden heart of matter itself! But I was startled from my inner reverie by the sound of the tent zipper. The sound was amplified and seemed in super-slow motion, as I distinctly heard the zipper being pulled down over each tooth. Someone was entering the tent unannounced!

It was Anton, one of the other people on the vision quest whom I had not gotten to know very well. I was too startled by his sudden appearance to say anything as he crawled on his hands and knees toward me with great deliberation, until finally he was kneeling right next to me. He was wearing skimpy little shorts and, astonished as I was by this sudden and unexpected intrusion, I noticed how muscular his thighs were. We were supposed to be alone for the whole of our vision quest, and I could not figure out why he was here. I raised my hand and touched his thigh to make sure he was real and not just a figment of my imagination. He was solid, really there, kneeling before me. I looked up into his eyes, and I felt almost assaulted by their penetrating boldness, by the pride I saw there, and the indignation I felt streaming from them.

Transfixed as I was, I finally emerged from my stupor and went on high alert. I knew he was here to rape me. I actually heard him telling me in my head, like I was reading his thoughts. "I am going to rape you, and then I am going to have to kill you." Doom descended, and in an instant I was overcome with fear and hopelessness. And then I woke up.

A dream! How could this have been a dream? I had been awake, hadn't I? Lying in my tent writing in my journal about eggs. For a moment I couldn't tell what was real. I could have sworn everything I had just "experienced" had happened. It felt so real. What concerned me, too, was why I had dreamed a rape scenario after having such a wonderful egg vision? A thought occurred to me, a memory really. I remembered back to a time in Australia when at a seminar a psychic had singled me out of a group of thirty women to tell me something she had seen in my emotional field. She felt compelled to tell me about an important message she had about a past life. "Your heart is troubled," she had said. "You have held a wound within your heart for lifetimes and it is time to let go and forgive. You were raped by several Native American Indians and then they killed you, and since then you have held a deep anger in your heart toward men, and the love that you seek shall not be able to come forth until you open your heart and forgive."

Perhaps Anton had been one of those Indian men from a past life. I really did not know what to think, for I was still confused about what had happened and in disbelief that I had fallen asleep and dreamed. It all felt too real. I lay back down and this time made a conscious effort to sleep, which I did fitfully. I don't know what time it was during the night when I awoke with a horrible dread running through my being. I heard footsteps crunching on the leaves as someone approached the tent. I quickly clicked on my flashlight and unzipped the tent just enough to look out. The glowing blob of a flashlight was moving toward me. I knew it was Anton! I leaped up, threw myself out of the tent and began running down the track toward where the group teepee was located. As I crashed through the undergrowth, I felt certain that the dream I had was a warning, and now Anton was really here, seeking to hurt me. I was in disbelief, and in panic.

I must have been off the path to the teepee, on some other trail, for ahead of me I saw a house with lights on inside. I made a beeline for it, in a desperate attempt to reach safety. I ran to the door and found it was open. I flew into the house, looking for someone, anyone. At just that moment, a small, dark-haired woman emerged from the bathroom, her hair still wet from her shower. Surprisingly, she did not appear overly startled, and simply stood there and listened as I breathlessly explained what was happening. Still, she didn't say a word, which even in my panic I thought was most odd. But there was something about her look: she seemed to know what was going on but her eyes held a power and a surety that kept me rooted in place. She began to draw the window blinds down, and as the last one descended, I woke up.

"Oh, no," I moaned to myself. "This can't be another dream!" It had all felt so real. I now didn't know if I was asleep or awake, and I couldn't prove to myself that I wasn't dreaming at that very moment. What was going on? I laid there in the dark, trembling in my sleeping bag, not able to identify what was reality and what was illusion and dream. I started to cry with fear coursing through me. How was I to know if I was asleep or awake? It was horrifying to me that I couldn't tell what was what. I was so paralyzed with fear that when the wind shook a cascade of raindrops onto my tent roof, I shrieked. The only thing I could think to do was to pray. I mumbled my prayer, at the same time trying to visualize the light of love and safety like an egg around my tent. I remember continuously saying to myself, "I am innocent, I am innocent. I am safe, I am safe." I couldn't stop crying, and I couldn't shake the fear and uncertainty of what was real and what was dream, and I found myself emitting a long, mournful shriek. The sound of my own pitiful voice brought me back to my senses a bit, and I remembered all my previous prayers, when I had asked to be released of any genetic or energetic blockages that might be impeding the flow of light and love through my being. Could this have been one of those blocks I am now facing?

I started to come around and realize what was really happening. My inner voice reached out and grabbed my attention. "Amalia! Get hold of yourself! Your fear is the very thing that has been impeding your freedom. It is the very feeling you now must embrace and allow to be fully expressed. Only then can you face the past that has been stalking you. This is it, Amalia. Now is the time. Embrace your fear and love it for the lessons it teaches you."

I felt the slow ebbing of the fear. Replacing it was the warmth of acceptance that my own mind, my own energy, had created this drama in order to teach me, releasing whatever it was within me that needed freeing. I felt a growing sense of wonder at how love seeks its way through fear, at how light seeks its way into the darkness and at how the past seeks its way into the present to be healed.

I now could rest. I felt proud that I had in some way "hatched" my fear, breaking through the hard shell of my heart. I realized that the woman who had been showering in my dream was the aspect of myself that was wise enough to not get caught up in the story or the drama of my wounded emotions. I drifted off to sleep with the certainty that I had finally gotten to the bottom of a deep wound, cleansed it thoroughly, and had even begun the process of healing it.

The next thing I remember was feeling Anton in my tent again, actually lying down peacefully beside me. With a long drawn out shriek I protested. "No!" followed by "Why is this happening again? This is a nightmare and I want out!" At that thought,

Anton's neck stiffened and his eyes hardened and begun to pierce my being with that same threatening look. I heard his thoughts again. "I'm going to rape you and then I'm going to have to kill you." I felt myself about to flee once more. Then I became lucid in my dream, saying to myself, "Hey, wait a minute! I am dreaming this now and I already dealt with this in my last dream. I've already journeyed into the realm of fear, embraced it, allowed it to show itself, and let it go with gratitude. I did my work! I am innocent!" With that pronouncement, Anton's eyes softened, exuding warmth and love, and he reached over and began to gently stroke my hair, shoulders, and arms. He touched me like one does a newborn baby, with caring and wonder. His eyes and his touch ushered me into the realm of love and security. I began to relax.

Again, the dream took an abrupt shift. In the midst of the serenity of Anton's touch, I heard the distant galloping of horse's hooves. I got up and unzipped the tent flap, and upon looking out, I saw a Native American man on a horse. He was a dark-haired Brave, a warrior whose face and torso were painted, and he was holding a medicine staff in his left hand. He beckoned me with his right hand, motioning me to follow him. I did not. Instead, I spoke in a strong and direct voice, "I am not going with you. I don't need you anymore. I am staying here." And in an even more assertive tone I commanded, "Go *now.*" The Indian said nothing, just looked at me and then quickly turned his horse and rode off.

I awoke again; knowing this time that I had been dreaming, and feeling grounded and centered. I could hardly believe the night I had just been through. Amazed at the clarity with which I remembered the dreams, and overcome by my confusion about what had been dream and what was reality. Dreams within dreams within dreams—I marveled at the process I had just endured. With the light of morning, I felt gratitude, honored to have been such an active participant in my own dreamtime. I contemplated how we each live in dreams within the dream. I thought that what had happened to me was not just the creation of my own unconscious, but perhaps a bleed-through into another portal. Into a timeless place where reality and illusion are no different, where love reveals everything unlike itself to be released and healed.

Thankfully, the remainder of the vision quest was restful. My major inner work was done, at least for now; my prayers had been answered. I was very pleased with the insight I had gained and felt renewed and cleansed. After the vision quest, however, came the peyote ceremony, and I wondered if I was up to it. Hadn't I done enough already? Peyote is a sacred plant to many peoples, especially those of the American southwest and South America. I had always held a place of respect in my heart for this sacred medicine, although I also admit that I had a bit of a romantic notion about it since I had read Carlos Castaneda's books. Peyote's visionary qualities were described as opening the window to the soul and to other dimensions. I decided to go the full distance and go ahead with the peyote ceremony to find out for myself what it might have to teach me.

The experience was anything but pleasant. In fact, it was a living hell. After questing for four days, which meant being alone in the open spaces of Nature, I found myself during the peyote ceremony, crammed into the teepee with all the other questers and many others I did not know who had joined us. The wood that was ablaze in the center pit of the teepee was shaped to represent a bird, perhaps an eagle or even more befitting, a phoenix that would rise from the ashes "after the death of the ego." Its head was facing south and around the pit was a crescent moon formed from pure white sand. Rattles and drums and singing filled the teepee, but none of them transported my attention from my discomfort. I felt stifled and almost claustrophobic. We were instructed to sit upright the whole evening, and it was all I could do to stay put and not flee from the teepee. The ceremony had barely started and I couldn't wait for it to end. I was tired and irritable, and to make matters worse, the man sitting to my left had a terribly loud voice and was singing the medicine songs out of tune. He was more than getting on my nerves—I wanted to annihilate him. I could hardly stand to be there, but I knew I had to stay. The ceremony would take all night. I somehow resolved to get my head and heart straightened out so I could not only bear it but also actually learn from the experience.

Soon the peyote was being passed around. I had heard that peyote tastes ghastly, but I wasn't prepared for the repulsiveness of its taste. The gruel-like mixture was foul, tasting so like a poison that my body resisted it as soon as it entered my system. Soon I was horribly sick; my energy and resistance were nonexistent- gone, and all I could do for the next few hours, was to sit on my knees with my head to the ground. Every few minutes I would attempt to sit straight and raise my head in an attempt to regain some measure of strength and grace, but I couldn't. I would collapse back down into a cowering bundle of despair. I just could not get myself together. Closing my eyes didn't help matters. With eyes closed I saw a dark pit of writhing rattlesnakes with the menacing "thThththth" sound of the rattlers. "This peyote is a poison!" I moaned to myself. "I want it out of my system now!"

Shamans say this is a sacred plant medicine, a gift from the earth, and that it will speak to you of its wisdom and make you well. But I couldn't see the gift in it at all. In fact, I felt sure it was a toxic poison that my healthy body was reacting to. I had been told that peyote will make you throw up, and that the act of purging is a form of "getting well" because you expel whatever in you that needs releasing and cleansing. Well, I certainly felt sick, and I wanted to vomit in order to feel better, but nothing came up. I was stuck in this continual spiraling nausea where every second was an eternal hell. All I wanted was for the sun to emerge and pierce the darkness. I knew that once the morning's light of day arrived, all would be well. But could I make it until then?

Hours passed and still there was no let up in my misery—or shall I say let out, for I did not "get well." Fortunately, a woman I knew, Monica, who was responsible for cooking the feast we would have after the peyote ceremony, entered the teepee and huddled in next to me, to my right. The peyote mixture had made its way around again. I made a decision not to take any more, and I was about to pass it on when she caught my hand and stopped me. "Amalia," she whispered. "Eat some more." I whispered back, "No, no way. It's poison!" She wouldn't accept my refusal. "The poison is in you," she insisted. "And it wants to come out. Eat some more peyote now. You have to, if you want to feel better." But I refused. Then Monica spoke full voice, not caring who could hear. "Amalia! Eat more now! I promise you, you will feel better. And you will move past this place where you are stuck." I could no longer hold out against her will and in courtesy to the tradition I took a tiny portion. I dry retched a few times as my stomach heaved, but nothing was actually expelled. I noticed that I was holding my breath, probably to reduce my ability to feel whatever it was that I was blocking. I knew that the more we breathe, the more we feel, but I obviously didn't want to feel anything at that moment. I also knew that breath is directly connected to Spirit, and the more you breathe, the more open the invitation of inspiring spirit into matter, increasing the vitality and aliveness in the body. Somehow Monica must have been surfing my wavelength because as I was thinking these things, she whispered, "Amalia, breathe!" I had to laugh to myself, not only at the synchronicity, but also because I could hear myself in her. I was the rebirther who was always advising people to breathe. Now the tables were turned. And so, I breathed.

With one deep breath I shored up my spirit and my strength. I focused my attention on the flaming fire pit and decided to survive this ordeal. I began to breathe consciously—to breathe into the sickness churning in my stomach, into the resistant roiling of my thoughts, into every nook and cranny of my being. I breathed new life, new spirit, and new strength into my body and new vision into my dragon eyes. I got up on my knees and stretched my arms toward the fire, calling its spirit toward me, asking for its alchemical cleansing. My inner voice urged me on. "Come on, Amalia. Be the love. Be the light. Let who you are spark forth like the fire before you. Get up from your knees and stand up for yourself, for you are a powerful woman."

I began puffing and snorting air into and out of my body like a fire-breathing dragon, I didn't care how I looked and was determined to make it through the ceremony with dignity. Something inside me gave way and I finally "got well." The poisonous feelings, beliefs, and illusions I had held deep within welled up from my stomach and I released it. I handed over the "sickness" I had held for so long into the flames. I felt great! I felt strong. I felt renewed. I soon even felt ecstatic. I was giving birth to the shamaness within. I was giving birth to the dragon energy that held the magic and wisdom of the earth. The eggshell that shielded my conscious awareness from realizing who I really am began to crack. I literally saw the shell fall to pieces around me and suddenly realized what all the egg symbolism was about; my true self was emerging. I could literally see my new and shiny egg shaped etheric field glowing around my physical body. Others in the teepee who had witnessed my long and arduous journey during this ceremony seemed to also witness my transformation. Through the glowing darkness one person, then another bowed toward me. Others were crying tears of joy for me, and a few others simply smiled at me. I felt connected to them all. I loved them all, each and every one, even the man with the horrid singing voice whom I had wanted to annihilate only hours before.

I had swung from feeling pathetic to perfection, from feeling terror to experiencing boundless love, from being imprisoned to being set free, from feeling resistance to accepting surrender, from being in hell to flying in heaven. I was struck by the realization of how I had been living—waiting, waiting for the light to pierce through the darkness, waiting for my knight in shining armor to make everything all right, waiting for the lifting of a deep, gnawing feeling of doom that lived within me. I now saw that I had to let go of control in my life. I had thought I was doing that, but I had to let go even more. I saw that I had to choose a simpler path, one less extreme in nature, less polarized in being—one where I was gentler with myself. I had to somehow resolve the dualities that were warring within me. Life can be easy, graceful, and pleasurable. Why wasn't I willing to live like that? The peyote showed me to myself now, in clear light and harsh truthfulness. All the judgments I had made about this plant medicine were now transformed into respect, reverence even, for the power of its vision and teaching.

As the ceremony finally came to an end, with the flap of the teepee opening to the dim light of dawn, I realized I had cracked the dragon's shell and I was reborn. I had taken my first breath with a new vision for a new life ahead. The peyote medicine had done its work to get me well and I was grateful for its lesson, but I knew that I would not partake of it again.

After the ceremony, we had a grand feast during which I was happy to feel my ordinary humanness, to simply eat and be merry. Later that afternoon, an opportunity arose for me to gather all my belongings and then be dropped at the airport. I would have liked to stay an extra day or two on the Big Island to integrate these powerful experiences, but an opportunity arose and I moved with the current as it presented itself to me. And so, with the peyote teaching reverberating through me like a dream, I boarded a plane and was whisked away, one-step closer to Sedona.

Chapter 5:

La Tierra de los Mayas.

After the richness of the tropical green forest and beautiful oceans of the Hawaiian Islands, I had to brace myself for the surgical-steel coldness and loneliness of Los Angeles. I felt engulfed by this concrete metropolis after the rural lushness of Hawai'i. I was glad to hear that INXS were in the city performing and inwardly smiled how the current of life had whisked me away so suddenly but in time to see "the boys." Massaging them, joining in on the party, and generally catching up on old times comforted and grounded me after the visionary ordeal I had just come through in Hawai'i. I enjoyed our days together and could have stayed with the band a little longer, but the call of Mexico was strong. I was eager to continue my journey to the Yucatán, where I hoped to retrieve the wisdom from the rock temples and practice my "secretarial skills" in preparation for Sedona.

The train ride from Los Angeles to Mexicali, a border town, was uneventful except for a strange synchronicity. During casual conversations with three different people at different intervals of the journey, I was warned off traveling alone in Mexico. The conversations each went something like this:

"Where are you going?"

"I am going to Mexico."

"Do you know how to speak Spanish?"

"Not really—a few words."

"Do you know anybody there?"

"No."

"Well, with whom are you going with?"

"Just me. I'm going alone."

Each of my seatmates then launched into stories of his or her terrifying experiences with bandits, cheats, or otherwise threatening people while traveling in Mexico. I didn't allow their fears to dampen my own sense of excitement about the journey, and I finally decided to remove myself from their "vibe" completely and go sit in another car of the train. I was no sooner settled when my seatmate spoke; making conversation that led, as was almost inevitable now, to his firing the same questions at me. I interrupted him midway through his sentence, rather rudely telling him, "I don't want to talk about it, thank you." Despite all the concern others were showing, I had little apprehension about this trip. I did make a mental note to make sure I kept my wits about me at all times, especially since I knew only rudimentary Spanish. Spirit might test me, of course, for such is the nature of all spiritual journeys, but I was confident that I was guided by Spirit in this Earth mission and so would be taken care of.

The two-hour train ride, terminated on the U.S. side of the border and a short walk over the border would bring me into the town of Mexicali. As I crossed the border into the land of the Mayas, I faced an immediate challenge: my menstrual flow started, two weeks earlier than expected. "Oh, great!" I thought to myself. "My first attempt to speak Spanish will be to ask for tampons or sanitary napkins!" I found a small convenience store, and after consulting my pocket Spanish dictionary, I managed to make the necessary purchase. I felt gratified and proud.

After freshening up, I caught a taxi to the bus station. I was not sure where I would head next, and since I was free as the spirit of the wind to choose a direction, I let chance direct me. I unfolded my map, closed my eyes, and let my finger pick a spot. Guadalajara. I was a bit startled and felt light-headed with a sense of déjà vu as I suddenly remembered a dream I had had some months back where the word "Guadalajara" had reverberated through my dreaming awareness and caused me to sit upright from my sleep in a jolt. I hadn't remembered that dream until this moment, and my skin went prickly as I wondered what else about my path was hidden in the recesses of my memory.

With just a rucksack, a couple of small duffel bags of belongings, and some light camping gear, I booked a bus ticket and set off for the two-day ride to Guadalajara. It was almost nightfall when we arrived, and I immediately found a clean and affordable hotel room. Before I went to bed, I felt the need to perform a prayer ceremony to declare my intention now that I was here in the land of the ancestors of the Americas. I was now actually stepping onto my path as a retriever of Earth wisdom, and needed to acknowledge my readiness out loud to Spirit. I lit a few small candles, a stick of incense, and some sage-herb, and then offered a simple prayer to request guidance. "Great Spirit, please guide me or bring unto me the prophets of this land. Connect me with the Wise Ones. I am not here as a tourist. I am here to do the Earthwork."

The next day, while exploring this handsome city, filled with vibrant culture, I found a charming vegetarian restaurant, where I connected with an interesting looking Mexicano. He had a long, dark braid trailing down his back and wore several carved talismans around his neck. He had a guitar strung over his shoulder and across his back. When we made eye contact, the recognition that

we were *compadres* at some unnamable level was clear. We introduced ourselves, me in my halting Spanish and he in his stilted
English. Luís was a musician who was part of an indigenous
Mayan ensemble, he was on his way to rehearsals, and he cordially
invited me to come along. My instincts were telling me that this
meeting was fated, so I agreed.

He led me down the street to a mansion that although now
faded and worn must have once been the most magnificent house
on the otherwise nondescript block. He led me inside and through
a labyrinth of rooms and halls and then up a rickety wooden
staircase that led to the roof. The vista of the city was magnificent,
but it was the group of seven musicians-four men and three
women, who caught my attention. As we joined them, I noticed
that they played traditional Mayan instruments and also had a
cache of music-makers straight from Mother Nature herself:
rocas (rocks), caracoles (shells), cachayotes (anklets made from
seed pods), and bamboo flutes. After quick introductions, they
began to rehearse, and their music was wonderfully lively,
evoking the freedom of Nature and celebrating their connection to
an ancient past.

After the rehearsal, one of the women, who seemed to be the
leader of the ensemble, invited me to participate in a Mayan
dance. I wondered if she knew of my connection to dance as she
gestured me into the dance circle. The sun was setting and the
moon was rising in all its' white splendor. What a perfect time to
dance! I accepted, and abandoned myself to the spirit of the
moment, dancing with several of the group members between the
worlds of the sun and the moon while the others played for us. At
the end of the dance, we sat around on the concrete rooftop floor and
caught our breath. This same woman, Clara, began to tell a story,
speaking in a low and almost solemn voice and almost continually
staring into my eyes, as if she were telling this story for my benefit
alone. I couldn't follow most of the story, since she spoke in

Spanish, but with the help of one of the musicians who facilitated the interpretation, I could decipher enough of it to catch the general story line. She was talking about the spiritual ones—the Wise Ones—who lived in a small community in the mountains just beyond the outermost reaches of the city. She was suggesting that I should visit them. She then turned to Jesús, one of the band members, and directed him to take down my hotel telephone number. That was it. The trip seemed like a done deal and I hadn't even been consulted.

I left the group in the gathering darkness, thanking them and Luís in particular, for a wonderful evening. Two days later I received a call from Jesús, but he didn't speak any English and talked in such rapid-fire Spanish that all I could understand of our conversation was the question, "Amalia, cinco hora?" I didn't know what to say to this question, since he was asking me to be ready to leave at five o'clock. Was he going to take me to the Wise Ones? Jesús had hung back and kept to himself when I had met him with the band, and I wasn't sure I felt comfortable heading off into the mountains with him. I didn't feel the intuitive connection with him like I did with Luís. Could I trust him? I didn't know. But I decided to go with the flow of fate, as I had so grudgingly been learning, but to keep on my toes, alert for any danger. "Si, cinco hora," I answered.

I was waiting for him in my hotel lobby at five o'clock. I had not packed anything to take with me, since the town was only one hour away and I assumed we would be returning later that evening. Jesús was late, and as the minutes ticked away I argued with myself. "Amalia, you don't even know him! You don't know where he's taking you or what trouble this could bring you." I remembered back to the four people on the train whom had each warned me about traveling alone in Mexico. My surety that Spirit was watching over me was quickly dissipating, but by the time Jesús arrived, I had convinced myself to take a chance on Spirit and head off into the unknown with him.

He was driving a well-kept, bright blue Volkswagen beetle, and a woman I soon learned was his girlfriend was in the front seat with her young daughter in the back seat. I got in the back and we drove off with hardly a word beyond stilted introductions. The car sputtered and spat as it gained speed, and the entire one-hour trip passed in stony silence.

Toward the last leg of the journey we drove through an old worldly village called Zapopán, quaintly dotted with a tortilla stand, a small market store, and a *zapatas* (shoe) repair store. A few scrawny cows languidly grazed the dry fields and every now and then a bicycler pedaled by, seeming in no hurry to get anywhere. We finally stopped in front of a high wooden fence with a huge gate that was patrolled by what I took to be a guard. Jesús exited the car to talk with the guard. I watched Jesús in his animated conversation, his hands repeatedly pointing toward me in the car. After about ten minutes, the guard opened the gate and waved us through. Jesús motioned for me to get out of the car and follow him.

As soon as we walked through the gate my sense of anticipation grew. Jesús explained that we had entered a spiritual community. With curiosity I took a fleeting look around to see if I could spot any of the "Wise Ones." Instead I spotted a flyer posted on a notice board: "Danza La Paz." (Peace Dance). It was taking place over the weekend and was starting that very evening, in little more than two hours. I was overcome with excitement—I wanted to join this dance. Dance is a strong passion of mine and so is peace on Earth, so it seems providential that I am here on the very evening of this special celebration. I caught up with Jesús, who had continued down the street without me and in ungrammatical Spanish with an English word or two thrown in, I told him that I must participate in the dance. "Por favor, Jesús. Es necessito yo participation in La Danca La Paz. Por favor! Es muy necessito!" I felt certain down to the marrow of my bones that this dance had been the reason I had been sent here by Luís's female bandleader. She had seen me dance, and she had known that I should be here at this special cerebration.

Almost as if a scriptwriter were writing the story of my life, Jesús called out to a woman who was just emerging from a building. She appeared middle-aged, handsome, with black hair upswept on her head. She seemed to glow with a kind and earthy nature. She was dressed simply in a white smock and white cloth espadrille sandals. Jesús introduced her as Celia. As he talked to her, I knew he was telling her of my desire to join the dance. She stared into my eyes. It seemed that every time I made a fateful encounter, it was recognized through the intensity of a stare. The woman simply nodded, and without comment Jesús turned on his heels and set off back toward the car to his girlfriend and her daughter. I was so excited about the dance that I didn't even notice he had left us until I heard the rumble of his Volkswagen as it drove away. At that moment I realized he was my angel, my courier to a ceremony I knew I was meant to be part of.

Celia was a woman of few words, but she immediately took charge. When it became clear to her that I had no clothes, not having planned to be away overnight, she explained that she would drive me back to my hotel to get my things. I was surprised to say the least, but had little time to think about anything since she was urging me to hurry with her to her car. The event was scheduled to start in little more than two hours, and the drive to my hotel and back would take at least that long.

As we drove, she talked more freely, although she offered only the minimum amount of information to get her point across. She had to repeat herself many times for me to understand and because of the Greek language behind me that only hinted at the Latin language, I could decipher every third or fourth word she spoke. She explained that a very special man would be arriving at the community that evening for the dance that will extend over the two days of the weekend. The dance is designed as a ceremony for cleansing the earth's energy and envisioning peace on Earth. Each day, there would be seven hours of nonstop dancing, and anyone who wanted to dance had to wear white clothing. I would need to wear a white dress.

I panicked as she explained the clothing requirements. I had no white clothing with me. When I explained this to her, she waved her hand at me, indicating it was not a problem. We would stop by her house on our return from the hotel and she would provide me with a white dress—she had many.

We made the round trip at top speed; in slightly more than two hours, having done more than I thought would be possible. We had not only gone to my hotel, where I had quickly packed a bag for the weekend and grabbed my sleeping bag, but we made three other stops. At Celia's small adobe house on the edge of town, she ran to get the dress I would wear for the ceremony. At a local store she bought two large tins of loose tobacco, which would be used as offerings to the earth during the dance ceremony, and at a bamboo grove along the roadway, we cut two several-foot long sections, or as Celia explained, "batons," which I would use in the dance. Celia moved like the wind, with a swiftness, efficiency, and grace that left me in awe.

When we got to the grounds where the dance was to be held, Celia led me to an open area where many people were camping and told me to claim an area for myself. She managed to procure a futon like mat for me to use beneath my sleeping bag. Then, since she had many details of the dance ceremony to attend to, she told me that she would check with me the next day to see how I was doing. As she walked away, it was obvious to me that Celia was a woman of some note. People addressed her openly but with an admiration that displayed their respect for her. After setting up my sleeping area, I followed the many participants through an open grassy area to the outdoor dining area, where we were served a soup of spicy vegetables and lentils, salad, and freshly made corn tortillas. Since I could not really participate in the many conversations going on around me, I became an onlooker, a witness to the unfolding of this most sacred of celebrations. I was impressed at the impeccable organization of the community and the layout of the ceremonial grounds.

After a short walk to let my food digest, I returned to my camp bed, which was out under the moonlit sky, and relaxed until the cool balmy breeze lulled me to sleep. I was awakened in the early morning by the trumpeting sound of a conch shell being blown. Many of the participants were already dressed in their white ceremonial wear and were heading in an easterly direction toward the ceremonial dance grounds. The sight was inspiring as they walked in unison, with confidence and gentleness, in the fullness of their spirit self. Their gaze was cast toward the rising sun, and the conch shell trumpeted majestically, calling their God-self into being. I could feel the intensity of their connection to the deep roots of their land, and for a moment I experienced ancient history come alive. But I indulged myself for only a few moments, as I, too, was to be part of the procession. I quickly dressed and calmly joined the formation.

As we neared the designated entrance point to the dance area, we walked through a cloud of smoke from burning incense, sage, and copal, which ritually cleansed our bodies and spirits. An elderly man waved a huge fan of eagle feathers down each of our bodies to complete the cleansing. We then filed into the dance site, forming a ring at whose edge several men drummed on a huge, handmade, skin-covered drum, sending a wave of drumbeats that sounded like thunderclaps reverberating across the open site.

The elder who would lead the dance, Luciano Pérez, locally called Tío (Uncle) Luciano appeared, making his way toward the fire pit at the center of the circle of dancers. He was the special guest Celia had alerted me to. He was fairly small and stout in physical stature, and his radiant presence filled the entire arena. With a single commanding gesture he signaled the drums to a halt and began his introduction to the Danza La Paz, the Peace Dance. He then explained the dance patterns we would follow, demonstrating the patterns with his hands. He instructed us to re-form into two circles, with females positioned in the inner ring and males in the outer. Without any fanfare except the resumption of the thunderous drumbeats, the dance began, and I quickly caught on to its weaving, serpentine movement. Round and round we danced, stepping resolutely, our bare feet stamping down to make firm contact with Mother Earth and our upper bodies swaying to the rhythm of our steps. The two circles of sixty Earth dancers wove in and out among one another in a dance of symmetrical simplicity. With each stomping movement, we connected our energy to Mother Earth, thanking her for her gifts and directing our intent to her cleansing and rejuvenation. There seemed to be an order to the dance, like the dance of bees; of silent communication, that conveys information. Soon the dancers began singing—more a chanting really—and joined their voices to the drums that beat with the heart of the earth. I was feeling transported by the hypnotic dancing motions, chants, and drumming. But as the sun began to rise into the sky, its heat quickly gathered force, and I, like most of the other dancers, was sweating from exertion. After about two more hours of dancing, Tío Luciano signaled a break, and we quietly retreated to the edges of the dance site, where we were offered water and sat on the shaded grass to rest. This was the pattern of the dance for the remainder of the day. Hours of dancing and chanting, punctuated by fifteen-minute rests and water breaks. Except for a little fresh fruit we were given at the end of the day, food would have to wait until the conclusion of the weekend ceremony.

As the day wore on, dancing became an act of will and stamina, for the sun was unrelenting, and the stomping action was hard on the legs and feet. At times, I questioned what I was doing there as the driving, repetitive motions of the dance dissolved my focus and weakened my perseverance. But mostly, I felt part of a seamless, holistic wave of group energy and not an individual with personal needs or desires. During that first day of dancing, which went on until late afternoon, I learned that the interweaving of one's individual intent into the larger group consciousness intent is one of the most powerful tools of manifestation. That where a group gathers with focused intention, this intention is magnified exponentially, more powerfully propelling the will of that intent into the world, in this case, for the healing and purification of Earth.

At the conclusion of that day's dancing, Celia came to check up on me, as she had said she would. She instructed me to make my two ceremonial batons from the bamboo we had collected. We were going to use these in the next day's dance. She provided me with colored string, shells, feathers, and beads to decorate the two thin, eighteen-inch lengths of bamboo. I wound colored string around each, starting at the base with red string and then changing to orange, yellow, green, blue, and ending with violet, representing the human chakra system and the rainbow that in Native cultures symbolizes all the different tribes of the world that we were dancing for. Then starting at the base of each baton again, I crisscrossed white string over the rainbow-colored string to represent how Spirit is interwoven throughout the whole. I affixed a cord that I strung with white feathers, little pebbles and shells at the base of the batons to represent both Heaven and Earth.

The second day of dancing began as a repeat of the first day. We lined up single file and moved toward the ceremonial dance area with the women holding their batons, one in each hand and the men their staffs. But once we were cleansed and had entered the dance site proper, I was surprised as a group of Aztec dancers charged into the circle. We were enveloped by a vista of bright-colored clothing and headdresses adorned with multicolored jungle bird feathers, some of which fanned upward and outward for up to three feet. Several drums began to beat in counterpoint rhythm, as the Aztec dancers created an intricate pattern of percussive movements. Like a storm that electrified the arena, we were spellbound as we stomped our feet in place, alternately thumping our staffs or batons on the earth and then raising them as we watched their wild dance. Soon other dancers entered the circle. They appeared to be small bands of four or five individuals representing various indigenous groups, and each had its own dance style and song. Sometimes individually and sometimes together, each band of dancers performed, often singing along with the drums. The spectacle increased as the pace of the dancing picked up, and I was astounded as I watched them move and listened to their songs. I could imagine them as the latest in a long line of such dancers, stretching back through history, each ancestral generation constant in its devotion to the earth, worshipping their ancient gods and goddesses, the sun and the moon, and the spirits of nature. They had arrived like a mirage in the desert, infusing us with strength and the courage to continue the dance. Their dances were a testament to my own deepening connection to the wisdom of the earth, from which I could draw strength during the day.

After half an hour, the guest dancers filed out of the circle, leaving us to continue our dance. As we moved in unison, our batons and staffs made a stunningly colorful contrast against our white ceremonial garments. We sometimes held one in each hand, or held them together horizontally at our waistline. We raised and lowered them, using them as energetic vacuum cleaners, sucking up energetic debris from Mother Earth's body and flinging it into the central fire pit to be purified.

At the end of ceremony, after another physically exhausting but psychically energizing day of dancing, I felt a tremendous sense of accomplishment and immense satisfaction. The ceremony officially ended not with the end of the dance, but with a ceremonial cleansing ritual. Small groups of us took turns in a *temezcal*, a purification steam bath much like a Native North American sweat lodge. The next morning I thanked Celia, whom I had not seen much of during the ceremony since we had each kept pretty much to ourselves, in retreat in our own inner worlds. She graciously arranged a ride for me back to Guadalajara, and then she left as abruptly as Jesús had; her mission with me accomplished.

I continued to travel throughout Mexico and came to realize that I had major misconceptions about Mexico. I had expected to find tumbled-down towns rampant with poverty or crowded cities festering from decay. While I was sure that Mexico, like every country, has its share of each, overall I found Mexico to be a complex mosaic of stark natural landscapes and an enlivening colorful culture. The countryside most impressed me with its bare-bones beauty, for each place I arrived at was more pristine in its allure than the place before. At one moment, as I was standing alone gazing out over a broad expanse of fields that led in the far distance to the purple haze of a mountain range, I literally fell to my knees in appreciation. While the Hawaiian Islands had been lush in their botanical excess, Mexico was bared to the bone, scrubbed clean of extravagance but true to its own stark grandeur. I felt that everything was right with my world—this was indeed the proper place for me to begin my work with the rocks. If there was wisdom to be retrieved from the stones, then Mexico was the place where they and I could begin our conversations simply and frankly.

My work with the rocks of Mexico began at the ruins of Teotihuacán, "The City of the Gods," which lay 25 miles northeast of

Mexico City. Built by the Toltecs, Teotihuacán was a primary center of learning and culture whose temples were built in alignment with the stars and the solar system by a people with an understanding of advanced mathematics, astronomy, and geometry. The Pyramids of the Sun and of the Moon dominate the complex. Representing the Great Cosmic Mountain, the Pyramid of the Sun is said to connect Earth to Heaven and to contain an entrance into a hidden world, into *Mictlan,* "The Underworld," from which will one day emerge the ancient wisdom that has lain dormant or been forgotten or ignored for so long. It is also said that within this stone temple, access to the Emerald Records are attainable, which contain the true Story of Creation.

I arrived at the ruins late in the afternoon, went straight to the Temple of the Sun, and climbed its long staircase to the apex of the structure, which is 200 feet high. My intention was to enter the stillness of meditation in order to see through the window of time and listen to the stones speak. The sun was strong, and I felt bathed in the solar rays as I attempted to extend my intuitive roots into the stone edifice to access any encoded wisdom. I had barely started when clouds moved in, seemingly from nowhere, and it started to drizzle. At first I was dismayed, feeling that I may have to stop the process, but then noticed how the sun-baked stone drank in the moisture. I felt that my metaphor of drinking up the life-giving messages of these stones was being played out literally, so I stayed put and observed the rain offer itself to the rocks and the rocks thirstily drink it in. I cleared my mind of any concerns for my own comfort. I felt embraced by both aspects of the natural world— the stone in all its stability and firmness and the rain in all its impermanence and fluidity. I allowed myself to experience the synthesis of opposites as the cool water met the hot stone. In the steam that rose from the stone, I recognized the transformational process at work, and I likened the rising steam to the release of any wisdom that might be encapsulated by these ancient stones. I leaned over and breathed this essence into my being, and then thought about the merging of dualities and how the marriage of opposites, (in this case water and stone), often reveals hidden wisdom.

I sat there, atop the Pyramid of the Sun, with the Pyramid of the Moon in view opposite me for a long time, until darkness began to descend and I had to leave—without actually retrieving any overt messages from the stones. I was grateful enough, for the teachings the temple rocks and rain had given me. I climbed down the temple stairway and headed toward the bus firm in my intention to return the next day—but once again fate intervened.

That night, back in Mexico City, I ran into two of the dancers I had met at Danza La Paz: Fernando, a young Mexicano, and Robert, his Australian friend. During the dance they had invited me to join them on a pilgrimage to Huautla de Jimenéz, a remote mountain village north of Oaxaca. They were in town looking for me, and they were leaving in a couple of hours. The bus ride to Oaxaca would take eight hours; we would then have to change buses, with another six-to eight-hour drive to the village. Was I up for the trip?

Was I ever! Fernando had explained that he made infrequent visits to Huautla de Jimenéz to pay homage to an elderly shamaness he had once apprenticed with. Her name was Aurelia, and she was the mistress of the sacred mushrooms that grew in that area. In fact, this was the same village in which amateur mycologist R.Gordon Wasson had had his first experience with the visionary mushrooms back in the mid-1950s. Through his reporting of his experiences, he introduced the world to María Sabina, the local *curandera*. Curiosity-seekers in droves had trekked to the town to find the mushrooms and María. It got to the point where María lamented ever having introduced Wasson to them, for the foreigners who clamored to the village mostly lacked respect for the sacredness of the mushrooms, which the indigenous peoples saw as sentient beings that could impart wisdom to humans. She eventually came to believe that the mushrooms were losing their power.

This trip was a rare opportunity to meet a local wise woman and I was not about to miss it, especially since Robert spoke fluent Spanish and could translate for me. The mushroom ceremonies were alive and well, and Aurelia was one of the keepers of that tradition, even though, as Fernando explained, she was also a Christian, and so had introduced Christian elements into her teaching and ceremony. While I was eager to meet with Aurelia, I wasn't sure I wanted to actually participate in the ceremony. My experience with peyote in Hawai'i had not been pleasant, and I was loath to venture into the territory of the visionary "plant teachers" again. Fernando assured me that I would not have to participate if I didn't want to, so I agreed to go, excited at the prospect of meeting this medicine woman.

The ride to Oaxaca, while long, was uneventful, but the final ride from Oaxaca to the village was plodding, and often perilous. The bus driver had to carefully negotiate long stretches of narrow, winding mountain roads. At some points, I could look out the window and directly over a cliff edge! I fretted over each swerve of the bus as it rocked back and forth around hairpin bends and I mumbled prayers for surviving the journey. It was early afternoon when we finally pulled into Huautla de Jiménez. The town was little more than a hamlet, with one small café and a few dilapidated stores forming a marketplace at its center. Mountain peaks ringed it.

We were hungry, so we went to the café for a quesadilla before we walked to Aurelia's house. She greeted us with a warm smile and waved us into her humble abode. She was a small, wizened woman with classic Mayan features, and she had a grandmotherly air that quickly put me at ease. We sat on wooden stools at a rough-hewn wooden table as she offered us cups of hot cocoa and homemade sweet bread. Once we had eaten again and she and Fernando had caught up with each other, she motioned us toward several small back rooms where she suggested we rest before the evening's ceremony. I dropped off to sleep with only mild anxiety about whether I should participate or not.

We were awakened about an hour later by slight nudges from Aurelia and the word, "Ahora!" It was time to prepare for the ceremony. She instructed us to go to the marketplace to purchase 108 cocoa beans each, ceremonial candles, several special dried herbs, and some fairly rare feathers that we would need for the ritual. Under Fernando's direction, we found what we needed at the marketplace and gathered the plant materials and special feathers at the edge of the jungle on the outskirts of town. When we returned to Aurelia's home several hours later, she ushered us into a small, dark concrete-floored room toward the back of the house, where an altar was adorned with photos of Christian saints, such as St. Paul and St. Michael, of Mother Mary and of Jesus Christ. Dried herbs were hanging by their stems in bunches from the ceiling beams, as were clear plastic bags filled with the cocoa beans we purchased from the market. The smell of burning copal filled the room and a few church candles were lit on each side of the altar.

We gave Aurelia the bundles of herbs we had picked, and she lit several of them and then blew out the flame, so the bundles were smoking. She smudged us one by one while she recited prayers. She occasionally stopped to sip some fluid from a bottle of infused herbs. With a mouthful of the liquid, she would run her lips over the area of our chests and arms while rolling the fluid around in her mouth. She would then pull back and spray the liquid through her lips onto the floor; as if she were releasing the negative energy she had pulled from our energy bodies. After these cleansing rituals, she asked us one by one to speak our names, and on so doing she addressed a saint, who would protect us during the ceremony. Finally, she laid out three plates onto which she measured out a portion of dried mushrooms. I was feeling scared, but knew that it was too late to back out of the ceremony. I asked Robert to tell her that I'd be given the smallest amount possible and he did, but she did not really adjust the portion of mushrooms on the plate that was to be mine.

We sat on mattresses on the floor, the only light in the room from the flickering of candles. We silently chewed the mushrooms, which were bitter and rubbery. I felt anxious, especially since Robert was my only real lifeline in terms of communicating and he was about to enter into his own visionary world. Plus, I felt closed in. The room was small and felt suffocating to me. I wanted more than anything to be out in the open air under the stars. I worked hard at calming myself, at stopping the chatter in my mind, and eventually I settled down, getting into a state, more or less, of trust in the process. I was in Aurelia's hands now—and in the hands of the mushroom spirits.

I didn't have a clear sense of time, but it seemed that very quickly my senses started to reel, my heart beat quickened, and my sense of balance faltered. Then I felt my sense of self begin to expand—along with my sensory perceptions. Where before I had seen only darkness punctuated by the dim light of the almost burned-down candles, I now began to see bursts of color, as if the air were erupting into showers of colorful dots. My head felt light, as did my body, and I felt as if I were lifting off the floor, expanding, escaping into the ether, which was alive with color and motion. Fernando must have sensed the shift in me, for he reached over from where he was sitting next to me, gently clasped my hand and held it as we eased down into a supine position on the mattress. Aurelia blew out the candles. And it was then that I panicked.

I suddenly felt gripped by fear. I didn't want to be in the darkness, it made me feel alone and unsafe. I felt the stability of my sense of self begin to founder. I felt my breath coming harder and faster. Aurelia was attentive to my condition, for she spoke to Robert, who translated: "Tell the girl not to worry. She will be all right."

I did not feel comforted by these words. How could I be all right when my senses were taking on a life of their own? I was losing control of my world, and more than anything I wanted light. I needed to be able to see, to orient myself. But all around me was darkness—the ghostly alive darkness of the mushroom realm. Plus, the room felt as if it were closing in on me even more than before. I argued within myself—that my mission was not to be in a small, dark room working with mushrooms but to be out in the wide expanse of Nature, firmly seated on a rock somewhere, listening for the voice of Mother Earth. Fernando once again squeezed my hand, and that gesture brought me out of my inner turmoil and my focus back to the mushroom ceremony.

I knew I had to stay present, in the now, and not be off in my mind somewhere else at some other time. I worked consciously to regulate my breathing, and as I did I felt myself relaxing. I don't know how much time passed, but the next thing I knew I was laughing, louder and louder, more and more heartily. The others also began to laugh, and Fernando once again squeezed my hand in acknowledgment, but this time his grip was powerful and over-whelming. I knew he was off on his own visionary journey and I now felt the need to disconnect from him. We each had to be in our own interior spaces, free from the need to keep tabs on each other through relating to the exterior. So I slipped my hand out of his and assured myself that I was strong enough to handle my own inner flight, confident enough to freely connect with the shaman within me.

I rolled over onto my stomach, and as I did so, it felt as if my "flight path" altered, too. I felt something like the directions within myself shift, and I was falling down, down, down, into an abyss, a void of darkness. "Oh no, not this!" I thought, trying to put the brakes on. But I continued to fall. I felt the energy around me as ominous, just as I had during the Hawaiian peyote ceremony. I was sure I had entered the Underworld. The colors I was seeing dissipated and then disappeared, seeping away into nothing more than a grayscale contrast of darks and lights. Somewhere in the distant recesses of my mind, I clung to the thought that I needed to shift my stream of consciousness from the dark toward the light of love. I knew such light glowed somewhere in this dark and threatening place. At the same time, another part of my mind was embroiled in a debate. One inner voice was asking Aurelia for permission to get up and go outside. Another inner voice was insisting that the value of the experience lay in remaining right where I was, in the dark and following the tradition of the ceremony. I so badly wanted to be out of doors that this inner voice won the debate and I groped around the mattress for my flashlight. I found it and turned it on, the narrow yellow beam falling directly on the altar at the back of the room and on the picture of Mother Mary. The artist had painted a large heart in the middle of her chest and a smile on her face. As the thought struck me that "this is the pure heart I seek to find," I heard Aurelia shift on the mattress next to me, pulling and tugging at a blanket to cover herself with and to block out the light. Fernando and Robert both groaned with discontent, and I found myself in amazement, thinking, "They've become mushrooms! They shrink from the light as if it could endanger their existence! But I want the light. This is my path. I've already done enough work in the realm of my shadows and of the Underworld. I well know that part of my life. These mushrooms are a poison to my being. They are not what I need!"

I simply stood up and walked out of the room, and then out of the house. As I breathed in the fresh night air, I felt renewed. I knew that I had just made an important choice—the choice to follow my own inner compass, which was leading me to the path of light, not of darkness. I was imbued with the new sense of strength, and I felt a deep remembering of who I am and what I was setting out to do in my life. I realized that in each moment I have a choice to experience my reality in a way that nourished and served me, and I needed to retain the courage to make that choice.

At that moment, the skies opened. I stood in the downpour and laughed at the seemingly orchestrated moment of the clouds' unleashing. I stepped back under the wide eave of the house and squatted down with my head curled in between my knees. I watched the earth takes its long drink.

Then the rain stopped as abruptly as it had started. As I took a few steps out from under the eave, two black dogs charged out of nowhere, stopping about three feet from me and growling menacingly. I was frightened, and it flashed through my thoughts that these were the hounds of hell. I made my stance as large as I could and stared them down. In my mind, I challenged them. "Come any closer and I'll abolish you. I've chosen the light. You of the darkness, back off!" Amazingly, they immediately cowered, their tails tucking between their legs and their ears flattening, and they slinked away, whimpering like helpless pups.

I walked to the edge of the thicket where the jungle began and crouched down by the roots of a large old, gnarly tree. I grounded my energy to Mother Earth and asked her for guidance and assistance. I felt the roots of my being slowly but surely penetrating the earth, moving down deep into her core, just as the roots of the old tree beside me had done. I felt myself bonding with the tree, merging with its energy. It had stood here, still and fixed through the passage of countless days and nights, and it had been flexible enough to bend against the pressure of fierce rains and winds and had the stamina to withstand long bouts of drought. It had been witness to the trials and triumphs of generations who endured this hardscrabble life.

Then I became conscious once again of the mushrooms I had ingested, and felt my inner voice rise within me. As I crouched at the edge of the jungle, I affirmed my willingness to allow the light of my consciousness to illuminate the depths of my unconsciousness, for there I knew, still lurked the fear and self-judgment and other opinions that held me in the dark and away from the light of my full power. I recognized this meeting place of these two worlds—the merging of light and dark—as a new doorway within the self, where the Emerald Doorway exists, the doorway to ancient, natural knowledge. With these thoughts reverberating through my being, I quietly made my way back to the house and into the tiny room where I was staying to write about my mushroom experience.

I see through the eyes of a Huautlán mushroom on this night. It wants to stay low to the wet, dank earth, watching the grubs and insects crawl in the dark and moist soil. It knows the darkness well, for it survives in the darkness, yet yearns for the light. Even though it exists in darkness, its consciousness is wide-awake and alert. Darkness is in fear because it sees itself as separate from the light; it wants to merge with the light but fears that once it surrenders and merges with it, it will no longer exist. This correlates to our fear, which makes us feel separate from love. We want to merge with the heart of love but fear our dissolution into it. There is a place for both fear and darkness, as fear wants to be embraced as part of the totality, not to be shunned as wrong or bad and hidden out of its existence. It plays an integral part in teaching us what love and light are, for how can we know what love is if we haven't experienced fear, it's opposite? How can we know light if we do not know the dark? Thank you, Huautlán mushrooms, for giving me the teaching of dark and light on this night.

On finishing writing the last word, I quickly fell into an undisturbed sleep.

The next morning, none of us spoke of the previous night's experiences. After a quick wash and a light breakfast, Aurelia directed us into the back room to complete the ceremony. She carefully counted out the cocoa beans we had bought and divided them into three piles, keeping a few for herself. She placed each pile into a plastic bag and then also tucked in the candles we each had bought; a few small, colorful feathers; and a picture of the saint that was watching over us. She twisted the bags closed and sealed each with a plastic tie, instructing us to hang our bag by a window in the light for one month, so the energy of this ceremony would find its way into the light during that time. She brought the ceremony to a close by smudging us once again with copal incense to cleanse our energy bodies.

I was relieved to be leaving. I vowed that this was the last time I would ever partake of any psychotropic substances. We thanked Aurelia, said our farewells, and caught a bus back to Oaxaca. We made the trip in almost complete silence, each of us in our own private worlds. Robert helped me get settled in a safe and inexpensive hotel, and then they left, each heading his separate way. I had elected to spend some time in Oaxaca, a city known for its art and culture. I was not on any time schedule and had no particular itinerary, and wanted to explore this cultural center of the Huichols and Mayans.

As with each of the places I had visited, this place held its own special charms, and exuded its own mysteries. I remember one incident in particular. One morning while I was finishing breakfast in the central plaza, I spotted a few white feathers on the ground nearby. I crouched down to pick them up and noticed there was a trail of them, so on a lark I left my table to follow the trail. Halfway across the plaza, I stopped, looked up toward the sky, and gave thanks, for I was thinking of the winged ones above, the angels that I was sure were watching over and protecting me. Just then I felt a tug at my skirt, and turned to see a little boy with a sweet, dirt-smudged face. He had a handful of the white feathers and from what I could understand of his Spanish, he was telling me I was an angel and my wing feathers were dropping off. He was handing them back to me! I laughed with delight, but before I had a chance to respond, a woman, his mother I presume, hurried over and pulled him away with her into the growing crowd of early morning shoppers and strollers. A man who witnessed our encounter and overheard the boy's comment came over and joked to me, saying that I was either an angel or a chicken! We both laughed, and this was only one instance of the openness and wittiness of the people of Oaxaca.

I seemed to meet the most interesting people during these long, lazy breakfasts at the plaza. One morning I met a charming and remarkable man, Guillermo Aldana. He spoke fluent English and was a photographer who worked for the National Geographic Society. He was traveling on assignment now, journeying throughout Mexico to various ancient ruins and indigenous sacred sites. He was, he explained, interested in capturing as best he could the wisdom of the land. He beguiled me with stories of his adventures and we formed a fast friendship. We met over several mornings, and our conversations often centered on the nature of rocks and the wisdom they carried. We weren't speaking in metaphor, for his visual appreciation for the rocks bordered on the philosophical and he did not scoff or even question my mission to retrieve their messages. During my month-long stay in Oaxaca, I saw Guillermo almost every day and I learned a lot from him—about Mexican history, geology, photography, and a host of other subjects. Most importantly, I took to heart his opinion that anyone seeking to capture the essence of a place must develop the patience to not rush the landscape, but to allow it to reveal itself in its own time. At one point, after telling him of my interest in the local shamans and of my experience with the visionary mushrooms, Guillermo offered his take on the subject of shamanism.

"Shamans are medicine peoples," he explained, "who through their inheritance and genetics are trained in the uses of Earth Spirit through plants, water, air, fire, space, and spirit. They have the will to heal the sick. They would use whichever element was more necessary for that person at his or her time of need. They will use the tricks of the trade to lure and captivate their audience. That means smoking grasses and herbs, drawing negative energy out with their breath, and rolling water in their mouth and then spraying it out. They know all this is hullabaloo, but they also know that they need to captivate the person being healed and make him believe in the healing process. If someone doesn't believe in his wellness, a shaman will create this theater by using all his tools so that the ill person will shift in consciousness. The more he performs his act and the more he activates the ambiance, the better the healing may be."

Guillermo agreed offhandedly with my assessment that in his own way he is a "photographic shaman": he sees the potential of perfection where others don't, waits for the right relationship between the light of the sun and the shadows cast by that light, and only then snaps the picture. He has his own bag of tools, selecting just the right lens and filter from a variety of choices to create the picture that will captivate his audience and even transform them in some way.

Guillermo invited me to join him on his photographic pilgrimages, and I often accepted. On many of those trips, as he and I sat patiently waiting for the conditions to come together for the perfect shot, he would talk of Mexico, of the land and the people. Sometimes he extended his musing over a wider scope, and one-day he explained to me how the gods were born into human culture.

"The first step of man's conscience was taken in prehistoric times through the killing of mammoths, for food and survival. After killing the animal, the cave man saw his own hands covered in blood and for a moment related his own experience to that of the dead animal. 'I killed for my family,' he must have said to himself. 'This beast might have been a mother or a father. Now its children don't have a parent to take care of them. This could happen to my family.'

"He then reached out and pressed his bloody hands onto the wall of the cave he lived in, in a desperate gesture that said 'Stop!

Don't kill me!' He tried to keep death at bay. He tried to prevent the revenge that may be waiting for him.

"So this hand symbol became a sign of protection and the cave man's conscience bore seeds, leading to the rudiments of religion. In prehistoric times, history revealed itself through these symbols, the unwritten words, from Africa, Mexico, America, Australia, and many other countries. One of the earliest symbols was the handprint in caves. Even cultures separated by thousands of miles and too many years to count, with no known contact with each other produced this symbol. Later many other belief systems retained this symbol and infused it with their own meaning. For instance, the Catholics took the figure of the hand as a symbol of protection—from the hand of Fatima, who was the daughter of the prophet Mohammed, to the hand of fate. The handprint was the first symbol of spirits and of gods being born from the other world into this world.

"From then on, the expression of this fear and belief became more and more sophisticated, according to each individual tribe, and was dependent on the environment in which they lived. They eventually learned to make the images of gods, good gods and evil ones, for their own use. They hoped to assume their power. In Mexico one of the oldest cultures belonged to the Tabasco, who lived north of the Mexican Gulf. Legend has it that this culture developed with the assistance of an outside influence—from space beings. It is said that the people learned to communicate with star peoples, and it was from them that they acquired their complex knowledge of the calendar and time. It was from this beginning that the Mayan civilization arose and spread.

"For the Olmecs, god was the jaguar. It was the most dominant animal in the region, the one they most feared and hence most respected. It personified cunning and symbolized transformation, so the Olmecs adopted the Jaguar God in order to protect themselves. Many tribes turned the most powerful animal of their region into the personification of their god.

"Many tribes revered animals as gods for their good aspects, which were respected, and their threatening qualities, which provoked fear. These animals connected them to Spirit because they could either kill or provide food for their families. The Aztecs, for example, revered and feared the serpent, and an Aztec shaman would let the snake bite him to increase his immunity and as a test—if he survived, he was seen as favored by the gods and so advanced to a higher level of his shamanic practice.

"The North American natives held the bear and eagle as their most feared or revered animals, and the Huichol Indians of Mexico held the deer as the most sacred of the animal kingdom. For the Huichols, the deer supplied them with food and clothes for protection, so the deer became the god of goodness. The shamans of this tribe would eat deer soup even if the deer was infested with maggots, because it would connect them to the Deer God, who would bestow blessings upon them."

As he paused in his explanation, I asked Guillermo about the nature of the owl and told him about the vision I had experienced during a massage back in Australia when I had shaken the talon of a twelve-foot owl, which had escorted me to the owl dreamtime. He obliged me with another mythology lesson.

"The owl traditionally is the symbol of feminine wisdom. It was the power animal of the Greek Goddess Athena, who held the power of wisdom. The owl's flight is by the light of the moon, symbolizing the feminine principle, and it sees into the darkness, bringing the wisdom of consciousness into the unconscious. The eagle, in contrast, is traditionally the symbol of masculine wisdom. Its flight is among the powerful rays of the sun, which is more masculine in its energy." As he spoke, I remembered the embroidery of a favorite black jacket I had when I was eighteen, one I had spent countless hours beading and stitching with the symbols of the celestial energies: on the right lapel I stitched and beaded the sun, and on the left, the moon.

Another thought also occurred to me: that the moon is the eye of the Goddess while the sun is the eye of God. We as humans are always immersed in the light of wisdom as evidenced by the marriage of the God and Goddess, through the union of male and female. I knew that the union of dualities was a major lesson for me, one I still had not fully learned.

During another of our photographic ventures, Guillermo told me more about the Aztecs and their beliefs.

"The Aztecs were a fierce tribe of warriors who instituted a ceremony that involved sacrificing a human heart to feed the sun, so that it would shine the next day. They also believed that blood fed their gods collectively. These gods maintained the cosmic order and had to be kept satisfied. But this bloodletting perhaps had other uses as well, for example, for the Aztecs, it was equivalent to their exerting their power as warriors and rulers over others.

"The Azteca came from the mountains of North Colima, southwest of Mexico City, and they were known as savages, as a mountain people who were trained to kill others and steal their property, food, and the like. Every year, when the mountains were covered with snow and the weather got too cold to stay there, these Aztec warriors traveled down the coast to Mexcaltitan, where they healed their wounds, got food, and generally strengthened themselves for the next season of warring. When they first arrived at the coast, much to their surprise they saw that the families there were living in harmony, happy with their lot, fishing for their food and making many beautiful handicrafts. Since there was an abundance of food, the women didn't have to work so hard and had time to express themselves through art.

"Now the story goes that the Aztecs had no power here, for everything was easily attained and freely provided and did not have to be governed by the warriors and rulers. In this kind of environment, the strongest tribesman of the Aztec tribe, the chief, and the most intelligent man—his counselor, had no power and so lost respect. They wanted to regain their power and their tribe's respect, so, the counselor of the Aztec chief saw that a storm was coming and he seized this opportunity, collaborating with his chief, to tell and warn these people that it was unsafe to stay there and that they must flee with the Aztecs back to the mountains. He told the tribe that the lightning spirit and the thunder beings and star beings had sat in counsel with their shaman and told him that the sun was about to disappear, which was true because it was going behind the storm clouds. He made up a story that all this had been told to their shaman by the gods. He warned his people: 'The first person who says no to returning home with us will cause the sun to hide, perhaps never to show itself again. The only way the sun can be convinced to return to the sky tomorrow is if we cut out that person's heart and offer it to the gods. Then the sun will agree to appear again.'

"But their story did not work. The people refused to go, and so the Aztecs began the ritual of sacrificing human hearts to the gods. Later, in approximately the year 1325 A.D., the Aztec peoples arrived in Mexico City, where civilization was already thriving. They saw the Aztecs as savages, as wolves from the mountains, but also recognized them for the powerful warriors they were, and so made an arrangement with them and trained them as mercenary soldiers. But the Aztecs fought for themselves under the dominion of their own god. Eventually they ruled all of Mexico until 1519 A.D., when their empire was conquered and destroyed to the point of near extinction by Hernando Cortez and his armies. Cortez, a Spaniard, created the "New Spain" upon the remnants of the indigenous civilizations. It wasn't until 1810 that the Mexicans became independent of that Spanish influence, and in 1910 a new revolution started, and has continued until the present time."

This was the history of the people of this land as told by Guillermo. I could not verify how accurate his rendition of history was, nor did I care to. I loved and honored the hours held in council with this remarkable man simply because in his own way he was a teacher preparing me for the mission I felt called to. With Guillermo I had the chance to talk of legend, history, and shamanism while in the embrace of the land itself, in the open sweep of a desert with a ruin on the horizon or among the stones of the ruin itself. There he performed his photographic shamanism, and prepped me for learning my own brand of patience with the spirit of a place and of the land. I traveled with Guillermo on and off for three weeks, until I was ready to leave Oaxaca and head into the Yucatán to practice—and experience—my own form of shamanism.

Chapter 6:

Deeper Into Mexico, Deeper Into the Earth.

I next ventured into a small town called Tule, an hour or so east of Oaxaca. I had heard there was an especially grand tree there noteworthy of seeing, called the Tree of Tule, purported to be the largest single bio-mass in the world, rooting itself in the earth some 3,000 years ago. The night before I visited this massive tree, I had a dream in which Mother Earth asked me to hold a meditation circle for thirty people at the base of the tree. We were to link hands to make a ring around the tree, stand with our backs against the trunk, and firmly plant our feet on the ground and lift our heads toward the sky, mimicking a tree's penetrating roots and leafy crown. Then we were to breathe in the energy of the earth and filter it up through our feet and into our hearts, filling our hearts with the knowledge, wisdom, and ancient stillness it contained. Our purpose was to free from our hearts whatever pain was locked there, and release it through the exhale in our breathing rhythm, so that we would become clear conduits of this life-force energy. Although I remembered the dream in vivid detail the next morning, I was uncertain whether I would actually carry out these dream instructions. All I could promise myself was that at the very least I would carry out the meditation and release ceremony myself.

When I finally stood before the voluminous tree, I saw how it would indeed take twenty to thirty people to fit around its massive trunk. The tree was directly in front of a chapel to *"la Virgen de Guadalupe"*—the Virgin Mary, and it stood in valorous innocence as it extended its branches toward the sun. The tree itself was protected from contact with people by a white picket fence that encircled it, but I couldn't resist reaching up to caress a branch and leafy tendrils that hung from the branches. Several large limbs extended down so low that I could rest my face against one, tenderly and with great respect for this ancient guardian. I began the rhythmic breathing—what I called Earth Breathing—which I had been shown in my dream. As the minutes passed, I felt more and more deeply connected with this huge, living presence, and I understood how this "Earth Breathing" is analogous to photosynthesis— of a tree's, or any plant's, natural and resourceful exchange of energy with the sun and the earth. As I opened my heart chakra and released any heavy energy I held there, I felt the earth's unconditional willingness to receive and then transmute negative energy into positive energy. I understood how by releasing our pain into the earth like dead leaves, the earth could recycle dead matter into new sources of nourishment for other living things, and so fuel evolution. I realized that this process of "Earthing" oneself is a powerful means of alchemy, of transmuting disease, (un-ease) into healing and harmony. I felt the wisdom, strength, and beauty of Earth, living, being, breathing and feeling with us.

When I had completed my meditation, I wandered toward the little chapel that was almost hidden by the wide girth of the tree itself. At the entrance, I was captivated by a statue of *la Virgen*

Guadalupe: she stood patiently with her loving arms outstretched, offering her luminous light of grace. Her cape was painted midnight blue and was rhythmically studded with painted white roses.

The chapel's caretaker, who was attentively sweeping the floor, saw my interest in the statue and came toward me, his eyes bright, as if lit by fire. My Spanish had improved to the point that I could understand most of what he said as he related the tale of how *Guadalupe's* cloak came to be covered with roses.

He explained that a Mexican Indian had a vision of a bush of flowers growing in a particularly remote mountainous region. Roses had not been introduced to Mexico at this time, so he was unfamiliar with this flower, but he was determined to search for this bush nonetheless. He combed the mountains for a long time until he finally came across the flowers he had seen in his vision. He took these roses back to his hometown and shared the vision he had seen. The very same night of his return, the cloak of the Virgin Mary of the church he belonged to had astonishingly become covered with white painted roses. At this statue here, and at others across Mexico, the people paint the cape of the Virgin with roses in honor of this miracle. As I left Tule that day, an inner smile melted deeply into my heart in honor of the dream-weavers of this ancient land, who follow their visions and offer them at the altars of our own inner shrines.

From Tule, I traveled to Monte Alban, a nearby ruin where I intended to record my first formal retrieval of Earth wisdom. This ancient Zapotec ceremonial city sits atop an artificially leveled mountain and overlooks the dry, expansive valley of Oaxaca. Like many other temples in Mexico and throughout the world, the ruins here were constructed over much older temples and ceremonial sanctuaries. Excavations of Monte Alban and of the other ruins that lie beneath it, have yielded treasures of gold, copper, jade, crystal, obsidian, turquoise and bone. I didn't know a lot about this ruin, as I preferred not to engage my mind, but rather to trust my intuition and energy at this and other sites. I was not a tourist at these sites, but a worker for the earth. So, when I arrived, I scanned the area energetically, to determine where I should settle myself, to feel the call of any rocks that were willing to share their wisdom.

I slowly walked across the grounds of the ruin, until I came across a neatly mown grassy area partially enclosed by an ancient stone wall. I felt the draw to rest here, so I squatted facing the wall and silently introduced myself, sharing my intent and asking permission to enter the world of the stones. I then turned and sat with my back against the wall, settling myself into the inner silence from which I could best hear the messages of the stones. It was not long before, just like at Teotihuácan that I felt connected with the stones and then it started to rain lightly. I was able to ignore the weather and stay focused with my inner vision, and in a few minutes I heard the voice of an ancient rock.

Whisper to the rain, let the murmurs of your heart be given unto the rain, for the rain washes away, cleanses and "re-vibrates" these murmurs and returns them unto you as new tones, to demarcate your voyages in life. It is when the rocks drink the water from the heavens above that the information afoot is absorbed. Water is mutable and flowing; it is under-standing and compassionate—it moves with understanding in its compassion of its obstacles. Rock is solid and concrete in its "seeming form"; but it too is compassionate and under-standing in its knowingness of itself. It doesn't need to do anything or prove anything, it just is. When water merges with rock, there is a resolution of duality, softness merges with hardness, mutability merges with concreteness, and mobility merges with the immovable. Heavenly tears merge with the desert rocks' longing, for when they come together and merge, the rock releases the information it is longing to give.

The language of the rocks surprised me; it seemed tinted with an old English and poetic style. Perhaps I had anticipated something more primordial? As I pondered this offering, I was able to weave together many of the threads from the tears in the fabric of our lives. I delved into the twin relationship between sound and silence, of sun and moon, of male and female, of chaos and order, of future and past, of cause and effect, of pain and ecstasy, and of light and dark. I remembered an astonishing insight I had once received while looking out of the window of my house in Australia. My gaze had landed upon a palm tree that Marcus and I had planted. The midday sun was strong, and it lent clarity to my inner sight. I noticed how the tree cast a large, dark shadow, and I realized that the stronger the source of light, the greater a shadow would be cast, also, that the denser the object, the more intense the shadow. I now related this insight to the human experience, whereby, the more light and love we invite into our lives, the more our shadows of fear and darkness will be revealed. If we judge and shun these fears and inner shadows, we push them down deeper into our beings and into our bodies, thereby creating more density. But if we embrace these fears and shadows, they then more easily or quickly are able to dissolve into the face of light and conscious awareness. This insight, along with the offering I received at Monte Alban, showed me that the sum of the parts equals wholeness, which is in itself the gateway to love.

That message satisfied me, and I spent the rest of my time in Monte Alban exploring the ruins but not doing any retrievals. I did not want to rush the process or become greedy for insights. In fact, as I left Monte Alban I realized that my time in Oaxaca was complete and that it was time for me to move on. When a friend Victoria, invited me to spend a weekend visiting Puerto Escondido, on the southern coast of Mexico, the invitation felt perfectly timed and so I accepted her invitation.

The coast was an energetic world away from the sacred ruins in which I had been spending my time. The throngs of local young people seemed lifeless, interested only in surfing and getting high on psychotropic drugs. I was saddened for these young ones, for it appeared to me that they had lost their inherent connection to their motherland. This augmented my own longing to connect with the spirit of the earth, so I spent most of my time at the shore and not in the town.

One day, while walking along the shore, I spotted an interesting formation of rocks looming like a small mountain in the far distance. It took longer than I expected to reach them, and as I wandered among them, I came upon a cave. Its interior was dark, and while it did not look especially uninviting, it did look uncompromising. Despite that feeling, I felt a pull to enter into the cave, so I stopped before it. The day had been sweltering and the coolness of the cave's entrance seemed a reward for my long walk across the sand so I decided to enter the cave. I felt sure it wanted to talk with me, but before I did, I asked its permission and when I felt I had received the okay to enter, I did so. It was spacious inside and, naturally, damp and very dark. I was no more than a few steps inside before I realized it was home to what sounded like hundreds of bats. The smell of bat urine and excretion snubbed my nostrils but I wasn't frightened. In fact, a curious thought occurred to me: I immediately wondered if there was a connection between these bats and the young people of this area. I felt a vampire-like influence had leeched the life force from many of the young people here. All they wanted to do was fly in the dark—surfing through dark tunnels of water or through the dark haze of drugs. The cave seemed insistent that I hear its message, so I took a deep breath to clear my thoughts. As I moved still deeper into the cave, I began to feel a little frightened. My curiosity was stronger than my fear, however, and I was eager to attempt a retrieval here in the cave—inside a rock!

As I settled myself upon a rock that protruded from the damp earth, I decided to ask for a revelation about the nature of this area and its people, although I was open to any information that the rocks wanted to impart to me. I turned to face the opening of the cave, facing the surf. My reasoning was that it might be important for me in this retrieval to be viewing the water, since this is the element that the people of the area were most intimate and involved with. I had a pad of paper and pen with me and took them out now and with only just enough light to write in, I silenced myself, ready to be the scribe for the rocks. Soon, I felt myself writing, my hand moving as quickly as possible to keep up with the information I was attuning to.

Here the bats communicate their darkest secrets and deepest desires to be part of the outer world. They hang on and cling to the roof of the cave, not ready or able to let go into the discovery of the world beyond their own. They slither their tongues, screeching at the possibility of a new world. Here they dwell in their cave of darkness, living in the dankness of their own excretions. These bats sleep with their eyes closed to the outer world, blind to the light of day. They work consciously at extracting information from the light—like vampires, sucking nourishment from the light, feeding themselves in the darkness. At the turn of day, when the rest of humanity is asleep, the bats communicate and confer about their extractions. They are communication siphons for some extraterrestrial beingness from another realm, and they release this information in the dark of night, when all static and interruption of energy is low and clarity for sending information is high. They, like everything else, have their jobs to do in keeping things in order, perhaps absorbing the negativity of people's consciousness

*and releasing it to the other side? They are innocent like
a fetus clinging to the uterine wall, extracting and absorbing
nutrients, pure in their form and intent. They know of the
dream world, of the void, where the darkness is all-knowing
and communication is made through the inner silence.*

When I stopped writing, I remembered something
Guillermo had told me: that bats are respected in the Mayan
culture for the protection they give, as they are the symbols
of death and rebirth and play a significant role in the cycles of
reincarnation. He had also said, that they protect the souls from
death as they travel into life again and are the gatekeepers and
protectors of the Underworld. Perhaps these bats are the protectors
of the young surfers as they travel from their "inner world" to
the outer.

I left the cave deeply moved by the retrieval, for I had
learned something penetrating and beautiful about bats, which are
normally among the most reviled and misunderstood animals in
the world. I was left intrigued by the part about the bats being
siphons for some extraterrestrial beingness, but decided to trust in
the information given.

The next day I was on my way back to Oaxaca to collect my
belongings and catch a bus to the state of Chiapas, where I had
decided my next destination would be—to the ancient Palenque
ruins. I always enjoyed the long bus ride between destinations, as
this provided me with privacy and time to recapitulate and integrate
my experiences. I also took this time to study Spanish by consulting
my pocketbook dictionary.

Once in Chiapas, I made some inquiries with some locals at the bus station about a safe but reasonably priced place to stay. The dominant opinion was El Panchan, a cabana complex with an adjacent campground that was within walking distance of the Palenque ruins. It also had a reputation for being the quietest and "most spiritual" of the three camping areas in the area. When I arrived at El Panchan I was delighted with what I found. The complex was set in a pristine jungle-like environment, complete with flowering shrubs, meandering streams with pools that held large fish, and stone walkways that connected the clusters of small guest cottages and cabana-like bungalows. What's more, the cantina there served vegetarian food and there was even a meditation temple. I knew I had found the home base of my dreams when I saw that two of the adjoining bungalows were named the sun and the moon. I took the Sun bungalow and situated myself comfortably, for I planned to stay for at least three weeks.

My reservoir of luck seemed to be overflowing when later that evening, as I wandered around the complex, I met an older man named Moisés. I could tell instantly that he was a man of wisdom, an "elder." I was not the only one attracted by his energy, and there was soon a small group of people gathered around him. His silver hair seemed to glimmer and his dark brown eyes shone with light as he told us that he had been a tour guide in the area for more than twenty years. He quickly launched into a story about the ancient Mayans and explained that Palenque is the most dramatic of the classical Mayan cities.

I couldn't wait to visit the ruin, and did so at first light the next morning. Upon entering the complex, I was taken aback by its verdant beauty, the lush emerald-green canopies overspreading the complex. "This is how the Garden of Eden must have looked," I thought to myself. Even though I was transfixed by the natural beauty of the area, my attention was almost immediately pulled to a grand temple that appeared like a white stone jewel nestled against the velvety green backdrop. This was the Temple of Inscriptions. I walked over to it, awed by its magnificence. It is a massive stepped pyramid of nine levels topped with a rectangular building with five doors. A grand stairway rises more than seventy-five feet from the ground to the middle doorway. Deep inside the pyramid lay the sarcophagus of the Mayan king Pacal Votan, after whom the city was named, and the glyphs and inscriptions throughout its interior were eventually deciphered, revealing details never before known about the ancient Mayans. In fact, three large panels of inscriptions there are the second longest Mayan inscriptions ever found and detail the descendants of Pacal Votan.

I found a place near the temple's base to settle in for my meditation, and I quickly and reverentially entered into the inner silence, awaiting any messages from these stone timekeepers. I felt the energy almost like an inner wind with an electric quality to it, keeping this temple and all the other stone edifices in this ruin alive and amplified with cosmic information. The message came swiftly and clearly.

> The sun, moon, wind, rocks, and water all contribute to Earth's electromagnetic current. The wind was especially revered by the Mayans as the god IK, and is the transporting element. Its magic accelerates our ascension to Gods' domain, just as the eagle uses the wind to ascend, as a messenger carrying its wisdom aloft and offering it to the central Sun God above.

I sat in silence after this short retrieval, allowing its simple power to reach deep within me. I felt it was only priming me for a much deeper connection that was to come. When I felt ready, I quietly opened my eyes, gave thanks to the stones of this temple, and wandered away, with no specific destination in mind. I next found myself at the Royal Palace, where Lord Pacal Votan and his family had once lived. A bas-relief in the stones of the temple showed the Royals with hooked noses and the flattened skulls so characteristic of the Mayans. The Palace area itself was a labyrinth of stone coated in green and yellow lichen and besides the tourists who wandered through, its only inhabitants were the parrots, lizards, hummingbirds, and howler monkeys that had taken up residence there.

Nearby I found the *Temezcal,* a Mayan steam bath, a place of purification much like the Native American's sweatlodge. I had read about how a chosen priest or priestess would sit in silence in the *Temezcal,* releasing his or her fears and sweating out his or her physical impurities in preparation for a sacrificial bloodletting ceremony. I decided to attune myself to these rocks, and was effortlessly transported through a doorway of the past. I saw myself in a past life, sitting in this lodge in silent preparation as a "chosen one." I was about to be cut, so that my blood would become an offering to the gods. My present self melded into that ancient self, and I felt my sense of separateness, of aloneness, but also of resolve. I was sacrificing my own desperate will for the will of the gods. As I tapped into my emotions more deeply I could feel the fear and excitement coursing through my body. To be a chosen one was a privilege! Through the offering of my blood to the earth and the gods, my entire bloodline would be brought honor.

I was abruptly thrust out of my meditative connection with the past by the eruption of loud chattering and laughter by nearby tourists. I tried to drown out these sounds by pressing my hands over my ears, but that didn't work. The magical connection severed, and I could not reenter the inner energetic space necessary for any further retrieval, but I was determined to try. I found myself becoming more and more tense, and as I struggled to shut out the external world and stay connected only with the interior one, I realized that there was a whole new way to retrieve information. I could become rocklike myself! Instead of becoming soft and receptive like water, allowing the information to flow into me, I could become in a sense "denser" and more "grounded." This stability allowed me to become still in a different way, sinking down deep into myself with fortitude and entering solidly into timeless silence from where the information was waiting to be received. I would delve under the noisiness where silence exists and would have to experiment with this new way of accessing the wisdom of the rocks.

I sat back against the rocks and let my mind wander over the history of this place and of my own sense that I had once lived here—and died here. I didn't know a lot of this site's history, but I had read that the Mayans had used blood sacramentally. The blood of the Royals, of human "chosen ones," such as the priest and priestess, and of such sacred animals as the jaguar, was offered once a year as a gift to the gods above and as nourishment for the earth below. I also had read that those who entered the *Temezcal*— who purified themselves in the steam baths in preparation for their sacrifice—were often given psychotropic mushrooms so that they could more readily access the mystical realms between life and death. Also, that they may have even been given herbal anesthetics for pain. The ceremony, from what I knew of it, did not sound pleasant, and it differed for males and females. The females would pierce their tongue with a sharp fish bone and let the drops of blood fall onto a rock altar, whereas the males would pierce their phallus.

I contemplated what an offering of blood might mean, what it might accomplish in the realm of the mystical and sacred. Perhaps, like a homoeopathic dose of medicine for the earth, even one drop of royal blood was enough to quench the thirst of the land and to bind humans to the gods. I could imagine a single drop of sacrificial blood seeping deep into the soil, gathering energetic force and running into the secret caverns and labyrinths throughout the earth. I envisioned it gathering even more force and plunging into the Underworld—deeper and deeper still—until it emerged somehow into the realm of gods—of the heavens. The Mesoamericans believed that the Underworld is a gateway to the spiritual world, where going inside meant going outside and going down meant going up. Life is a great circle—a great circulation! What seems to be linear or dual is circular and singular, like pain leading to ecstasy, bloodletting turning into life-getting.

My thoughts were electrifying me, and I felt almost dizzy. Enough! It was already early afternoon and I needed a break, so I headed back to my cabana, where I lazed in the sun and wrote in my journal until early evening. Shortly after dark, Moisés showed up in the open courtyard and a small group gathered round him as he entertained us with his historical stories, myths, and legends. I went to bed that night eager to return to the ruins. I planned to go back in the early afternoon and to stay until nightfall, evading the guards and remaining in the ruins after dark so that I could sit in total silence with the rocks and the jungle away from the chattering crowds. Even though the rocks had just taught me a new way to go inside to access the silence without the disturbance of tourist's clatter, I felt I could go deeper in a quiet environment. I drifted off to sleep hoping my plan would work.

I arrived back at Palenque at about two-thirty in the afternoon and immediately went back to the Temple of Inscriptions, where I climbed the stairway to its top. Not knowing exactly what this particular temple's purpose was, beyond being a tomb for a Mayan king, I decided to rely on my instinct, trusting in my openness to receiving the information of its life giving energies and historical currents. At the top of the steps was a hoard of Japanese tourists. I was taken aback at the frenzy of activity: they were snapping pictures, jabbering almost nonstop, scurrying here and there. They lacked any sense of sanctity for the ancient site, never mind for its sacred energies. I felt saddened by the gulf I observed between the bustle of the tourists and the quiet reverence and magical aura of this stone temple. I felt tears spring to my eyes, and a longing overtook me—a desire really, to hug the stones and wail and to let my tears stream into the stone floor. I felt as if through my reverence for the site I might somehow make restitution to the spirits of the place for the boorishness of the tourists. I was thankful for yesterday's lesson about how to recognize the silence within the rocks even amid the stir of the "normal" world, and I began to connect with this silence. Almost immediately, I could hear something calling me. A voice from the depths of my own heart? An echo from the ancient stones? I wasn't sure but I trusted the process and followed the call as I began the descent into the heart of the pyramid. Carefully I made my way down the steep stone steps to where the funerary chamber of Lord Pacal Votan himself lay almost seventy-five feet down inside the temple. I felt a growing connection to his energy, and almost in spite of myself I heard my inner voice call out: "I am coming, my lord. I have arrived, I have arrived."

The monolithic sarcophagus was richly decorated with carvings, and a large relief carving showed Lord Pacal reclining in some kind of strange chair or, as some believe, in a vehicle, perhaps even a space vehicle. His clubfoot was clearly depicted in the carving. Although I shared the area around the tomb room with many tourists, I felt wrapped in a cocoon of silence, as if I were alone with this ancient and royal beloved one. I was completely mesmerized, and felt that I had entered into a different reality zone—a place that was paradoxically timeless, yet guarded by ancient timekeepers. I felt a strong attachment, even love, for this Mayan royal. I sat down on the cold stone floor by the entrance of the tomb. The sarcophagus was cordoned off to prevent damage from curious tourists. I knew almost immediately that now was not the time for me to attempt a retrieval. I would come back here at dusk, at the meeting point of two worlds, day and night, at that mysterious "hour of power." I quickly scampered back up the stone steps and wandered the ruins for several hours.

As the sun began to set, I was at the edge of the temple complex, by myself and partially hidden by the thick jungle vegetation. I managed to evade the guards as they herded the last of the tourists from the immediate vicinity. Then I just waited, meditating in the shadows of the jungle, aligning myself with the energies of this magnificent site. I felt waves of gratitude wash over me, and I got the idea that I needed to prepare myself further by actually cleansing myself. Not far away was the Queen's Pool. I undressed and stole over to it, its waters crystalline and cold, and the area surrounding the pool overhung with greenery and small, cream-colored lilies. As I immersed myself, using the power of my intent to cleanse myself spiritually, I felt flickers of energy, as if there were many beings around me. In my mind's eye I suddenly saw many small water nymphs flitting around the pool, imparting to it a feminine water energy. I felt accepted, welcomed, blessed by these energy beings. I inwardly asked what I acknowledged to be the Lily Spirit, if I could pick a lily to wear in my hair to visit my Lord Pacal. She granted my request. After I tucked the lily in my hair, I quickly finished my cleansing prayers, retrieved my clothes, and tugged them over my still-wet skin. Then I headed for the Temple of Inscriptions, feeling very present in the moment, completely aware and open. As I climbed the stairway to the temple, I felt certain that I had once, in a past life, been a priestess in service to Lord Pacal and that I had received training in dance and the earth mysteries here in this very temple complex.

As I neared the top of the temple, the entire stone edifice was awash in moonlight. The relief carvings on the walls seemed to dance to life. I was alive with anticipation—until I reached the top of the temple and found that the entrance door to the stairway leading down into the tomb had been locked. I stood there in the darkness for a few minutes, suddenly overcome with anxiety. The shadows seemed to darken, and for a moment I wondered if I would have had the courage to descend in the dark into the tomb room. But my loss of certainty lasted only a few moments. I knew that I was connected to Lord Pacal and that our energies could merge no matter how far the physical distance between us. I turned and exited the temple and sat on the uppermost platform with my back resting against the temple stone. Moonlight washed over my face. I closed my eyes and entered the silence within. Soon the stones began to speak:

> We are the children of the universe; we come from afar, from another world, at one you have not yet reached. We have come to seed your planet with the knowledge of the One who emanates the light of information. He has come to anchor this information and let it unravel from his being like a holographic spiral staircase. You receive this transmission in a gentle, unobtrusive way, your DNA alerted and fed this encoding system of informative light that leads you back toward your Great Central Sun–God. This spiral staircase of light is the sacred geometric route back home—your path to ascension. Lord Pacal is an Ascension Lord, a Lord of Light; his physical body is buried far down in the density of his stone tomb, which itself acts as an anchor of light that infiltrates into the deep recesses of darkness. This is a necessary step in resolving duality in preparation of the Ascension process. This spiral staircase of holographic and geometric "light mats" (info-mat-ion) is soon to unravel completely, to expire, leaving you with little time left to find your way home; the light is dwindling, the sun is setting, and soon, your journey will be guided by the moon within your souls.

When I was present to myself again, I spoke inwardly to Lord Pacal, "Thank you my Lord. We will meet you in the Oneness through the ascending staircase when we truly arrive by your side." As I prepared to leave, the thought occurred to me that Lord Pacal could very well have been the Christed luminary for the ancient Mayans. I also realized that my visits to these sacred sites are my way of visiting the sacred sites within myself. It is my way of journeying deep into the recesses of my own body, deep into the density of my own history, and into the density of my bones where the DNA, the sacred spiral of information about my own lineage, resides. It is within, that I—and we all—can access the past. The way is along the spiral staircases of light that unravels each of us into the nowhere-ness (now-here-ness). Likewise, the stones encode the blueprint, the DNA, of Earth's history. The natives of America saw the rocks as the bones of the earth, which hold together the physical structure of Earth's body and the place where history is stored both geographically and spiritually.

At Palenque, something shifted within me. For more than fifteen years, I had, as a naturopathic doctor, treated people body, mind, and spirit. Now my ministry had shifted, to listening and learning from the earth, from the bones of the earth, from the sacred echo of the collective past. I was indeed becoming a record keeper, and I finally felt ready to make the plunge into the Yucatán proper. Spirit often seemed to direct me to my next destination and now this parting was no different. As I prepared to leave the El Panchan hotel, two women I had met there—Sandy and Suzie— offered me a ride to Chetumal, the last city in Mexico just before the border of Belize. From there I would find my way to Guatemala and the famous ruins of Tikal.

Sandy and Suzie were companions, and were two of the most hilarious women I had ever met. They made the most unlikely couple. Sandy was a large-boned, physically intimidating woman who looked as strong as a rugby-player and as outlandish as a "motorcycle mama." She wore her dark hair closely cropped to her skull, and her arms and legs were festooned with tattoos of eagles and panthers. Her dress was masculine: green army-type shorts, a T-shirt, and combat boots. Suzie played counterpoint. She was as dainty in stature and build as Sandy was looming and large. She was always well put-together, from her tightly fitted summer dresses to her perfectly applied make-up and her coral-painted fingernails and toenails. She also had a thick southern accent that I enjoyed. These women were rare jewels indeed—one a diamond in the rough and the other a delicate pearl. Energetically, I thought of Sandy as the Indian Chief and Suzie as the Southern Belle. They were an unlikely pair, but they fit together perfectly. I was eager to be part of their combined "aura," for everything they did seemed to be tinged with laughter and delight.

The first day's drive was restful, as Sandy did all the driving. We had a wonderful time chatting and telling stories of our travels and adventures. The day flew by and before I knew it we were pulling up to a small, unappealing motel—the only one in the area— to spend the night. I fell asleep almost right away, but was rudely awoken by my throbbing wisdom tooth. I knew immediately that this wasn't a minor problem, and my spirits sank as I thought of having to find a dentist in some out-of-the-way Mexican town. As the night wore on, the pain intensified. I tried everything I knew to quell the pain, including Reiki healing, Foot Reflexology and bathing the tooth with Tee Tree oil, a "fix-it-all" essential oil that I always carry with me when traveling. I used all my skills as a healer, but to no avail. I even tried to "talk" to the pain, to see what it was trying to tell me. All I could come up with was that my "wisdom" was going to be extracted from me in a painful way. So much for the easy access to Earth wisdom!

As morning approached, I broke down from the pain, falling to my knees next to the bed and praying for relief. As the sun came up, I felt the back of the pain had broken, and I was overcome with a feeling of familiarity about what had transpired. Why did this scenario feel so familiar? Why was it that I seemed to have to have these dark nights of the body-mind-soul only to find relief with the arrival of the light of day? I thought back to the agony of the peyote vision quest in the dark of the tepee and the visionary mushroom journey in the darkened mountain house. The only answer that had any appeal for me at all was symbolic—that I was undergoing a series of "birth" traumas, that I was somehow struggling through a kind of dark birth canal trying to be born into a new world of light. By the time I met up with Sandy and Suzie to resume our journey, there wasn't a trace of pain left in my wisdom tooth, for which I was thankful.

We hadn't gone much farther on our way before we stopped for a short visit at a small ruin, whose name I have forgotten. It was of unimportant stature, but we were drawn to stop there, so we did. I spent a few minutes sitting in stillness with the rocks, choosing to rest my back against an adobe wall with an arched top. At one point I looked up at the wall above my head and was startled to notice a large bee hive hanging from it. Bees are high in my rank of personal animal totems, and I was happy to be close to them again.

On the walk back to the car, I caught a motion in my peripheral vision at the edge of a tree line and jerked around to my right. I glimpsed a dark-skinned man wearing a tunic woven with Mayan designs walking through the trees. He was hurrying along, but I could see him well enough to note the colorful headdress he wore and the strange sandals with straps of leather that wound up his calves. I couldn't be sure, but it looked like he was carrying a pick-ax or some kind of other pick-like tool. I wondered for a moment if I had just experienced a time shift, as this figure seemed to me more akin to something from Mexico's remote past than to its present day, but I didn't dwell on the thought. That is, until I got back to the car and began to share notes about the ruin with Suzie. She described seeing a man in the ruins dressed exactly like the man I had seen along the tree line. "He was wearing a headdress of some kind," she described, her voice tinged with confusion.

"And tie-up sandals!" For some reason, I didn't mention that I, too, had seen the man. Somehow the sighting seemed private and sacred, and I couldn't shake the feeling that the Yucatán is a place of the Time Lords and Timekeepers, where time zones are thin and even overlapping.

That night we stopped again, but this time at a grand, lovely hotel situated along Bacalar Lakes, whose waters were proclaimed to contain healing properties and exhibit seven different shades of blue. After stretching my legs by strolling along the lake's edge, I retired to my room. This night turned out to be a repeat of the previous night—I was awakened by intense pain from my right wisdom tooth. The pain was nearly unendurable and I didn't know what to do, but I had to get out of that room. Perhaps I was slightly delirious. All I know is that I felt trapped in that room and needed to be out in the fresh air. In the hall I found a stairway that led to the roof, and I climbed it like a drunkard, bereft of coordination and wanting only the moon as companion to my pain.

When I was on the roof, I looked up at the soft glow of the moon and lost my rational mind to her. "Please, forgive me, my queen," I pleaded. "I hear your call. It beckons me to awaken from my dreams. Only through my delirious fever and pain do I hear you now, deep within the pain of my being. I cry from a pain I didn't know was there. Only from there do I hear your call." Suddenly I understood that I was not talking to the moon, but to Lord Pacal's mother the Queen via the moon, and had realized a mistake I had made, back at Palenque. I had honored the Lord by visiting his tomb, but I had virtually ignored the Queen, his mother. "I know not what became of me to run to my Lord Pacal's tomb!" I admitted. "I eagerly paid homage and respect to him and bypassed and neglected your humble tomb—a tomb of underlying beauty and wisdom that goes deep into the bosom of all women." I was listening to myself talking to the moon, but I seemed outside myself, as if another me were talking. I heard myself launch into a lament for womankind. "Women who have suffered through the initiations of love. Women who have sought the ends of this earth for balance, harmony, and the completion of a sacred union between the genders. Speak my queen! My mind is broken open by pain, and my heart is open to receiving your wisdom and communications."

I heard the moon reply on behalf of the queen.

The reason the people of Earth don't feel me as they do Lord Pacal is because I have completed my part of the mission. My work is done on this planet, and I now wait for my Lord, my counterpart, to complete his. The illumination he carries is a strong one, which still sheds light on your path home to our Great Central Sun. I am waiting in darkness for my Lord, so that the sacred marriage can travel through time and journey towards its completion of balance—the masculine and feminine principles joined hand in hand, the most prominent duality your Earth still has to embrace. Through the last breath that my soul has to expire, it is hard to keep my consciousness connected to my soul as it longs to return home. With my consciousness anchored in the Underworld, I, too, assist the process of ascension with the knowingness and remembrance of the true soul marriage of man and woman upon this earth, the true completion of this mission in this millennium.

I was confused by the message of the Queen Mother. She seemed to speak of Lord Pacal as her beloved one. Perhaps this was only my pain speaking, in a delirious and jumbled kind of wisdom—a wisdom pain that may have too truly revealed the confusion lying in my own tomb of despair.

I don't know for how many hours I sat on the rooftop watching the moon sail across the ethereal ocean of the night sky. By the time I finally retraced my steps to my room, the toothache had subsided. Once again I tried to make some sense of what had just happened and why I had nearly lost my mind to the pain. I decided I must have been manifesting physically what I had been holding in emotionally for most of my life. For so many years, through my childhood with demanding parents and then through the tumultuous years of my marriage and my demeaning husband, I had held my tongue, set my jaw to hold back the anger. For so long as an adult I had resisted speaking my truth, so as to be a patient and kind "spiritual person." But now, despite all my emotional releases of the past few years, I was still physically manifesting my emotional pain, this time through my aching wisdom tooth. "Wisdom is the tongue of my ancestors," I said to myself, "and I'm now compelled to find my 'wise-dom-ain.'" I liked my word play, but I was bursting with questions: Why is it that suffering and pain seems to precede the birth of wisdom? Does being wisdom-filled first require the breakdown of control? The disintegration of the self-made image? Or is it that pain helps us reach deeper into ourselves to find peace, or even to strive higher toward the divine for guidance and assistance? I had no answers, and slept fitfully the rest of the night.

The next morning I was awakened by the sounds of quarreling. My traveling companions were having it out and I could hear them through the wall of our adjoining room. I didn't really know what was happening with them, but only a short time later Suzie came to my room to let me know we were all on our own. They were each going their own way, and I would have to find my way as well. I wasn't sorry. After my strange night on the roof, I was ready to be alone, with no one to look out for but myself. After I paid my room bill, I walked to the town's only taxi station, and while waiting for a taxi I silently spoke to my wisdom tooth, which was still smarting. "Please hang on until I get to the United States. If I'm going to have a tooth extracted, at least let it be done in a civilized dental clinic, in a country where I can speak the language fluently and have my needs met." Soon a taxi pulled up and I was off to Chetumal. From there I hopped a bus for the ten-hour trip through Belize and into Guatemala, where I planned to visit the ancient city of Tikal.

Along the banks of a lake called Petan, in the Guatemalan state of El Remate, I checked into "El Mirador del Duende" (meaning the view of the elfin and goblin realms,) a self sustaining ecological park that had been recommended to me by several tourists and locals whom I had consulted. The park contained a charming string of freeform white stucco bungalows run by a man of Mayan descent named Manuel De Soto. Manuel had a wild, gypsy look about him, with roguish dark hair and a gold hoop earring in his left earlobe. He spoke fluent but heavily accented English, and I spent my first evening there mesmerized by Manuel's stories, which were crammed with interesting historical data and so made listening to him a little exhausting. I felt breathless from trying to keep up with his lightning-quick train of thought. When I finally got to bed late that night, I felt as if my inner wiring had somehow been rearranged. After a few moments of breathing deeply to catch up with my sense of self, I was met head-on by mandalas of ethereal hues of pink, green, purple, orange, blue, and white. One of these complex geometric shapes traveled toward me—and then through me. As soon as that mandala disappeared behind me, another formed before me, one of equal beauty and complexity. It, too, drew toward me and then through me. Faster and faster they came as the process repeated itself. I felt that instead of my stepping through doorways of light, doorways of light were passing through me. Then the scene shifted, and I was hurtling out through space. I thought that perhaps these mandalas were templates of light and that inner/outer space was opening to receive me. I felt myself being propelled outward into another dimension and felt as if I were about to spontaneously combust. As the sensation intensified, I must have panicked, for I sprang up, nearly leaping out of bed, sure I had just saved myself from immolating into nothingness.

Later that night I remembered having a dream. It was of the Pleiades, a star system popularly called the Seven Sisters and important to the spiritual systems of many ancient cultures. In my dream this constellation was brimming with tiny stars that flowed outward from it into space, traveling in an orderly stream across the sky. I followed them, and danced the star-wisdom within me along their path of light. Then one star far ahead of me in the stream of stars separated out and soared back toward me. I extended my index finger to touch it, and as our energies connected I was infused with light. I jerked from the stellar shock, like a child who had stuck her finger in a light socket. I remember thinking, in my dream, of the movie ET, when the little boy and the alien touch fingers, tip to tip.

I awoke in the morning with this star dream still emotionally electrifying me. I was sure that this land of the Mayans, this land that I was coming to know and feel intimately deep within me, was a bridge not only into the earth but also out to the stars. I remembered the carving of Lord Pacal Votan sitting in his strange vehicle. Perhaps it was a star-ship. Perhaps he was indeed a star voyager.

It was with the energy of these strange and affecting reveries still lingering in my consciousness that I set off for Tikal, which has the reputation of being an "unsettling" ruin. I did not know much about this ruin, as I was making it a point to stay as objective and unschooled by logic as possible so that I could be a better and purer retriever of Earth's wisdom. But the descriptions I had heard from people I ran into, on the bus and at the hotel, were that Tikal could be "dark" and "intense." This rather surprised me, for Tikal is touted as the most magnificent of all Mayan ruins. It was a sprawling and wealthy city that covered six square miles and was home to more than 100,000 people and the seat of power for the lords of the Jaguar Clan. When I arrived there, although I was making an effort to not be influenced by others' experiences, I, too, found the energy rather "heavy."

I made my way to the tallest structure in the ruins, the Temple of the Two-Headed Snake (shown on maps as Temple IV), which towered as high as a modern skyscraper above the roof of the surrounding jungle. I was perspiring as I made the challenging climb up its long stairway, stopping halfway up at the tomb building before continuing on. At the top, I found a quiet niche where I could partially screen myself from the tourists, and there I prepared myself for a retrieval.

Here in this lost city of timeless suspension is the anchorage of light. Rocks are indeed great anchors of light; they contain so much information that is packed so tightly with light energy that they appear solid and dense, but they are not solid and dense—in their seeming remoteness and darkness they actually embrace the light. Their light energy is anchored in its extreme opposite of darkest density, which in its absorption of experience reveals information: the language of light and know-ledge, (a ledge of knowing). The silence is deafening and if you listen in stillness, delving into the internal depths of your own inner sanctuary, you hear the inner voice of silence, which speakes of no-thing and every-thing. This omnipresent temple, this temple of the two-headed snake, holds the balance of light and dark. The interplay of the two is evident, the merging and fusion has been done, the resolution of duality manifest.

I found the messages about the union of opposites, the integration of duality, the light revealed in the darkness, and the knowing that emerges from silence to be apropos for a temple named "Two-Headed Snake," and I wondered what other information was awaiting retrieval at this magnificent ruin. Although I wandered among the site's many temples for several more hours, I did not feel called to attempt another retrieval. I decided to head back to the hotel.

While waiting for the bus, an elderly, petite, and soft-spoken man struck up a conversation with me. I had developed my Spanish to the point that I could understand him fairly well, although I had more difficulty speaking the language. His name was Andrés, and he seemed determined to tell me all he knew about another ruin, Uaxatún, the place of *ocho piedras* (eight stones). He explained that Uaxatún is the oldest of Mayan cities so far excavated and is the place where the Mayans were thought to have consolidated their culture, developed their complex calendar system, and perfected their glyphic writing system. He said the ruin was isolated and quiet—off the tourist circuit—and he described the site as having a "feminine quality." I didn't know why he had brought up this ruin or why he was going into so much detail about it. Was it a message from Spirit that Uaxatún should be my next destination? I was not surprised when the old man next told me the ruin was only sixteen miles north of Tikal and he would be happy to serve as my guide. I was unsure if I should take him up on this offer. I thought back to my initial train ride into Mexico and how three different seatmates had warned me to be careful about traveling alone in Mexico. I had pretty much ignored their warnings, so I was mystified as to why they now seemed to rise to mind. I did not intuit any danger, and there was nothing overtly threatening about this gentle-spirited man. I finally accepted his offer, drawn by the prospect of visiting the rocks and connecting with the land there.

I followed Andrés onto the bus that would take us to Uaxatún. The sixteen-mile ride took over an hour because of the deteriorated condition of the wet, muddy road that wound through the Guatemalan jungle. The bus was old and rickety, and its engine seemed to always be straining. I wondered if we would ever make it to our destination and felt great relief when we finally did. The bus pulled into a quaint and remote village, and Andrés led the way from its tiny center to his tiny hut of a house, where he introduced me to his wife and three children of which I was happy to meet. The village had few amenities: only one ramshackle restaurant that contained rough wooden chairs and tables, and a one-room classroom. Classes did not seem to be in session, and Andrés told me I could hang a hammock in the class-room and sleep there. Pigs, hens, and roosters roamed the open fields surrounding the town, where the children played among them. We made plans to tour the ruins early the next morning.

Dawn brought a flood of sunlight that glinted off the jungle canopy, making this emerald world almost vibrate. The ruins were not far, and Andrés and I walked to them on labyrinthine pathways through the glistening jungle. I listened as he offered his knowledge with grace and generosity. I couldn't understand all of his Spanish, but that didn't bother me, as I was more intent on connecting with the ruins energetically than intellectually.

When we got to the ruins proper, I told Andrés that I wanted some time alone to connect myself with the energy of the place, and he graciously wandered off so I could have my privacy. I found a large rock and sat atop it, sinking my energetic roots into the earth and finding that place of silence within. The rocks of Uaxatún spoke to me.

The rocks here are the loyal and ancient keepers of a living myth. Together with the surrounding jungle, they suspend time, opening us to the timeless zone of the Mayans. Here the rock walls were once lined with jaguar pelts, quetzal feathers, snakeskins, precious jade and caracoles, all symbolizing the Mayan gods, who were revered. The honored warrior wore quetzal feathers and serpent skins in commemoration of Quetzalcoatl, the greatest of Mayan gods, who is carved into the face of a rock tablet and so forever guards these temples and this royal domain. The sacrificial circular stone altars record the taste of blood and fear while the wild jaguar records the stirrings of the Underworld. The small ceremonial dens are where initiate priests, priestesses and royals spent three days in isolation, preparing their consciousness for their voyage and initiation into the Underworld. This initiation was the bloodletting ceremony, where a fishbone spike was used to pierce the females' tongues or the males' penises so that their blood could spill to the earth as an offering of gratitude to the gods and to the earth itself for the gifts of life and fertility. The initiates of this world, of Uaxatún, of the place of the eight stones, had the utmost dedication to the gods and goddesses. The rock here that is vision-scaped into a turtle, shares the history of knowledge through the knowingness of both the Under-world and the Outerworld. When the turtle immerses itself in the world of the ocean, into the unknown depths of our unconscious, it retrieves messages from the silence that resides deep in our own beings. On its return, the turtle raises these messages back to the land of the known, to our conscious Outerworld.

I came out of my meditation feeling that the rocks had provided me as much information as Andrés had. I soon joined back up with him, and he led me to one of the many astronomical observatories in the ruin. These temples to the stars, he explained, are almost always four-stepped pyramids that were precisely aligned to the cardinal points of the compass. Here the astronomer-priests would spend countless hours over innumerable years, one generation after another, calculating the paths of the heavenly bodies, especially the sun and moon, which they thought of as celestial beings. I knew from my meditation that not only the ancient priests knew the secrets of the stars and of time. The rocks did, too. This knowledge was not for a chosen few, but was for us all if we only had the patience and the openness to listen. The nature of rocks themselves is that they are the keepers of knowledge. They are the expert record keepers, the witnesses through time— past and future—of sacred events. They are imbued with the culture of place and also instill the place with culture.

Once again, I sat silently to meditate. I leaned back against the base of one of these ancient observatories, and I retrieved the following history.

The priests here would catch the stars and planets with their eyes and store these holographic im-prints in the temples of their own minds. These mind templates were then grounded on Earth in the bodies of the priests and in the rocks of their star observatories so that a future race could access, and behold, this knowledge. The Jaguar Priests, priests of the Underworld, would stay awake all night when the moon eclipsed the sun, praying and chanting in fear and in the hope that their god, the Sun, would return unto them.

My inner and energetic retrieval was soon displayed in stone before my very eyes as Andrés showed me the jaguar heads carved into one temple pyramid. There were eight jaguar heads, two on each pyramid face. The jaguars in each pair were situated one lower than the other. The lower one was carved with its eyes closed, symbolizing the eclipse, the onset of darkness, and the descent of consciousness into the Underworld. The higher jaguar was depicted with open eyes, on guard, watching for the return of the sun, for the return of consciousness from its journey to the depths of the Underworld. As I examined the carvings, I remembered that Guillermo had told me that jaguars can see in the dark and so were associated with astronomers in the Mayan world.

Later that morning, Andrés took me to a temple where priests and priestesses would perform ceremonial dances for the royal family. He left me alone there, so I could once again connect with the temple in private. Since I was already awakened to my connection of sacred dance, I did not want to miss an opportunity to connect with the ancients through movement. I climbed to a platform high on the temple and constructed a simple altar, in preparation for my dance. I decorated a small area with some flowers that I had gathered nearby and carefully placed two rocks I had been carrying with me on my travels. They were from sacred sites of central Australia, which Marcus had given to me to guide my journey. One was from Ayres Rock (Uluru), an Aboriginal ceremonial site for both men and women. The other rock was from the Olgas (Kata Tjuta), regarded as a powerful male site. I first held the Uluru rock in my left hand and the rock of Kata Tjuta in my right. Then I connected through them to the ancient Aboriginal Dreamtime and anchored that energy into the Mayan temple. Then I placed the rocks on the altar. I had some incense in my bag, so I burned some copal and sage, and honored the Four Directions. Finally, I was ready to pray through dance. I found myself dancing my story, communicating to the spirit of the land of my journey that led me to this temple. With long arms swooping up to the heavens above, head raised high and with my bare feet pounding the stone floor, I delivered my soul intent to the Gods and Goddesses. This was an initiation into a journey of sacred dance, that I knew I was to present to the peoples whom I would inspire and teach.

We left the ruins soon after my dance, both of us content to remain quiet, satisfied that we had shared the energy of a very special place. That night I slept in a hammock in the schoolroom, my dreams transporting me back to the temple grounds, where I communed with turtles and jaguars.

Chapter 7:

The Yucatán Transmissions.

Traveling back into Mexico on my way up into the Yucatán, I made a stop at Bacalar Lakes Hotel to revisit the lake's healing waters. My wisdom tooth on the other side now began to screech with pain. "Oh no, not now," I pleaded silently with it. "Please wait until I get to the United States. The dentists there will be safer and more civilized." But the thought of going through another night of delirious pain motivated me to find a dentist immediately. After making some inquiries, I was referred to a dentist in Chetumal, which made me cringe since I considered it one of the worst cities in Mexico.

The dentist's diagnosis was expected: both wisdom teeth needed to be extracted. He administered pain medication through what felt like four blunt and brutal needles, and before the extraction procedure had even begun, I was shaking with pain and fear. I silently called on all of my angels and troops of medicine guides to assist me, but I felt dreadfully alone as the dentist approached with the pliers. They looked like something he might have taken down from his garage wall. He used them to begin muscling out the first wisdom tooth—pulling and yanking until he was sweaty and I was fighting to remain conscious. With every yank at my tooth, my entire body lifted up off the chair, but the stubborn tooth relentlessly refused to budge from my jaw. Finally, mustering all the strength he could, the dentist twisted the pliers and yanked for all he was worth, and the tooth finally gave way. He held the bloodied culprit between the tips of the pliers to show me why it had been so difficult to extract—it was shaped like a cashew nut! Needless to say, this was among the most horrifying and painful experiences I had ever endured, and it was with relief that I heard the dentists explain that he could not extract the other wisdom tooth right away. It would be in my "best interest" not to attempt it today, he kindly explained. As much as I wanted to be finished with my tooth pain, I also did not want to undergo that torture again, so I thanked him and got the hell out of there.

I was bent over with pain as I hailed a taxi. The driver pulled over and as he opened his door to assist me, two young men passed me on the street. They stopped and asked if they could be of assistance. They introduced themselves as Tom, from England, and Michael from the United States. I filled them in about my dental adventure and told them I was headed back to the Bacalar Lakes hotel. "We are heading there, too!" they exclaimed, and offered to escort me and keep a close eye on me until I recovered. Tom jumped in the back seat with me. He had English schoolboy good looks, but beneath the strong lines of his face was a character that was shy and awkward. I whimpered like a small child on his shoulder during the ride. Even though I could sense that he was not used to this sort of emotional display, he kindly comforted and reassured me that all would be well.

Back at the hotel, I sat on the veranda of my room holding my cheek and trying to endure the pain. The view of the large cerulean-blue lake and the twilight sky cast in shades of orange and pink were spectacular enough to distract me somewhat, but eventually the pain won out. Once again I was forced to consider why I was undergoing this ordeal. Twice now at Bacalar Lakes I had been nearly flattened by pain from my wisdom teeth. What was all this about? An answer arose like a retrieval from my center.

The pain is here so that you may meet it with conscious awareness. There is a severe blockage in your being, one that inhibits you from experiencing your natural inheritance of ecstasy, bliss, and joy. This is yet another opportunity to sit with the pain, take responsibility for it, go into the core of it and come to know what is deep within you that is finally being expressed. Go into your center, where oneness exists. Go into the core of the pain where ecstacy dwells. Welcome the pain as a release, for it no longer needs to linger in the looming shadows. Once brought into the light of consciousness, fear and darkness can no longer exist.

This message reminded me of the sacred mushrooms' wisdom, which had been about the resolution of duality. I had been working on this issue for so long that I had thought I surely had resolved it, but apparently had not. So, over the next few days, I worked inwardly, while also healing my body, taking baths in the healing springs and allowing the restorative powers of Nature to work their magic on me. Tom and Michael also visited, and in a few days my gum felt better. My other wisdom tooth was not bothering me, and I felt renewed emotionally. It was time to continue my journey.

I caught a bus to Tulum, which lay on the northern tip of the turquoise coast of the Yucatán. Once I settled in there, I immediately went to the ruins, eager to resume my work with the stones.

The Tulum ruins are perched high atop a cliff overlooking the Caribbean Sea. Although the city had once been called Zama, it became known as Tulum, which in Mayan literally means "wall," because high walls surround it. This city was once a major link in the Mayans' extensive trade network as both seafaring and land routes converged here. The Mayans had built the walls as defenses against Toltec invaders.

My introduction to the ruins was at its ocean-side entrance. The first thing I saw was a large snake, some kind of constrictor, whose jaws had partially engulfed a rat, slowly pulling the doomed rodent to its death, inch by agonizing inch. I stood motionless watching this primal scene and got the feeling this was a sign of some kind—perhaps even an omen—of what my time in the ruins might be like. I took a deep breath as I moved on, into the ruins proper, and felt again, as I had so often before in the land of the Mayas, that I was entering a state of primeval nature. I was stepping back in time, or, more accurately, entering timelessness itself. The stone walls here are light gray from the encrustation of salt blown up in the wind from the water below and the ruins themselves were cloaked by a mythic energy that was at once both pure and innocent and yet animated with potency and vibrancy.

I settled myself inside the wall and almost at once connected with the stones.

The rocks and stones here guard the gateway between the Underworld—the unconscious, the unknown realm of the deep ocean and the outer world—the conscious realm, the seen world of our terra firma. They are condensed memory banks bridging one world to that of the other. All the information from the unconscious world not yet passed through into the conscious is kept here for safekeeping until mass evolution reaches a level of being able to accept this information into conscious awareness. The rocks release this information by emitting their encoded energy data into holographic thought forms, stamping the templates of geometric patterns, which trigger and activate our own holographic DNA memory banks. These encoded messages are like a correct numerical code that opens a locked safe, giving access to stored items that are ready to be utilized. Those that have traveled the energy doorways within their own inner passageways receive these codes unconsciously, becoming conduits for this information, much the same way as the temples do. Throughout time, this information becomes integrated and grounded within the knowledge of their own body. Once grounded, this energy is released into the morphogenic field (the energetic blueprint of form) around them, thereby triggering and reactivating others who intersect their paths.

This compellingly abstract message seemed to reverberate throughout the ruins as I wandered the grounds. Some of the Tulum temples have high stone pillars that are capped with tablet altars, raising the sacred word to meet the gods above. As I walked throughout the ruins, I sensed that the Mayan's awareness of embodiment of form and matter equaled their deep connection to their God-state selves. These temples seemed to me to be the outer manifestation of the Mayans own inner divinity. They no doubt conceived of their bodies as conduits for Spirit, and it appeared that this is what these stone temples were embodying— the form within which Matter and Spirit merge into something more magnificent still. Standing among these stone edifices, I could imagine the awe they must have inspired in the ancient Mayans, and I understood how in building these temples, the people may have been commemorating the fusion of the physical and spiritual.

Inspired by my psychic connection to the entire complex of temples, I settled myself once again to attempt another retrieval. I softened my breathing as I entered that still center within. On a long exhale, I felt propelled back into the memory banks of Earth, which revealed the impregnation of Spirit into matter, where Spirit—the spark of life itself—embodies the manifestation of itself. On the next inhale, I felt my spirit ignite and the energy rush fueled my passage to the stars above. I felt connected to the Pleiades, and tuned into its stellar frequency. I then received the following transmission.

The star beings of this constellation used the city of Tulum as a lighthouse, storing stellar light on the site, so that its light could infuse those entering the ruins—much like the fireflies, which absorb the light of day and emit this light into the darkness of the night. Once a person is struck and infused by this force of light, the bridge between the worlds of consciousness and unconsciousness, of sea and land, of sky and earth, and of man and woman is made. This path into union, alights them toward a safe journey home, where the heart of all things lay.

Upon opening my eyes, the first thing that fell under my gaze was a lighthouse! At least it resembled a lighthouse. It was positioned at the far edge of the ruins, closest to the ocean. It seemed amazing to me that I had not noticed it earlier. I took this sighting as confirmation for the transmission. (Later I discovered that, that particular part of the ruin is sometimes referred to as "The Lighthouse.") My voyage to the Pleiades had rocketed me high into space and yet had also pulled me deeply into the earth. I pondered its significance, but decided that I should be connecting not with my intellect but with my instinct. So, I closed my eyes and reestablished my heart connection with the ruins. Soon I heard the rocks speak again.

Only by being willing to meet the Underworld, the unseen world where fear resides and is blinded by the light of truth can you be given access to the doorway of the heavens inside you. It is one of your earthly missions to initiate darkness, fear, unconsciousness and matter, into light, love, consciousness, and spirit. By embracing bodily fears and accepting the material self, we come to know this as one of the most profound journeys through the darkness of matter into the reaches of love and light. Only then shall we respect the purpose of fear as a passageway and healing into the oneness of sacred union. This assists Earth in making her debut as the royal province of the universe. She will then be acknowledged in her full glory, as the Emerald Jewel of the multi-verses and her crown will herald the edification into the Heart of Oneness.

The stones of Tulum were speaking to me in ways that those of other Mayan ruins had not. Perhaps the prying loose of my wisdom tooth has unleashed a new ability within me to listen to the wisdom of the rocks. I spent two weeks exploring Tulum. During that time, several observations in particular seemed important. The first had to do with the dogs of the ruins. I spent a lot of time alone in the ruins and noticed that four dogs seemed to be residents of the site, living there permanently. I suppose the logical explanation for their presence was that they were homeless and so had claimed the ruins as theirs, but I felt a different connection with them. They were gentle and often basked in the sun, stretched out on the ground or a stone and soaking up the solar energies. I connected with them at an energetic level and intuited that they were representative of our need to protect the energies and information within us. Just as the Mayan guards and warriors had once watched over the city, alert in their watchtowers for any "oncoming enemies," these dogs, too, were guardians and warriors. I thought of Annubis, the black dog that protected and guided the ancient Egyptian goddess Isis. The dogs of Tulum felt as sacred. They embodied the feelings of loyalty, love, and protection of the highest order.

Another observation I made at Tulum had to do with the stars. I had been drawn out into the heavens and specifically into the constellation of the Pleiades, and I later learned that the Mayans believed themselves to be from the star nations. They actually carved star emblems atop their temples. Moreover, on the facade of a doorway lintel of the Temple of the Descending God at Tulum is a male figure sculpted with his head pointing down and legs spread, knees bent and feet together, appearing to be descending headfirst from the heavens. He is thought to be a deity who seeded the culture that was centered here at Tulum. Because of my observation of the dogs at Tulum, I wondered if the Mayans might have come from Sirius, the Dog Star. Or perhaps even from the Pleiades—speculation certainly, but intriguing nonetheless.

I also bonded with another creature of the ruins—the iguana. The iguanas were hard to spot as they blended in perfectly with the gray stone as they sunned themselves on temple rooftops. They sat completely still for long periods of time, and I imagined them entranced by the dazzling rays of the Solar King, captivated by the force and power of the great Fire God of the sky, the Sun. Momentarily one would scurry along the roofline, as if purposefully heading somewhere, only to stop suddenly, freeze in place, and turn its head toward the sun. One day, I decided to tune into their world to see what their purpose might be.

The lizards love rocks, scurrying along seemingly eager to get to their destinations when in the snap of an instant they freeze to hold time still. With their backs arched and heads pointed toward the sun in a knowing and wise stance, they look to the distant horizon witnessing a dimensional reality different from ours. The forms they see are geometric and linear in configuration. While you see the outer forms in shapes as objects, they see inside the form-they see the energy patterns that create the forms. They are one of the last vestiges of the prehistoric era, and they know about time and space. They are timekeepers. They have traveled from afar, and they come without judgment or discernment, but with instinct. The lizard species were seeded on Earth to bear witness and calibrate its energy patterns, seeing into its holographic templates, for they are information transmitters for their extraterrestrial colleagues, much the same as the bats are. Holding time to witness the stillness of the desert heat absorbing the rays of the sun, they become the store-house, the powerhouse, and the mitochondria of the sun's energy. This, in turn, gives them the ability to see through the eyes of Solar Priests.

As much as I loved Tulum, after nearly two weeks there, I decided it was time to move on. I caught a bus that took me an hour or so north up the Turquoise Coast to Playa del Carmen, a beach resort. It was known as a "party-party" town and I could see why: it was filled with young people, most of whom were good-looking and darkly tanned. It was a colorful town with "good vibes," no doubt because there were festivities happening every hour of the day. What had called me here was not the fun, but the "magical cenotes" that I was repeatedly urged to visit. A cenote is a kind of well, an underground passageway of limestone caverns and chan-nels into which rainwater drains. Many of them are filled with pools of crystalline water and phantasmagoric rocks, stalactites, and stalagmites. I could hardly wait to attempt a retrieval in one.

It took only a few days in Playa del Carmen before I met someone who could allow me to explore a cenote. Roy was an American who owned a large parcel of land that had a large cenote on it. When I told him about my desire to spend some time in a cenote listening for the voice of the earth, he offered to take me to the cenote on his land in a few days time, when he would be driving over to do some maintenance there. I could hardly wait.

When the day arrived, I jumped in the back of Roy's pick-up truck, since his co-workers were up front in the cab with him. As the wind whipped through my hair during the drive, I used it as an energetic tool to sweep away any old thought patterns or emotional blocks that might prevent me from fully engaging the cenote's message. I then sent out a silent message of my own to the cenote, announcing that I was coming to visit and commune with it. I was excited and humbled at the same time; I was going to walk through the magical womb of Mother Earth, into her secret chamber, her innermost sanctum.

When we arrived, and after Roy had sent his helpers off to begin their work, Roy walked me across his property to the cenote. The land was parched and dotted with spindly cacti, small shrubs, and outcroppings of limestone rock. I marveled at the prospect that under the dryness lay a wealth of water. Roy had been in the cenote only a few times, but he had cleared a path through the tunnel into it. As we approached the entrance to the narrow tunnel, he handed me a flashlight and made sure that I felt confident going in alone. I was prepared—I carried a small knapsack on my back that contained water, notebook and pen, sage, a towel and a pullover, candles and matches.

Assured I was okay, Roy turned and waved his hand in parting. He would be expecting my return in a few hours. I turned and faced the dark mouth of the tunnel. A ray of sun suddenly beamed down, illuminating the entrance. I took this as an invitation by the nature spirits. With no hesitation and a great deal of humility, I stepped into the opening of the cenote, then lit my sage stick and smudged myself to purify my body, mind, and spirit. The tunnel to the cavern sloped gently downward, and I could easily follow it. I soon had to turn on my flashlight, and in a few dozen feet more the tunnel terminated in a cavern at whose center was a large pool. The surface of the black water was as reflective as glass, and for several minutes it held me mesmerized by its beauty.

Finally, however, I slipped off my backpack, clicked off the flashlight, and stood with my eyes closed, quieting my mind and opening my heart to the spirits of the water. No sooner did I feel the initial pull of connection, when I was overcome with a need to immerse myself in the crystalline pool. I went with the flow of energy, asking permission of the spirits to follow this impulse. I not only felt the water beckoning me, but I also felt as if the spirits of the pool had been awaiting my arrival. It felt right and proper that I should immerse myself in their liquid world, and so I quickly disrobed and stepped into the water. It was not as cold as I expected, but its temperature did not matter anyway. I was swept beyond my body, completely immersed in my energetic connection with the water spirits. They reached out and I could feel a swathe of energy direct itself toward my heart. I felt it tenderly wash through my heart, cleansing my emotional body. I don't know how long I stayed submerged to my shoulders in the pool, but eventually I felt the cleansing was complete. By the light of my flashlight, I put my clothes and sandals back on, feeling refreshed and renewed in body and spirit. I was baptized by the Earth Mother and was now ready to connect with the rock spirits.

As I shined my flashlight around, I noticed that the tunnel continued into the depths of the cenote on the backside of the pool. I decided to explore deeper into the cenote before attempting a retrieval. With each step into this passageway, I offered a prayer of thanks for being here, in the belly of the Mother. The tunnel was chilly and damp. Stalagmites jutted up from the tunnel floor and stalactites of varying widths and sizes hung from its roof, dripping water on me as I slowly made way into the shadows. Before long the tunnel opened into a small cavern that contained a narrow pool of water and a natural walkway that ran along its side. I made my way around the pool to the back of the cave. As I switched off the flashlight, blackness engulfed me. The silence was complete, leaving my senses free to easily connect with the spirit of the cave and to find my way among the spaces deep inside the stone.

I sat in the darkness, in the stillness, giving myself over to the cave, but could not maintain the fullness of my feelings of reverence. Slowly, fear began to steal into the spaces around me and within me. I felt an odd fusion of creepiness and awe. I was aware of the dualism of my feelings, which helped me to focus on the pleasant connection instead of the uncomfortable one. My sense of calmness increased, and a visceral, more ecstatic connection strengthened, until I found myself in a state that I can only describe as one of "no-thingness." I felt encircled in grace, while I also literally felt pulled toward the "void of creation." My mind did not exist here, and slowly my physical and intellectual self began to dissolve. Then, just when I felt that I was vanishing into "nowhere-ness," I pulled myself back and grabbed hold of the last vestiges of my "self"—back to physical awareness.

I clicked on my flashlight, sure that if I did not quickly reorient myself to the real world of flesh and blood and rock and earth I might be forever lost in this otherness. I emotionally steadied myself, thinking that I had been astrally traveling to an unknown destination from which I might not have known how to return. With that thought, a rush of wind swept over my head and I heard a whooshing sound. It took seconds for me to realize it was bats! I sat down cross-legged and placed my hands upon the rock floor, marshalling my willpower and trying to maintain a measure of calm. I had succumbed to my fear so many times before. Now, I was determined not to.

After a few minutes, when silence and stillness returned, I turned off the flashlight. Almost immediately, I felt a bat dart by, only inches from my face! I steeled myself, refusing to turn the flashlight on again. I had to go into the center of darkness to reach the light that dwells within. I had to trust myself and the spirits of this cavern. Another bat flew by. Then another and another. I felt I was being tested almost to the limits of my emotional endurance but I held steady. Slowly, slowly, I regulated my breathing, allowing myself to re-enter that grace-filled state I had felt only moments before. Soon, I was fully enveloped in its majesty, in its mystery. My sense of self began to shift, and instead of sitting upon a cold rock floor, I felt I was enthroned within the earth and that a royal domain of spirits sat in witness, in silent sovereignty, with me. Abruptly, an immense current surged through my body, and I felt showered by an electro-magnetic energy. I knew, with no doubt, with no question, that this energy was somehow "activating" me, cleansing me in still deeper ways.

I was ready to receive a transmission. But no transmission came. Instead, my inner eyes were alight with images—dolphins, bears, bats, serpents, jaguars, cats, and eagles. They paraded by of their own volition, and I was simply a silent, if startled, witness. I knew with certainty that the energy of these beings resided here, that this cavern was a template of some kind, like a creation nursery that anchored the energies of these animals deep in the bosom of the earth. This nursery was a royal domain, and was ruled by a queen, an Earth queen. No image of the queen arose in my mind's eye, but I was certain of her presence. I surrendered my love to this queen, realizing in a flash of insight that she was the same one who resided in the throne of my own heart. I felt touched by her hand of grace, wrapped in her mantle of beauty.

I sat in that grace-filled space for nearly half an hour before I felt myself returning to the dimension of the physical. I clicked on my flashlight and prepared to leave. As I returned up the main passageway, I gave thanks for the energetic cleansing I had received. I felt as if I were still somewhat in an altered state, and as I followed the path back out of the cenote, my right arm suddenly reached out toward a ledge on the passageway wall. It was as if my arm had a mind all of its own, and before I knew it, my hand closed over a six inch spire of crystal, encased in calcified limestone. The first image that came to mind as my brain registered what I held in my hand was that this was a crystallized tear that had been shed by Earth herself and that it was a totem gift for me. I stopped, closed my eyes, and asked if it was all right to take this chunk of crystal with me on my way out of the cenote. I felt, rather than heard the affirmative answer, and sensed that I had a mission—to return this gift from the darkness of this inner world to the light of the outer world.

As I exited the tunnel, squinting in the late afternoon sun, I felt as if the crystal was a scepter from the Queen's parlor. I offered a prayer to the great Mother, the true Royal Highness, Earth herself. I called all the parts of myself back into my body, in case some parts of me might still be sitting in the "throne room" of the cavern. At that moment, too, I thought, for no apparent reason, of the cave medicine of bear, representing in Native American symbolism, the "going-within place," a place of hibernation and protection. With that thought, I looked up from my prayer position to see the image of a bear perfectly formed in the salt-encrusted outer wall of the cenote. At that moment, too, a bat flew from the cave and winged past me. I felt the electric surge of the magical. I was intoxicated by the energy, by the silent unfolding of beauty.

It took me quite a few days to integrate this deep and powerful experience, and during that time I did not attempt any more connections with the rocks. Instead, I spent the next few days "playing" in Playa del Carmen, and then I headed east—to pay homage to the magnificent ruins of Chichén Itzá, which is considered one of the crown jewels of Mayan temple complexes.

I entered Chichén Itzá on the morning of the spring equinox. This was a special day for thousands that would make a special pilgrimage to the ruins, for as the late afternoon sun strikes the main temple of El Castillo, "The Castle," a shadow of a giant serpent moves down the steps of the pyramid. The shadow is of Kukulcán, the ancient name for Quetzalcoatl, the great Winged Serpent God of the Mayans. The sight is magnificent. Moreover, the stepped pyramid has other interesting and magical qualities. For example, if you shout at the base of the pyramid, a shrieking echo returns. This is said to be the call of the Quetzal bird, sacred to the Mayans, which also represents their collective spirit.

Because I anticipated a crowded equinox day, I arrived at the site at six o'clock in the morning. Still, I was surprised to find only a few visitors there. I made the normally grueling ascent of the pyramid's steep stairs without undue effort, instead feeling overcome with reverence as the morning sun cloaked the temple in a wash of soft light. I was eager to attempt a retrieval before the crowds came. When I reached the top of the pyramid, I stopped to catch my breath and to survey the magnificence of the ruins, which were spread out in clear and majestic view from this height. Miraculously almost, I was alone at the top of El Castillo, so I prepared for the retrieval, wanting to take advantage of my good luck. I silently introduced myself to the stones, cleansed myself with the smoke from smoldering sage, and then greeted the four directions, starting in the east. Then I sat against a temple wall, closed my eyes, softened my breathing, and inwardly greeted the stones. "I am Amalia, wisdom-keeper of the stones. I come to you in the peace of love and light to hear your ancient wise tongue. I acknowledge who you are and come to you in reverence and humility at receiving your wisdom." I quietly settled into the stones' domain, in that intense stillness and deep silence, and what unfolded from within me was most out of the ordinary—it was not the voice of the stones, but the images of their myth.

In my mind's eye, I saw a turning wheel of light, each spoke of which led to a tablet of light that was covered with ancient Mayan carvings. Second by second, the wheel turned clockwise, clicking off a brief segment of time as it turned. Each tablet contained information and knowledge about a specific segment of time. I was startled by what I was seeing and my eyes flew open.

I realized that I had been shown the codices of the Mayan calendar, each one a storehouse of information, a stone tablet coded as part of a grand Mayan library. I had not received any words. Like my time in the cenote, this retrieval had been visual and imagistic rather than verbal and auditory. As I sat there, contemplating my vision, I began to understand that the rocks themselves are like pages of the codices—like the Emerald Records that anchor the wisdom teachings of the earth. As I rose, giving thanks for this vision, and started the slow climb down the precipitous pyramid, I wondered how this temple and this entire complex of temples must have looked during its prime. At the base of El Castillo, lay four large serpent heads carved at the corners of the pyramid face. Their hungry mouths wide open. They were off limits, but I wondered if I should enter one anyway. The pull into the stone temple, into the heart of its stone self, was compelling. "I am a wisdom-keeper of the stones," I argued with myself. "Surely, I am permitted to enter. They long to connect with consciousness, for this is the way they can evolve." I cautiously approached one of the serpent mouths and leaned my body along its giant stone tongue. On this day especially, when the sun was positioned perfectly to make the serpent come alive and slither in shadow down the face of the pyramid, entering into the heart of the mystery seemed not only appropriate but also necessary. I closed my eyes and remained still. With my inner vision, I noticed that the rocks of the pyramid seemed to be wavering, moving in place in a fluid and rhythmic motion. "The rocks are wavering like water," I said to myself. Then I was able to see a distinct zigzagging energy pattern in them. As I was submerging myself in their energy, I was startled out of the vision. I do not remember now what snapped me back, only that I abruptly came back to myself.

As I climbed out of the stone serpent's mouth I considered the meaning of seeing the rocks as "watery." The first connection I made was to fertility, and how land can be made fertile only through watering. The serpent, too, is a symbol of fertility and in some cultures is associated with rain. In addition, because it sheds its skin, the snake signifies a new beginning or renewal. I later read something in a pamphlet that confirmed the validity of my vision. Chichén Itzá breaks down into Chi, which means "mouth," Chen, which means, "water," and Itzá, which means "magician." From my perch in the mouth of the stone serpent, the stones of the pyramid had magically wavered like water to my inner eyes.

I felt I was off to a good start at Chichén Itzá, and decided to continue my exploration at the Temple of the Warriors. This is a massive structure that is surrounded by the Plaza of the Thousand Columns, where hundreds of stone pillars rise into the air. I wandered into the Plaza, noting that each column was made of multiple "sections" that were each covered by relief carvings that appeared to record Mayan history. As I wandered among the columns, I felt pulled to one in particular and sat on the ground with my back resting against it, ready to enter the silence within to understand the meaning of this temple. A thought entered my head like a message from Spirit—each pillar represented the spine of a warrior, and each section of a column represented a vertebra. Together they formed a complete backbone, which itself contained a portion of the history of individual Mayans and their collective history as well. A question entered my mind, abruptly and unexpectedly, as if it had been inserted into me from outside myself: "Where's the blood? Where can I get a cup of blood?" I was startled by this inner voice, and wondered from where within me or outside of me it was originating. I thought of the blood sacrifices I knew the Mayans had made. Perhaps it was the memory of the land itself that I was sharing. The Mayans had offered blood to both the sun and the earth. It was an offering for fertility, for life itself.

Feeling uncomfortable delving into this blood image, I decided to resituate myself, so I got up and meandered along the temple grounds, out of the plaza, and over toward a huge well. This, I knew, was the Well of Sacrifice. This sacred cenote is one hundred and eighty feet across and its sides drop steeply down for eighty feet to a vast disk of water that is covered by emerald-green algae. This well had played a significant role in Mayan ritual. The name Chichén Itzá might even refer to it, as one interpretation of the meaning of the name is Magicians at the Edge (mouth) of the Water (well). I had read that archaeologists had recovered pottery, gold, fabrics, jade, opal, obsidian, copal, bells, and even the skeletons of children from the bottom of this well. The Mayans believed that Chaac, the God of Rain, resided in the well. Thousands would journey here by foot from all over Central America to participate in ceremonies for this rain god, as rain was crucial for survival. Children and young adults, especially males, were the sacrificial gifts the people gave Chaac to encourage his return gift of rain. I had later read in a book, that those who were to be sacrificed to Chaac, often had their bodies painted blue and were given sacred herbs and psychotropic mushrooms so they could easily commune with the spirits. They were taken into the temazcal, the steam bath, for further purification and then adorned with gold and jewelry of precious gems, including obsidian, opal, and jade. Finally, they were lead to the well and thrown in. If the person survived the fall and rose to the surface of the water alive, he or she became the new king or queen.

I did not feel called to attempt a retrieval here and since tourists were beginning to arrive, I wandered the ruins until late afternoon. When it was time for the ceremony of the serpent's descent, I made my way back toward El Castillo. As I did, I noticed a weird-looking, bulbous hive of some kind hanging from a tree branch. My curiosity won out over my reason, and I touched it. A swarm of wasps flew out and I was stung repeatedly. The pain was intense, and as I stood there trying to recover from my fright and deal with the pain, a young man hurried over. He quickly introduced himself as Juan Manuel, a local Mayan. He pulled out a box of matches, and began to moisten match heads with his tongue. He then pressed the wet heads of the matchsticks to each wound and assured me that the sulfur would quell the pain. As he ministered to me, I flashed back to the morning, when I had reclined along the stone tongue of the serpent's head. I felt sure that I had committed a violation of the temple, for which I was now dearly paying the price. The moistened match heads did help the pain, and I thanked Spirit for sending me a rescuing angel.

I made my way to El Castillo and found a place at the edge of the crowd to sit and watch the spectacle. The grass was sparse and stiff with dryness. This land was crying for water, and I prayed to Chaac to restore it once again. Then the magical display began, and I joined the crowd in hushed silence as we watched the shadowed serpent begin its slithering journey down the temple stairs. Legend has it that this serpent of the sun descends from the heavens to receive the offerings and prayers placed in the mouths of the stone serpents that adorn the corners of the temple. We watched the serpent's descent with reverence and awe. We were witnesses to a sight that had been held sacred through history. Our spirits seemed connected to the collective spirits of the ancients. I am sure I was not the only one to feel the weaving of time and energy as the serpent finally reached the lowest point in the pyramid, where the gifts were accepted and would be returned to the Gods. At that moment, it began to rain. Perhaps Kulkucán had accepted my silent prayer for the earth! I retreated under the overhanging branches of a saber tree and stood silently, still in awe at the unfolding vision that had so truly enveloped me.

Chichén Itzá had been one of my most magical experiences to date, even though I had not undertaken or received any substantive transmissions there. My next destination was Uxmal, which is considered one of the finest examples of Mayan architecture and was a flourishing city of more than 25,000 during the late classical period of the Mayans, from about 600 to 900 A.D. I caught a two-hour autobus ride across the Yucatán Peninsula to Uxmal. The village around the ruins seemed untouched by time, and although thousands of tourists passed through, it seemed unaffected, frozen in time with its horse-drawn carts and streets lined with weeping willow trees.

The ruin itself is a huge plane, covered with buildings of odd shapes and sizes. The magnificent Pyramid of the Magician is the dominant temple, its wide stairway especially steep. Unlike most of the other ruins I had visited, Uxmal emitted a feeling of ghostly emptiness, as if its secrets would be forever undecipherable. It was thought to have been home to magician-gods or perhaps the site of a Mayan Mystery School. Even its legends are out of the ordinary. One claims that a witch from a nearby village succeeded in hatching a child from an egg. The child had fully grown in one year, but was a dwarf. The ruler of Uxmal felt threatened by this odd child-man and ordered him executed if he could not perform three tasks. The king devised impossible tasks, one of which was that the dwarf builds a temple in a single night. Much to the King's dismay, the dwarf succeeded in all the tasks, and he was crowned as king himself. The temple he built overnight was the Pyramid of the Magician—the oddest most imposing structure in the ruins.

The Pyramid of the Magician is actually a structure made of five temples joined on an elliptical base. It is made of gray stone and has little ornamentation, except for the giant mask of the rain god Chaac, whose open mouth serves as the entrance to the west side of the pyramid. Rising approximately one hundred feet into the air, it is the tallest temple at Uxmal and its stairways rise especially steeply on two sides. As I slowly climbed my way toward a platform about two-thirds of the way to the top, I felt particularly cautious, and very thankful when I safely reached the platform. I settled myself and prepared for a retrieval. I felt sure that this peculiar stone temple had wisdom to impart and I was eager to listen. It took longer than usual, but finally I heard the stones speak.

The magician plays with the illusion of dualities. He merges the two seeming opposites so that another reality is revealed-one that the mind cannot yet fully comprehend and therefore sees as magic. The mind is committed to the separation that is duality, locking in frames of reality from its limited perspective of fear, of this is this and that is that, as if the two sides of the brain were competing to determine which is better, more powerful, or more correct. Yet, the reality is, that the two hemispheres of the brain cannot function powerfully and correctly when in separation and competition. Full function and correct observation are achieved when the two work together, offering to each other their gifts and power. Only then can they walk through the doorway into union, through the corpus callosum, the meeting spot at the center of the two brain hemispheres. The mind knows of duality and separation; it feels safe in this duality, which makes the truth elusive. It does not know that real safety lies

*in the actuality that nothing is separate, that everything is
connected in the oneness. The magician opens the door and
dissolves the walls. At first the mind fights for its apparent
reality, but eventually it indeed surrenders to the truth.*

The Pyramid of the Magician was resonating with power,
and I felt fully enveloped in that power, but I also sensed that
this transmission was only a precursor of deeper truths that Uxmal
held. So, I thanked the stones and carefully made my way down
the stairway, and wandered about in the ruins, waiting for the pull
of energy to another temple. That pull came as I followed the signs
to a structure called the House of the Old Woman. Legend has it
that the "old woman" who had once dwelled here was a sorceress
and the adoptive mother of the dwarf who built the Pyramid of the
Magician. It is a partial stone structure, sitting atop a craggy hill
and difficult to reach as there was no clear path leading to it. I
found the going slow, as the rocky earth shifted and crumbled
beneath my feet and the spiky weeds pinched me through my
slacks and socks. I persevered however, reaching the ruin with a
sense of accomplishment. I felt the stones calling me, and I was
not going to miss this opportunity to listen to them. I was sure that
here, in this stone ruin, many secrets lived, for this was not a place
for the fickle or foolhardy.

I was met at the doorway to the small stone building by
a swarm of bees. I could hear a warning in their mass buzzing: "We
are the guardians of this place. Enter at your own risk." I thought
back to the wasp stings I had received only days before at Chichén
Itzá, and I felt a healthy respect for the keepers of this sanctuary.
I halted, introduced myself silently, and explained what I was
doing here. The bees seemed to back off, so I quickly entered.

It was dark inside, with pockets of light coming through the
ruined walls, and the air was dry and still. A vulture was perched

high atop one wall, where the roof was gone and the afternoon sun streamed in. It stared at me for a moment, before flying off, and I had the uncanny feeling that it too was a sentinel, keeping vigil, awaiting the old woman's return. I settled myself as I usually did on the ground, but this time with my back against the stone wall. I trused that by dissolving myself into the space around me, becoming unobtrusive, and by traveling into the realm of the rocks with reverence, the stones would welcome me. But as I sat in meditation, nothing came. I could not hear the welcome of the stones. I was patient, but still, after what seemed like a half hour, I was still not picking up any energy from the stones.

I was about to abandon my attempt when suddenly my mind seemed to light up with images—startling and fragmented images that were sexual in nature. Accompanying the images was a disconnected feeling, one of searching, of looking, of seeking—as if the will of the old woman were flitting around, not sure she was home, not sure if she could return to rest here. And then nothing. No images, no feelings. The connection was lost. The secrets and mysteries of this place were not going to reveal themselves to me. The rocks were mute. Perhaps they were respecting the powerful sorcery of the old woman, keeping her energetic legacy silent and private. I could not know, but I felt as if my being here was a violation of that privacy, and so I left.

As I picked my way through the thorny weeds and down the unstable face of the hill, I wondered about what had just happened. It had been an unusual experience. The stones had never been so possessive of their secrets. As I made my way back through the ruins, I came upon a tour guide and asked him about the old woman's house. He did not offer much information, except to say that there were numerous carved stone phalluses in the area surrounding that ruin. Their meaning was a mystery, even to archeologists. I had not seen these phallic stones, at least not with my physical eyes. Although I had sensed them intuitively and seen fragmented images of them in the sexual visions, their meaning was a mystery to me, too. This whole scenario just added to the oddness of Uxmal, as inexplicable a sacred site that I had ever visited.

I did discover one other interesting connection with this attempted retrieval, however. I learned that bees loved these temples; building hives in the crevices of the stone walls. Some temples even had beehives carved into their lintels or walls. Bees had become a theme in my life. I had encountered them on the Big Island of Hawai'i, throughout my travels in the Yucatán, and now here in the House of the Old Woman. I was curious to know if there was a deeper meaning behind my encounter with bees, so before leaving Uxmal, I chose an out-of-the-way spot in the ruins and sat in meditation. I asked the rock beings for their counsel on the matter. "Why are the bees here? What is their part in this world?"

Bees work for the royal one, the Queen. Many bees build their hives as a temple for the Queen, in which to preserve the heritage of the royal lineage and in guardianship of the inherent knowledge. Bees work incessantly for the Silent One at the center, who has the instinct to keep the state of affairs balanced and amenable to the Gods. The hive is a template of the Mayan Kingdoms, where many busy workers constructed temples of worship for their royal kings and queens, high priests, priestesses, and lords. These were places from which the highest, clearest communications from the gods were heard and then put into service for the people and their lands. The work of the bees here continues, anchoring the game plan, the regional working template for a progressive future.

When the transmission was over, I thought back to when I had left Australia. It seemed so long ago—a lifetime ago. On the night before I left, my beloved friends had gathered to bid me farewell and together sung a song called "The Pollen Path." I thought this ironic now. I remembered some of the words to the song: "Beauty before me, beauty behind me, and beauty all around me." I understood that the path inward, the path to the golden pollen place within, is like the descent into the hive, where the honey is made. It is the golden path to Earth's inner royal chamber; it is the Beauty Way of the Navaho Indians, who offer corn pollen to honor the earth and pray for the fertility of the land.

As I finally left Uxmal, I knew that my journey through Mexico and the Yucatán was complete. The Beauty Way of the southwestern United States was calling me. I was finally ready for Sedona, the original destination of my dreams way back when in Australia. At the end of their historical cycle, the Mayans had journeyed out of Mexico and into North America, to the very area where I was now ready to go myself. There they had intermingled with the Hopi natives and birthed the Anasazi—the Ancient Ones. One of the main reasons I had chosen to travel throughout Mexico had been to glean an understanding of these ancient ancestors of the Pollen Path peoples, of the keepers of Earth Wisdom. Like the bees, I had gathered up the pollen of the past and was ready to make honey. I had learned how to listen to the stone people, to trust their wisdom and counsel, to find my own heart in the heart of the earth. One day I knew I would share that richness with others, but for now, I was still in an intense apprenticeship with the stones. In Sedona, I knew my education would be furthered; although I had no idea just what new lessons were awaiting my arrival.

Chapter 8:

Sedona on the Rocks.

A lengthy but comfortable bus ride took me back through Mexico and into the United States. I enjoyed traveling by bus, as it gave me time to reflect and integrate what I have just experienced in preparation for whatever was to come next. My journey through Mexico had turned out to be enlightening and full of memorable surprises. From the gorgeous old hotels to the humble *posadas;* the pristine beaches I had walked and the crystalline water in which I had swum; the modest and warm-hearted peoples I had met and come to call friends; the noble heritage that still fed the spirits of these proud people; the temples and stone edifices that had either offered up their wisdom gladly or still stubbornly clung to their ancients secrets. No, I had had absolutely no trouble at all in Mexico, despite all the warnings I had heard prior to my arrival there: "What! You're going by yourself, a single woman?" "What! You don't know the language?" "What! You don't know anybody there?" These had not been my challenges. Instead, I had been challenged by the still foreign places within my emotional body, places that competed for my attention by aggravating my teeth, by calling wasps to sting me, by cajoling my fear. Mexico had beguiled and tested me, inside and out. I did not expect Sedona to test me. But on this assumption I was wrong.

First came Los Angeles, my jumping-off point for Sedona. Who had not heard of Los Angeles, or been tempted by its promise of glamour and vibrancy? But as soon as I touched the energy of this City of Angeles, I felt aversion. It felt empty, wounded, and weary. I was staying in a modest hotel just north of the city, and spent the first few days trying to more sensitively examine my rather negative energy response to it. Mexico had been open, natural, rural, alive, and ancient. But for all its frenetic activity, Los Angeles felt crowded by its own emptiness. I struggled to connect with the spirit of the land, and I knew it was not the miles of asphalt and the towers of steel and glass alone that were keeping me from succeeding. The drain of energy came not only from the relentless manmade environment but also from the energy environment, or lack thereof, that its people created. I was struggling not to make judgments, just energy observations—and what I felt was an intense estrangement between the people and the land. Los Angeles felt like a city of shadows to me.

In Mexican shamanism, *Mictlan,* the lower world or under-world is considered a necessary aspect of the sacred Whole. It is not a place of darkness and negativity, of evil or desecration. Instead it is, psychologically speaking, the potently transformative depths of the subconscious and dreamtime; and cosmologically, it is a repository of the primordial creative energies of Earth and even of the Universe. Los Angeles felt like a type of underworld to me, but not one that was held sacred. Here, there was an undercurrent of pointlessness. For all the vibrancy of the city, for all the incessant chatter of the television screens, for all the superficial perfection of the "beautiful people," the city was like a dream lost in the night, its meaning evaporating like mist in the moonlight, because it had nothing or no one to ground it, to claim it, to honor it. If Lost Angeles was a city of angels, these were angels who had forgotten they had wings and could not imagine they could fly. Simply put, the city lacked grace.

Not wanting to linger in Los Angeles, I expedited my travel arrangements to Sedona. I had caught wind of a Prophets Conference that was to be held in Phoenix, Arizona, which was only two hours south of Sedona, so I arranged to travel there first. I remembered an Australian friend's recommendation about how I should undertake my circuitous journey to Sedona. "Go to specific health or spiritual-based conferences that will enable you to meet a few key people that could point you to the right people and places for Sedona." This was an opportunity to follow that advice.

The Prophets Conference offerings ran the gamut from fomal lectures and workshops, to sacred arts and performances. Although the conference grounds were overflowing with people, I had no sooner arrived when I bumped into my dear friend Tara and her husband, Francis, whom I had met in Maui. Another enormous surprise was that Ariel Spilsbury, whom I had spent much of my time with in Maui and who was a treasured teacher to me, was at the conference, too. We celebrated our reunion and spent much of the conference together. The real reason Spirit had directed me to the conference, however, was not to learn new information, but to discover an important connection to Sedona, just as my Australian friend John had suggested would happen: I was delighted when Tara and Francis offered to personally deliver me to Sedona. They had heard about Sedona being a highly charged place, a sacred area of energy vortexes on the earth that amplify spiritual energy. So they took this opportunity to make a short pilgrimage to pay homage to the spirit of the land and to ensure that I was escorted in the finest manner.

I had always envisioned making a solo entrance into Sedona, but here I was with Tara driving me there, with Francis not far behind driving with a dear friend, Elizabeth whom I had befriended at the conference. It was appropriate that Tara was leading the way, since she is a woman who by her very nature initiates movement and stirs others to action. I had told her of my adventures so far and also recounted some of the earth retrievals. She was enthusiastic about my Earth mission, and as we drove through the desert now, she reached over and squeezed my hand in silent acknowledgment of my finally nearing the destination my dreams had foretold years before. We did not talk much during the final hour of the drive, and in that sacred silence I remembered back to all the "signs" I had received back in Australia about the red rocks and my becoming a "secretary" for the earth. I was amazed how quickly time had passed: could it really be two years since the energy of Sedona had first hit in my stone circle? I felt a deep calm in both my body and spirit as we neared Sedona. I was ready for whatever experiences lay in store for me. I had no inflated expectations, despite my awe at the series of synchronicities that had led me into this adventure in the first place and the mysteries I had touched along the journey.

At one point as we approached Sedona, the road swept around into a long, sweeping arc and as we rounded the pinnacle of the curve, I caught my first sight of the famous red rocks. The desert lay bare before us, except for the clusters of spiny cacti: saguaros, ocotillos, and mesquite. They seemed scrubby; emotionless sentries holding their posts under the golden haze of the sun. But the burnt-orange rocks seemed brazen in the way they called attention to themselves. What swept the breath from my body was the impact with which my amorphous dreams came flooding into geological reality. The mystery subsumed into substance. I felt the rush of memory made manifest, a quick, spontaneous running of my emotions like a river through my soul. I felt as if I had dreamed myself to life.

I slowly rolled down the window and reached my arm out. I opened my hand and spread my fingers wide. I felt the pressure of the hot air and I pushed back against it, gently. Having made physical contact in this way, I closed my eyes and opened myself energetically to the sacredness of this land and to cast the threads of my own energy down to the land. I made a silent request that the roots of the land receive me. "I am here rocks, I have arrived. I have come to do my Earthwork. You have called me and I am here. With all my intent I will do the necessary work." I leaned my head back against the headrest and wondered what Sedona would require of me, and what challenges and wonders lay waiting for me. I was not sure where I was to go and what I would do, except allow myself to be led by Spirit. The guidance began almost immediately upon our arrival into the heart of Sedona.

Tara had been kind enough to leave me to my thoughts, and she had driven in silence into the center of town, stopping finally at a health food store where we could purchase something to drink. Francis and Elizabeth pulled up right behind us, and we all entered the store—where in the middle of one of the store aisles Elizabeth ran into an old flame. She introduced us to Rahelio, a handsome, longhaired Native man who worked as a "Sacred Earth Guide." When he heard that I was on a quest for Earth knowledge, he looked deeply into my eyes and said two words, "Rachel's Knoll." This was a place where the locals went to meditate and watch the setting sun. It was only a fifteen-minute drive north of town and we decided to drive there right away.

I felt the energy of the knoll immediately—a penetrating primordial energy that sank deeply into the earth. I stood alone at the highest point on the knoll and surveyed the rocky expanse. Megalithic rocks of imposing height and heft, stood like ancient giants proclaiming their domain. Their weathered spires had eroded into odd shapes, which with only a little imagination became the faces of mythic beings. As my eyes swept along panoramically, I could not decide if the rocks were solidified spirit beings or Spirit solidified. I was awestruck. I had seen many magnificent landscapes, but none of what I had seen or energetically touched so far had prepared me for the heart connection I felt here.

As the sun sank in the late afternoon sky, the rocks cast shadows like rich red robes. I walked off by myself and sank to the earth deeply, closing my eyes and attuning to the rocks. A high-pitched drone seemed to enliven the silence, and I wondered if this was the signature sound of Sedona. I came to tears easily in this most tender of energetic states, in this heart-of-self to heart-of-land connection. And yet, for all the heartstrings the land seemed to pull in me, I felt that the spirit of the land was keeping itself at bay. Somehow the connection was not yet deep enough to penetrate my soul. I felt as if the land was embracing me with one hand and keeping me at a distance with the other. My eyes filled and the tears forced themselves slowly under my closed lids. I was not sad. What was the emotion? Longing? I felt a longing to enter into the world of these red stone wisdom keepers, but despite our heart connection their world felt too far away for me to ever reach with any depth. Had I come all this way for nothing? Had I endured so much only to be denied access when I most desired it? In that moment I did not know.

With my eyes still closed, I opened my arms to the earth and from somewhere deep within me a sound emerged. It was a cry, a sound filled with power but also supplication to the mystery. I let this deep tone loose into the wind—my soul cry for connecting to the spirits of Sedona. I heard the cry roll down the knoll and resound through the canyon. This was my sonic entry call, and I felt my spirit follow the rush of sound. I felt my energy free itself from my body, released like an eagle into an updraft that pulled my energy body into some kind of nonphysical union with the land, rocks, and sky. As my spirit flew across the land, I felt myself received by these spirit energies—and by Sedona.

Just as quickly as they had arrived into my life, Tara, Francis, and Elizabeth left again to continue their journey back home to Maui. Once again I was on my own, and the challenges began. Despite my "reception" by the spirits of the land at Rachel's Knoll, the larger energy of Sedona was not yet ready to accept me fully—or perhaps it was the other way around, and I was not yet ready to contain easily within my being the energies of Sedona. As had become a pattern for me upon first connecting with a new place, my emotional self was the first part of me to lose equilibrium.

I had found a small retreat center and rented a room for a few weeks. The days moved lazily, like passing clouds, but I felt anything but relaxed and calm. Everywhere I wandered in the town I felt disconnected. In fact, the town of Sedona did not feel much different from Los Angeles. "The people here are lifeless," I heard my inner voice saying, in disbelief. "They're out of their bodies." This is not what I had expected. In addition, the township was little more than a spiritual shopping mall. Everywhere I turned there were gaudy signs pitching material things, especially spiritual paraphernalia. There were psychics in booths on the street and set up at café tables in many stores. There were salespeople pitching everything from vortex tours to excursions, to sites known for their UFO activity. I was sick to my stomach at what supposedly spiritual people had done to Sedona. They were offering to take people to meet aliens when they, in terms of their relationship to the land, were aliens themselves.

I began to dislike everything about this place—including the rocks. I was also confused by my own feelings; for my feelings of disappointment and judgment went against everything I believed, including the Christian admonishment of "Thou shall not judge," a belief by which I tried to live my life. The judgments however were coming in unrelenting waves and although I knew they were, at the deepest level, about myself as much as about the environment in which I found myself, I found it difficult to control my feelings. Sedona was getting to me, and I looked deep within to try to understand my emotions. "Can I be this psychologically fragmented? This out of touch with the rhythms of myself?" I asked. I believed I was supposed to be here. Hadn't the trail of synchronicities been leading me to the red rocks of Sedona? After all the hardships and challenges I had overcome, wasn't Sedona supposed to be my "promised land?" If so, then why did I feel so distanced from the people and the land?

I tried to go easy on myself. Although my inner vision was obscured and I could not seem to focus on anything, least of all my mission as "secretary to the stones," I tried to just let the flow of my emotions run unimpeded. Blocking them, I knew, was useless. While I was not yet ready to connect deeply with the spirits of the land since I felt so disconnected from my own sense of self, I did try to make a stronger and less judgmental connection to the town itself. A few days into my stay in Sedona, I found myself in the "Temple Room" at the back of a metaphysical store called "The Eye of the Vortex." I was stretched out on a cushiony mat on the floor, just lying there and allowing myself to be, when the thought occurred that I should attempt a "retrieval" of myself. As strange as it sounds, I felt compelled to try to intuitively connect with a familiar molecule of myself, one that might be floating around in the ethers. "If only I could find one molecule of my self that feels real and stable and sure, I will be able to latch onto it and reel myself back into cohesiveness," I thought. I sat in silence, if not meditation, for a long time, but I was unable to grasp onto even such a tiny piece of myself. I felt completely alone and disconnected to my sense of self. Over the next few days, I tried using many of the metaphysical techniques I knew to try to draw myself together or ground myself, but none worked. Finally, feeling close to despair at the emotional and spiritual black hole I felt myself being sucked into more and more deeply, I called Marcus, in Australia.

"Marcus, I've spun out, I've lost it!" I moaned into the telephone receiver. He did not need a lot of explanation to know what I was talking about. In a calm and authoritative voice he soothed me. "Now Amalia, I know who you are. You are a powerful and strong woman. You will be fine. You are just clearing the past so you can get on with your job." Just the sound of a familiar voice raised my spirits. We talked for a few minutes more, and by the time I hung up the phone, I felt much more hopeful that I was on the right track here in Sedona.

That simple phone call helped turn the tide of my confusion and detachment. Slowly, over the course of three or four days, I felt more myself. The surety of my mission began to return, little by little, day by day. It took a full two weeks for me to realign my vision, restore my confidence in my service to the earth and finally, set out into the deserts and canyons around Sedona to meet the ancient red rocks.

The power places of Sedona have their own unique way of clearing our impurities, regenerating our cells, and realigning our vision. The landscape here contains energy vortex upon energy vortex, and once you surrender yourself to the rejuvenating energies of one of these special centers, you are changed forever, no matter how subtle the shift. Richard Dannelly in his book *Sedona: A UFO Connection* explains that on entering Sedona for the first time, a blowing out of every chakra can occur, leaving you with a feeling of confusion, of being unable to follow your own thought patterns and doubting your own mental processes. I felt that I had personally experienced such a blowing of my inner fuses after my time at Rachel's Knoll. Dannelly also writes that Sedona's vortexes activate ancient knowledge that has been encoded in your body so that you can bring the information to consciousness and can even activate this cellular information in others, even after you have left the power site. His message resonated with the knowledge and insight I had gained from my Earth retrievals.

I learned that a vortex is the unifying principle between two opposing spins of energy, which contain one or both of two types of energy: feminine or masculine. The feminine vortices are magnetic in nature, and the quality of their energy is nurturing, helping one to feel more deeply and to align with the meaning of "being" more fully. The masculine vortices are electric in nature, and their energies enhance action, helping one to become more expressive and assertive. They have the energy of "doing."

I began to see how the vortices of Sedona could be seen as something like a cosmic washing machine. If you allow yourself to engage fully in the transformative power of the sacred space there, you are run through an energy wash and spin cycle. When the spin cycle is complete, you come to stillness in a new state of inner cleanliness, with a lot of the old debris washed away from your physical, mental, emotional, and energy bodies. In that more pristine state, you find within yourself a profound stillness and silence from which you can better listen to your intuition, the messages of the cosmos, and the advice of Spirit. I felt that Sedona was certainly putting me through the emotional wringer! Perhaps starting the retrievals was not only the right move for me, but perhaps the only move I could make in order to truly regain my inner stability and composure.

From my first few trips out to the vortices of Sedona, I knew that my judgments had been misplaced. Whatever had overcome me had certainly been about me, as Sedona had reflected my own sense of separation. Once I was able to give myself over to the land, I understood why the ancient Anasazis had made special journeys to this area of the Southwest to undertake vision quests, to seek council from the spirits, and to undergo sacred rituals and initiatory ceremonies. They never lived among the red rocks themselves, for they knew that this was a sacred place of worship.

Now I knew that as well. The more time I spent out alone on the land, the more I felt reconnected to my mission with the stones, and I quickly fell in love with the area.

It took several weeks of spending long days on the land to feel truly restored to myself and ready to attempt an actual retrieval—to deeply connect with the sentient energy I felt coming from the stones and mesas. I decided to begin by revisiting Rachel's Knoll. I went in the early morning, when the rocks that were so strikingly orange-red in the sun were instead a pale and tawny orange-brown from the shadows. I sat high upon the rock ledge overlooking the valley of the rocks, which coalesced into a complex of ancient temples, prehistoric birds and ancient faces and entered into the familiar inner silence, making room within to hear the Ancient Ones speak:

Beyond time, when we together shared the mysteries of the circle wheel, we each knew our rightful place in that wheel of life. We respected and honored the placement of others, because we had once stood there ourselves or were going to move into that part of the wheel in time. Each position in this wheel offered merits, lessons, and initiations. We knew what to do and how to be-have, as we were participating in the cyclic ordinance of Great Spirit itself.

We were a race of peoples who stood as towers of light, as lighthouses, as way-showers. Our hearts pulsated in direct synchronicity, in rhythm, with the Great One, the overseer who witnessed the many evolving grand wheels in time. The love we experienced was born out of the union of all that exists—of knowingness and of wisdom.

Our libraries and teachers were the rocks, our sweet euphoric nectar the sun's rays streaming forth from our great central sun, pouring into the mouths of the caves *where we dwelled. The rain was our healing—streaming from our creator's eyes and heartfelt vision, melting and pouring the love from the heavens above to cleanse and humble ourselves.*

Every single action was a cermony, a commemoration of God brought into the manifested moment, revealing itself in the purity of the intention of Creation, to re-member, re-collect and re-cognize with the divinity and knowingness of who we are. Thus we brought all of our past selves, our multi-dimensional selves, together into one unit of consciousness, into present-time awareness.

Our circle has been broken; the movement within the grand wheels of life has been forgotten and longs to move in the oneness with "All that Is" once again. It is in the movement of oneness, in the flow of this great wheel of life, that we can truly reclaim our God-hood and be free to play in this sacred garden, the Garden of Eden, Heaven on Earth. We are the Ancient Ones who have been holding the memory of the past to yet again restore the Grand Wheels of Time.

In the days after this transmission I felt more surefooted and reconnected to the land and my mission as "secretary" to the stones. I was invited to stay at my friend David Cosmo's home in the nearby Village of Oak Creek, and began the hunt for a car. I had spent six months in Hawai'i and six months in Mexico, and I judged that I would spend at least that length of time, if not longer, here in Sedona, so I needed to get settled. Little did I know at that time that Sedona was to claim me for nearly five years! But now, with only a half-year's stay in mind and in my budget (I was still living off the proceeds of the sale of my house and business in Australia), I sought to make myself somewhat more comfortable and grounded in the community. I bought a four-wheel drive, to go anywhere that I wanted in this often forbidding, although beautiful land.

For my first real foray into the desert, I decided to head toward Hopiland, the reservation of the Hopi Indians. In a very Australian sort of way, I felt ready to reinvigorate my connection to indigenous roots. So, I packed my car with a tent, firewood and kindling, a pot and pan and food and water, and a backpack filled with personal items, such as clothing and my journal. Then, with a little courage and a sense of grand vision, I drove northwest toward Hopiland, ready to immerse myself in this land of dry earth, scrub brush, piñon pines, and ochre mesas.

After four hours of driving, I spotted a small sector of red rocks that stood out among the golden sandstone escarpments. They seemed to be somewhat tilted, reminding me of the Leaning Tower of Pisa. Even though they were not as grand or majestic as Sedona's twisting spires of rock, this grouping drew me in like a magnet. I carefully maneuvered the four-wheel-drive off the road and steered it across the hard packed desert, dodging clumps of cacti and small rock outcroppings. I was wary about making this unexpected detour because the sky was already exhibiting a tinge of sunset orange and I had to find a safe camping spot before nightfall. "Indian Territory," I had been told, could be fairly dangerous for a white woman traveling alone. While I was cautious, I also remembered all the warnings that had come to nothing during my trip to Mexico. I pulled over and sprang out of the car. Possessed with a great longing to touch my stone brothers, I ran with outstretched arms toward the rock face, my heart beating in my chest and hot tears springing from the corners of my eyes. My rational self was urging me on more important things, like making a camp, but I ignored that voice. Instead, I gave myself over to the rocks, pressing my palms and the cheek of my face against the cool roughness and sobbing with abandon. An inexplicable rush of sentiment coursed through me, and I abandoned myself to it. I felt that I knew these rocks, that I was being reunited with a long-lost beloved, who had been stoically and patiently awaiting my return. I hugged the rocks for the longest time.

Then I climbed up the steep slope exploring the escarpment. About one third of the way to the top, I spotted a cave like nook, and I scrambled in, and sat in its cool shadowy interior. I leaned over and kissed the rock wall to one side. I felt compelled to connect with the voice of this space, so I addressed the rock spirits aloud and with an overtone of excitement in my voice. "Majestic, grand pillars of knowledge, ledges of knowingness. Here there is patience, stillness, beingness, silence, and depth. Hello! I am back! I love you rocks! What is it that I may be doing?" Immediately, I heard the answer.

For a start, BE in your stillness. Be the conduit through which you watch your world revolve around your centeredness. Be the meeting ground between Heaven and Earth and know yourself as the lighthouse that you are! Hold your evolution in the palm of your being and stand forever present in your awareness. Ancient one, how long has it been? Intergalactic one, who has traveled the star-ways to find her place here in the rocks, what journeys have you undertaken?

Rocks here on Earth are the ancestors of the stars in the heavens above; they are the crone beings of new stars being birthed. Stars are the magnificent reminders of the ascension that occurs through the pathway of density and physicality of the rocks, which have a-send-ed their light of information to the heavens above. Rocks carry the hidden frequency of stars; they are the anchors of stellar energy, holding the light of each star and grounding it here on this planet.

Here on planet Earth, rocks embrace the elements of fire, air, water, and earth. Fire is captivated by the alchemical transmutation of the rays of the sun's light, which holds within it the memory of the sacred flame within the heart of every being. Air is captivated in the pores and portholes of the caves, which hold the empty filled space of timeless evolution. Water is drunk in from the rains to soften the hardness, shaping the flowing current of forms that rocks enfold. The earth element is captivated by the density of matter, creating the anchors of our planet, which maintain its structure and holds the form, to ground the light above.

All together, the elements of our planet have created the bones of the earth, to hold us in place, to hold the structure of form, of our home. They are the storehouse of the genetic information of our evolution on this planet, such as the bones in your bodies, which also store genetic ancestral information. The rocks are crystallized stellar energy, reminding you of your ancestry and your connection to your future galactic selves. It is when we become— and come to be-all that we are, that our past merges in the present, whilst recognizing our future selves so that we can return home to ourselves. With this returning, comes the gift of patience, stillness, beingness, silence, and the knowing of the depth of our love for planet Earth.

I opened my eyes, feeling calm and at peace. "Thank you, Rock Beings!" I shouted. "You who are the true masters of evolution through time and space."

Feeling satisfied, and even satiated, I got back into the car and decided to drive closer toward the Hopi reservation instead of camping out there in the desert. I felt I had been pulled off the path so that I could experience this first, intimate, and even passionate reunion with the Red Rocks. Camping here no longer felt necessary or proper.

It was just a short drive to the mesa top where the Hopi villages began. Hopiland was as ancient as it was dry and isolated. The area and its small villages are simple, even stark; its isolation keeps it relatively free from the corrupting influences of modern society. As I drove slowly up the mesa, and as night descended, I was alert to the slightest activity around me. There was not much going on, at least not to the visible eye. There was no obvious or welcoming place to camp and as darkness had all but veiled my sight, I called upon the vision of the night owl to assist me. I asked to be guided to the right spot to lodge for the night, a place that would be safe and close to the rocks. On my way down from the mesa, I noticed a small dirt road veering off to my right, and I felt pulled to follow it. It was a crooked, dark road, but it led me to a large rocky knoll with a flat area at its base. It seemed a good place to set up camp. The rock face was pockmarked with small, round caves that revealed their dark hollow interiors in the shadowy moonlight. "Hmm, these caves are stacked like a beehive," I thought to myself. "This surely must be the right place for my camp."

I quickly unpacked the car and made a small fire. The temperature in the desert had been dropping steadily, and I took a moment to warm myself. Then I prepared for a ceremony to align to the energies of the land. With a stick, I drew a circle in the soil around my camp area, setting an energy boundary for protection. I lit a sage stick and smudged myself, and my immediate surroundings for purification and then completed the ceremony by honoring the six directions: east, south, west, north, Father Sky, and Mother Earth. I made up my sleeping-bag bed close to the warmth of the fire, then sat by the fire and cooked up some rice and vegetables and a then prepared a hot cup of tea. The sky was now pitch black, and the moon and stars were brilliant. I looked up and across the rock face of the knoll and could just make out the small beehive caves. I took a few deep breaths. The presence of the caverns behind me caused me to shudder, and with a full exhale I released my anxiety. Drowsiness soon overtook me, so I nuzzled close to the fire and went to bed.

The next thing I remember is awaking with a start, feeling as if I were swirling downward inside some kind of energy spiral or vortex. I was reeling with vertigo and was overcome by sudden sharp pains throughout my body. My bones felt as if they were on fire. "Oh, my bones!" I cried aloud. "It's so painful." I groaned as I pushed myself into a sitting position, and that is when I noticed electro-static flares of orange and purple light radiating from my hands. I was scared. What was going on? I felt as if I were engulfed from the inside out in some kind of frozen fire, an electric-like heat that was firing itself through my bones and out my hands. The air itself seemed charged. I did not know what to do. I stood up to move my limbs and rub them hard to increase my circulation, but the pain of coldness that went deep to my core left me standing motionless in the night. I looked up into the night sky and saw a white star flare across the heavens-but it was shooting upwards! I was thoroughly spooked, but at the same time, I felt overcome with tiredness. I wanted to crawl back into my sleeping bag, but it wasn't enough protection for me. So I quickly scooped up my sleeping bag and blanket and hastily made a bed in the back of the car. I huddled up in the sleeping bag feeling safer and warmer there, even though my body was still tingling with the after effects of the strange energy that had filled me. My hands were no longer glowing, but the air outside still felt charged. I called upon the spirit of fire and breathed it into my bones and body to warm up. I gradually lapsed into a state of calm but heightened awareness. I heard my own inner voice speak to me. A type of retrieval was beginning.

> *Fire is of electric energy; it releases light and energy like the sun. Water is of magnetic energy; it retains energy and absorbs the light of fire, like the moon, which absorbs the light of the sun and reflects it back out. Humans contain both electric and magnetic energy; we magnetically absorb the light of love and then electrically give it out, expressing it through our actions. Earth, too, contains electromagnetic energy; it absorbs and magnifies the light and rays of the cosmos and then radiates this energy out to the world through the gifts of love, abundance, and nourishment.*

The voice faded as the pain in my bones intensified again. I was shivering with cold and pain, and I began to panic about my safety. I thought about starting the car up to turn the heater on but was so pained by the cold that I couldn't move. A thought arose that my car had a central nervous system not unlike my own, as if it were, for all its mechanical reality, also a living entity. I had made a connection from the car to the process of ascension. The inner voice arose once more.

> *Starting up a car engine whilst it is still frozen could crack a head or a seal. You need to let the warmth of the sun and the light of day, heat and warm the body of the car, so no damage can be done. The same is true of our bodies. Light and love is the fuel, the energy that can slowly melt our frozen core. When we "ignite" ourselves with light and love we accelerate our vibration, allowing access to higher states of being and to other dimensions.*
>
> *Ascension is about inviting and drawing the light of love down into the density of our physical bodies, merging Spirit and Consciousness with Matter and anchoring it here*

on our planet, Earth. We become lighthouses, beacons that signal the way to our homeward path, calling others to follow us, inspiring and igniting and activating others as we have ourselves been inspired, ignited, and activated. The light we harness in our bodies becomes the fuel that feeds the transmutation of density, making us lighter and so able to ascend. We help the earth too, for the more light we anchor into our own bodies, the more we raise the vibration of the light frequency of our planet. We can assist Earth in her ascension to a new dimension. Earth needs us not to abandon her. She needs us to remember our agreement to assist her in birthing herself as the jewel of the universe—as the "Emerald One".

I must have fallen asleep in the midst of that rumination, for I next found myself awakening in the brilliant sunlight. I felt warm—right down to my bones. I got out of the car, stretched my body a little and then looked at my immediate surroundings to see what may have contributed to the weirdness the night before. I realized that I wasn't equipped enough to withstand the elements of the stark and isolated mesas of the Hopiland region, so I quickly packed up camp and within an hour I was heading back to Sedona.

I stayed close to home that day, pondering my adventure and the ascension insights. I went to bed early, but I soon awoke to excruciating pain in my back. My upper back had completely seized up, but also was alive with spasms of pain. I could hardly move, so I rolled over onto my stomach and tried to breathe into and through the spasms. I heard a dreamlike voice in the space between my breaths.

The contraction in your back is like the winding in of an energetic key that is storing information in your bones. Bones, like rocks, store information. The energy here in Sedona is so compacted that it will either assist in centering you or spin you right out and expel you. You need to slow down and stand in the stillness that lies at the center of the spin.

I lay unmoving for a long time, considering the counsel I had just received, although I wasn't sure from whom or where it had come. I finally managed to get up and move around a little, although I still had to deal with the back spasms for a few more days. Unlike with my tooth pain, at least this time I understood what was going on at an energetic level. That knowledge helped me bear the discomfort. I was invited to slow down and stand in the center of all that spins around me, and to ground my energy and thoughts into stillness.

When the spasms slowed and then finally disappeared, I was ready to resume my work as a secretary to the earth. I drove to a magnificent range of red rocks, steering my vehicle cautiously and slowly so that I could use my energy and intuition to seek out my next retrieval. At one point I stopped in the desert and through squinted eyes tracked the land, looking for ruins. I was interested in gaining knowledge about my own lineage to this ancient landscape as I was sure that in a past life, I had lived here or somehow otherwise been connected to the land here.

The ruins in this area are not easy to sight, as they are well concealed either by being built well into caves or perched high on the rock mesas. As I carefully scoped out the landscape, my attention was caught by a pyramidal shaped rock protruding from a nearby ridge. It looked like the stone shoulder blade on a red-earth torso. To the lower right of it, I spotted the dark outline of a cave opening—it was shaped like a turtle. Suddenly I recalled a dream I had about a week before. I had seen two "flanking rocks"—each looking very much like this "shoulder blade" stone. In the dream, I had intuitively understood that when a person walked between the two closely spaced rocks, the rocks could read the person's energy capacity. In a similar way that a credit card is passed through the card reader to show that you have sufficient funds, the rocks were able to tell if you were qualified to receive the information and energy contained within them. Although I saw only one rock, not two, protruding here in the desert, I wanted to pass between that rock and the ridge so that my energy could be scanned through the resonant field of the rocks. I also wanted to explore the "turtle" cave. In fact, I felt drawn to explore the cave first. I intuited that I should pay my respects to the spirits of the land there before I passed by the flanking rock for my "readout."

The climb was challenging. I had to skirt dry and brittle bushes, prickly pear and agaves, spiky reeds and weeds. There was a lot of loose stone on the steep ridge, so the footing was slippery. Despite my determination and focus, the climb was too steep to safely make it to the cave. I was not disappointed, for I knew that everything in this hike was in divine order and that something else more momentous lay in store for me. I attuned to the ridge, letting it draw me one way or the other. I began to follow its magnetic pull and before long I found myself descending to a large, platform-like rock. It was nearly circular and must have measured twenty feet in diameter. I had not noticed it at all when I had scoped out the ridge earlier, and I found that quite odd. But here I was, and I was going to make the most of this gorgeous and isolated site. I decided to perform a ceremony, and I dug into my small knapsack for several items I had spontaneously packed in it that morning. First I took out my Aztecan *chachayotes*; ankle bracelets made from the seedpods of the *Ayoyotl* tree. I had purchased them in Guadalajara, and I knew that when the Mexicans danced, the sound of the seed rattles represented the shaking tail of a rattlesnake. I took my hiking boots off and tied the seedpod rattles around my ankles. I next pulled out a string of myrrh beads that were gifted to me in Maui, which represent strength and protection and strung them around my neck. Finally, I took out two rocks that had come from sacred sites in Australia and held one in each hand. I was ready for my ceremony, which would be one of sacred dance. Silently I introduced myself to the energies and spirits of the land, announcing my arrival and then offered my dance as a gift to the spirits of the land. With rhythmical movements and swift spins and twirls, I addressed the directions of east, south, west, and north, along with the sun and the pale crescent moon that rode the sky above. I danced the sharing of my heart and love of the land, raising my head high toward the summit of the distant mountaintops and pounding my feet to drive my intent all the way into the rock-solid ground below. I summoned all that I had come to be, while also storytelling through movement my long journey to these red rocks. With movement, gesture, and even with voice, I opened my communication with the Ancient Ones of this land.

"I have arrived, you who have called me here, from across the seas of time. I have come a long way and have traveled my Earth-Walk in consciousness and in anticipation of meeting you. You who have awakened me from my dreams. I have finally arrived. I initiate an opening to receive your messages. I am here to speak my truth and invite you to speak yours. I, Amalia Camateros, am here as a messenger of Spirit, a storyteller for awakening the myth into reality. I come to you in the safety and protection of love. I am here to retrieve your communications and take them back to the peoples of this planet. It is time now to awaken from your slumberous hibernation through time to activate, to merge and communicate with these humans. They have put in their time, throughout time, to understand the mysteries and access the doors and gateways of the kingdom of Heaven on Earth. They have offered their blood, sweat and tears with their blind sincerity. It is time to share with them the TRUTH. I call to awaken you now."

I moved from my dance into a place of balance and stillness and quiet, letting the swirl of the world around me come to a standstill at the center of my own heart. I sat down on the warm rock slab, closed my eyes, and waited. There in the darkness behind closed eyes I saw the molecules of existence within me implode toward my center, into the depths of conscious awareness. A chaotic interplay began between the molecules of light and the dark canvas of myself. The light and dark finally merged, and instantly I felt as if I were moving, traveling through a tunnel of pure beingness. I heard myself shout, spontaneously and surprisingly: "Wake up! It's time now!" Then I heard my voice as if it were someone else's, drop to a whisper. I made a request for myself and for humankind. "Speak to us, rocks. Speak to us." The rocks immediately complied with my request.

Open up the space inside you to allow this new frequency of information in by dropping the heavy load. Christ was said to carry this heavy load for you 2,000 years ago. The heavy cross he carried up the hill personified the burdens of physical density and mortality. He then handed this burden up to God Spirit as an offering to free mass consciousness into the awareness of spiritual divinity and immortality. It is safe to let go of the old constructs of reality. You have used them since you first walked this Earth plane and to what avail? By dropping and releasing the past, you come into the knowingness of now—and that is all there ever was, is, and shall be. The past, present and future creates a circle, an eternal cyclic pattern that holds you to the illusory experience of reality, as you know it. The past becomes the present, which becomes the future, which becomes the past and so on. "NOW" within the circle is the keyhole to open the door into the truth of reality. This place is known to you as the void, that place that you are so afraid to dive into, the place where once entered, there is no control and holding on to the old reality constructs. This is the place of true initiation, where access of all information is available. It is the center of the web of creation, where Presence is waiting to be received, retrieved, and renowned. At first this place is judged and experienced as darkness, fear, and the unknown, however, once you allow this to pass and you fully embody these feelings with conscious awareness, you then pass these "gates of hell" and enter the "Realm of Heaven." Light, love, and knowingness await you here. It is not until you embrace your fear that love can truly enter. By dropping the load that blocks the open space, you allow space for the love you seek to enter. You have feared that by dropping the load you will lose yourself, and you fear that the little love that is in you will escape. But actually, by unplugging the density and letting go of emotional band-aids and holdings on, the open space becomes a vessel for the new information of light and love to inhabit you, which becomes the knowledge of who you truly are.

Throughout every present moment of our stillness, we are here to remind you that it is the merging place of one polarity, with its seeming opposite, that creates the totality. It is not one or the other, but both seeming dualities that come together in holy matrimony to become the union of all that it can be and is.

The voice of the rocks faded, and I slowly opened my eyes. The sun was about to set. It was time to go. I raised my hands, with my palms facing the rocks in a farewell gesture, "I love you, rocks!" I called out loud and clear. Then I made a slow and careful descent back to the path and to my car. I was lost in thought about the message I had received and I drove almost in a trance. At one point I looked up toward the darkening sky and saw two eagles flying in and around each other. Their dance was captivating, and I stopped the car to watch. I stepped out into the cooling air and watched in pride and appreciation as the eagles danced on the thermals. I thought of my own dance, and I felt connected to the movement of these regal birds. It was as if they were returning to me the gift of dance I had only just offered to the Ancient Ones.

Although I had journeyed long and hard to prepare myself for Sedona, and I had a series of spectacular retrievals, overall nothing seemed to be going as planned. Not a day, after my magnificent retrieval on the stone platform and after watching the eagles dance for me in the sky, I was sidetracked by pain yet again. My remaining wisdom tooth on the right side had me howling once again. It was like what I imagined birthing pains to be: there were long intervals between blasts of searing pain that nearly took my breath away. I was thankful I was in the United States, and that I could get the treatment I preferred, but I was not at all happy to be suffering again. I was forced to once again confront myself. "Why am I in pain? What has the pain to say and teach me? Why is this pain so familiar to me?" I called a dentist and as I waited for the time of my appointment, I tuned in deeply to my soul to try to elicit answers from my Higher Self. During my meditation I received the insight that wisdom teeth are like the bones of our body and the rocks of our Earth, which contain the DNA store-house—that place where the wisdom records are kept. In this sense, whatever we store away in the back of our memory banks or whatever we suppress of our expression gets compacted down into the back molars. When it is time to mature and achieve a measure of wisdom, this repository stirs and wants to be set free from its shackles.

As thought provoking as this insight was, on the physical level I could find no compassion for my wisdom tooth or the pain. I was in agony and I saw little value in my suffering. The American dentist I called, saw no reason for my suffering either, and when I went to see him he administered a general anesthetic and extracted the tooth without my feeling a thing. I thought I was finally back on track, and through the worst of my difficulties, when a few days later the gum around the pulled molar became extremely sensitive. Soon I was howling with pain again. I went back to the dentist and he discovered that I had a "dry socket." He explained—as if I already didn't know—that this is an extremely painful condition that often makes the pain of an impacted wisdom tooth look mild in comparison. Over the next few weeks, I treated my miserable tooth wound with natural remedies and was soon back to full health and off exploring the desert again.

One of my forays after my painful hiatus was to Boynton Canyon, a site that is said to contain many vortices. A legend of the Yavapai and the Apache peoples is centered on this sacred ground. The story goes that "First Woman," who was called Komwidpokuwia, or "Old Stone Woman," founded Boynton Canyon. She was originally from a place called Montezuma's Well, where the Yavapai were living. Her father, the chief, knew that a great flood was coming, so he sealed First Woman into a hollow log, along with some birds and food, and allowed her to float off, figuring that wherever she landed would be the place where the new world could be safely re-created. She was swept away by the rising waters, and eventually landed in the highest dry spot—what is now Boynton Canyon. There she made her home in a cave, and the world started anew.

The "old stone woman" that lay hidden in the cave of my own soul urged me to seek deeper for my ancient roots, so I set out to find a ceremonial cave that I was told was hidden in the landscape of time; perhaps this was the cave that Komwidpokuwia had called home? I drove to Boynton Canyon. Then, with a paper containing obscure directions in one hand, a bottle of water in the other, and my white buckskin medicine bag over my right shoulder, I followed a trail along the sheer rock walls into the deeper stratum of the canyon. I noticed a smaller path, partially concealed by the limbs of some juniper trees that veered in the general direction of the cave, so I followed it up over the rocky boulders and dry washes and onto a small plateau. I had a sneaking suspicion that the cave was one ledge above where I stood, so I followed my instincts and climbed to the next plateau. There I spied a cave. I did not know for sure if it was Komwidpokuwia's cave, but it was a cave nonetheless. That was good enough for me.

From the entrance to the cave, I could look out over the glimmering emerald treetops that dotted the otherwise dry landscape in thick clumps. Other than the bluebirds whistling and scuttling throughout the piñion pines and juniper trees, and the occasional butterfly fluttering along, all else remained still. I sat with my back against a charred, blackened wall just inside the cave entrance, and upon closing my eyes I was swept downward, to the ground of my being, into my own ancient memory. I felt that I had sat here long ago, while the fires of the First People kept vigil or prayed during their ceremonies.

I entered a meditative state, but soon was roused back to more conscious awareness by a sudden realization-vision that the ancient Anasazis, who I could sense in some other time or dimension were sitting here right now by a fire looking out of this very cave. They shared the exact same evolution and consciousness that I was experiencing now. I could feel and see these ancient people sitting around me in an unbroken circle of union. Each and every one of them was an aspect of myself that I had come to know. They were my tribe, as were the rock people, and as were the winged ones, who could so easily consult with the moon as their spiritual guide, with the rocks as their teachers, the sun as their creator, and with the stars as their navigators. These Earth tribes lived and commemorated life as a grand ceremony, everything to them had a perfected purpose—everything! I felt that I was sitting in ceremony with them now, that this was my vision quest, that I had been drawn here to return to a teaching I had once known but had long forgotten—that in the language of Nature, in the space of silence where no time exists, the same wisdom of consciousness is eternally present.

Suddenly I sneezed, the sound like a whip cracking open the space of silence. I realized that this sneeze, too, was perfect, a lesson about the need to "let go" before "taking in." The sneeze had released a part of my energy that had longed to fly free through the rocks. With this release I felt my awareness expand wider still. I was in perfect resonance with the energy of this cave and the spirits of this place. I felt the urge to rise, and so slowly I rose to a standing position and bowed to the stones, in appreciation and gratitude. I turned and followed the cave wall for a short distance, moving slowly deeper into the cave until I found myself standing in front of what appeared to be a doorway that was naturally carved into the rock wall. I heard words. "Come in.,"

"How?" I ask.

"Open the door within you."

"How do I do that?"

"Open your heart."

I breathed into my heart and almost immediately, I felt myself as an energy being spiraling down into a still point, to a "rock bottom" place within myself. But at the same time, I felt my sense of self-of being-expanding, outward from my heart center. I was a larger "self" than I had ever experienced before. I felt thoughts drift through my awareness; words that were mine and not mine. "I am one with my tribe. They are each and every one of them a part of me. I am not separate. There is no need for any words, for we are one. We are one. Aho Mitakuye Oyasin."

I do not know how long I remained there, in the depths of the cave, in the rock bottom place of my own heart. But it must have been a good deal of time, because when I emerged from my center back to more normal awareness, the cave was almost in darkness. When I got back to the mouth of the cave, shadows had descended over the land.

I quickly gathered my things and emerged from the cave, looking around for the trail that would lead me back to my car. I could not see it. There did not seem to be a trail here at all. For a moment I panicked, but quickly, I regained my composure, knowing that if I had made it up here, I could make it back down. Once I was thinking clearly again, having got past the punch of fear, I remembered that the trail was under me, on the next plateau down. Feeling relieved, I decided to bid my farewell to this special cave by leaving my "mark" here. Among other items I carried in my personal medicine bag was a white chalky stone. I withdrew it now and drew a large spiral onto the rock flooring. I often did this to ground my connection to the rocks in commem- oration of my journey and to release the stored energy within the rocks to enliven their frequency. Then, as night began to descend, I found the trail on the plateau below the cave and headed back to my car.

About halfway down the trail, I came across a small, dry riverbed. I stopped there for a few minutes to tune in to the memory of its running waters. I inhaled the memory of wet rocks and as a consequence felt as if I were quenching my own inner thirst to connect with the soul of the land. A brief but intense current of magnetic energy, the energy of this once-flowing stream, passed through me. As it did, I felt as if this wet wind discharged excess electrical energy that I had stored in my bones from my earlier "fire in the bones" experience. I felt cleansed from the very marrow of my bones, and I sank onto my hands and knees, touching the earth and thanking the memory waters of this stream for cleansing me. When I opened my eyes to stand up and leave, I saw, not inches from my face, a tiny white feather, no bigger than a fingernail. I picked it up and received it as a gift from Great Spirit. White feathers have throughout the ages been a sign of the gift or presence of Great Spirit, as are rare white animals, such as the white elephant, dolphin, owl, tiger, rhino and white buffalo. I stood up to go, but immediately knelt down again, as if something from the earth was tugging me back down and close to it. I turned my head to the right and my eyes fell on a tiny red stone that was gleaming in the deepening shadows. It was perfectly round and smooth, quite unlike the other rougher and larger stones around it. I picked it up and gently held it with the feather between my thumb and middle finger at the height of my heart. Through this magical encounter of earth elements I saw that the red rock symbolized the root chakra at the base of our spine and the white feather symbolized the crown chakra at the top of our heads and that the heart, the emerald center, was the place where the two polarities could be merged. I gave thanks once again. The moon was plainly visible now, and I looked up at it. I heard its voice speaking to me. "Amalia, this is the way to walk your Earth Walk—as light as a feather and elevated as an angel, connected to the heavens above, and as grounded and anchored as a rock, connected to the earth below. Heaven and Earth united."

As I resumed my trek back down the now dim trail, I thanked Mother Moon, whose bright rays were now lighting the way for me. Everything about this trek was turning miraculous, and the surprises continued as I approached the bottom. I had been watching the trail closely, placing my feet carefully, when I found my attention pulled upward toward a formidable rock that stood powerfully in the distance, its strength almost as palpable as its solidity. As soon as I laid my eyes on it, a wandering star meandered across the sky directly above it, and then that star shot upwards! I instantly remembered the odd upward shooting star I had seen at the Hopiland region, and I felt goose pimples arise on my arms. I could not help but think that these two stars were not stars at all, but were starships. Whatever they were, I felt blessed to have witnessed these two mysteries.

I continued walking, but only a few steps further down the trail, almost at the bottom, I hit a pocket of uncannily warm air. I stopped and my eyes snapped heavenward. I saw the "wandering star" again. Was it the same one I had seen just moments before? I wondered. I couldn't know. The words "as above, so below" entered my head, and I bid my farewell to this area, to these rocks, knowing that this day I walked, as the Navajo say, in the "Beauty Way," with my head connected to the heavens above and my feet grounded and surefooted on the earth below. And in between, my heart was beating the rhythm of oneness.

Chapter 9:

The Ancient Ones Speak.

For many weeks after that hike, I thought about my relationship with Sedona, or rather with the spirits of the land called Sedona. I had been in Sedona many months now, and my relationship with the spirits was, to use the obvious metaphor, "rocky" at best. One day I was literally at-one with this land and the next I was struggling to feel connected. Finally, I decided to seek an answer, or at least some insight from the land itself. I walked out under the night sky and asked the spirit of the stones several questions about my purpose here in Sedona.

"Why did you call me with such fervor?"

Because you were forgetting who you are and what you came to do on this planet. You are an Earth Keeper, an Earth Wisdom Carrier; this is why you are so hell bent on being "grounded." Being grounded is carrying the wisdom and knowingness of who you are, in the present moment. It is an anchoring of all your summed-up evolution carried in awareness and consciousness and brought back into the physical body, NOW. An Earth Wisdom Carrier needs to be grounded in order to carry Earth's information and pass it on to awaken the sleeping masses. Earth Wisdom Carriers are the movers and the shakers, just like when the earth quakes, to release her built up accumulated energy; it moves and shakes the limited vantage point of mass consciousness.

You are here to re-mind humans of their ability to be their totality, all in one package-the body. It is not about leaving the body to ascend. It is about bringing the all-ness of who you are into a grounded and anchored way. Like the merging of spirit and matter that creates the experience of life on Earth. The experience of life creates the knowingness of the self; the knowingness of the self is the knowingness of all that is-and that is God.

"Why have I been called here to the rocks of Sedona?"

Because here, you will come to know yourself and become self-realized, thus offering a larger opportunity for the humanities of this earth. Here you can slow down enough to hear the messages, requests, and missions for you to carry on and then out. Your message and opportunity is to remain grounded while reaching the highest realms of Spirit. The more grounded you are, the greater is your ability to soar to the highest planes of existence, as you have created a launching pad for your spirit to return home safely, into your body. You are a messenger between the worlds, *retrieving information from the rocks and handing it over to raise the spirit of the people. In creating this link, the invitation of merging Spirit into the physical becomes your return ticket home. When your soul's passage returns home to you in the awareness of your body, then you can make your choice to return home to Source and the conscious dissolution into Oneness.*

These "answers" were enlightening and I felt I more than understood the messages, but I still wasn't feeling the spiritual equilibrium that I was seeking. Still, the information reaffirmed my deep commitment to following my path, however circuitous and odd it might appear. The messages were not new to me, but they enlivened my belief—my experience—that rocks are living reminders of an integral part of ourselves that we have long forgotten, of a precious part of us that is inherently rich in ancient wisdom. We have become disconnected from the heart of the earth, an epicenter at which wisdom lies in its stillness and anchors us to our experience of our body on this planet. But our hearts have become hardened, our emotional centers dense as stone, and for the most part we have closed our selves off from our connection with the energies of the natural world. This disconnection is our primordial wound. The cure is to soften our center, so we can dissolve the boundary that separates "what is in here" from "what is out there." At the level of Spirit, nothing is separate, and if we enter the caves of our hearts, we find we can hear the voice of Mother Earth, and also the Universe, for these expressions are one and the same.

This fundamental truth—that we are not separate from our environment, or from anything—is as old as the most ancient wisdom traditions. Yet, perhaps it was, as many Native Americans termed it, "new old" knowledge—something we had forgotten and now needed to retrieve from the deepest recesses of our own memory banks. The rocks can help. Their powerful subtle energies can encourage, and perhaps even accelerate, our evolution as humans—but as humans who are more than our bodies—as universal beings. I was more sure than ever that we are so drawn to rocks and sacred sites precisely because they are repositories of ancient stories about ourselves and our connection to the natural world; they are our environmental and evolutionary memory banks. By touching our awareness to the stones' awareness, we access divine Earth energies and cosmic information. Cultivating the sensitivity of our attunement to the rock kingdom enables us to once again read these subtler energies of the earth, thereby accessing the archetypal realm from the sacred sites within ourselves. This vibratory feedback loop can then encourage our own evolution, both physical and spiritual, perhaps even encouraging the rock kingdom's evolution, for as they are sparked with the conscious mind of man, the connection towards a higher potentiality is thus enabled.

The ancient indigenous peoples, who are a voice of the earth, said "as above, so below." They looked to the stars and to the earth beneath their feet—for learning their lessons, for these realms are reflections of each other. The stars spoke to them of a stellar wisdom that streamed forth from other galaxies into this world, and of the brilliant light that guided their dreams and visions. The mountains taught them to stand their ground, to create a strong base upon which to begin their ascent to the heavens above. The trees and plants spoke to them of drawing nourishment deep from the bosom of Mother Earth so that the fruits of life could be offered up to the altar of the God. The rocks spoke to them of the ancient wisdom that has been buried in the bones of the earth and in the soil of man's consciousness. Anyone can hear the messages and whispers of Nature when their heartbeat is attuned to the heartbeat of Mother Earth. The rocks, the "silent ones" of the natural world, have profound messages they now want to impart. When we attune to the silence of Nature, we can hear the inner voice of this "EarthSpeak."

My life was becoming a living library of knowledge and as sure as the sun would face the day I, too, would continue to trek out to the rocks to excavate the dark jeweled spirit of the earth. No matter how many challenges were presented in my daily life, I was committed to doing the "Earthwork," and it was with this tenacity that I set out to Faye Canyon for a retrieval.

Faye Canyon is a landscape that charms with its fairytale-like atmosphere, where the landscape shifts from rocks as massive as temples to delicate spires to grassy and shady nooks that stand in sharp contrast to the otherwise dry red terrain. I followed the main path into the canyon, feeling overcome with "fairy" energy. This was a first, for the desert regions are not where one would expect to feel fairy energy. Still, it was unmistakably there, and it lent a feeling of gaiety to my hike. I walked until I felt pulled to a particular area. This time it was a huge rock ledge jutting from the canyon wall just above the path. I climbed up and sat in the middle of the ledge. After spending a few moments admiring the stupendous view, I closed my eyes and sank into the center of my heart, but this time, instead of picking up a transmission from the rocks, or the earth, I heard an inner voice I could only claim as my own, although it seemed foreign to me at the same time. As I listened, the sense grew that this was my own "inner earth being" speaking—a voice that was mine, and Earth's simultaneously, for in truth they are one and the same.

I am one who, among others, is holding the emerald-green rods of light. Pegging and grounding these rods of light into the earth creates a launching pad so that the Emerald Green Ray, which represents the higher heart of Love, has a place to enter and land. I am acting as part of this gateway, as a grounding rod for this energy, for its entrance and for the new birthing of the heart of the higher soul of Earth.

This birthing takes place in the heart of the body and soul of humankind and thus also in the heart of the earth itself. The green of the heart, infused with the cosmic light of the silver moon and of the golden sun, unify to create a shimmering Emerald Green elixir that fills the royal chalice—of "The Heart of Oneness." As we allow this infusion of emerald light to light our doorways within, we expose and diffuse the dark corridors of our passageway for an easier journey back home to our God selves.

The more we allow this light in our own consciousness, in our own heart and in our Earth, the higher the vibration can comfortably reside within us. An easy landing is an easy birth, which becomes an easy navigation through the journey of our lives.

It had been a long while since the "emerald" image had arisen in my life. Back in Australia, it had been a signpost of my opening to my soul work, to being a secretary of the stones. During this retrieval I had sensed this striking color in the form of a uraeus— the headband worn by Egyptian initiates that has the head of a cobra snake at the center of a golden ring. This sits in the middle of the forehead, the place of the third eye, the eye into our inner selves that sees out into the cosmos. During the retrieval, I had felt this color at my third eye and felt that I was looking through the eyes of an emerald green snake. Beyond these visuals, I had also received insight into the meaning behind the words of the trans- mission and began to feel my own connection to mythological time, when figures of snakes were carved at the entrance of caves, the guardians who test us with a riddle we must answer before we are allowed access to the jewels hidden within the dark and deep. I knew the answer to the riddle could neither be right nor wrong, for the answer is the fusion of opposites, the total that is more than the sum of the parts. It was by descending into paradox that one emerged beyond duality, and in so doing, one moved through the Emerald Doorway into the heart of the earth and of the self.

Despite my insights into my mission with the rocks and my call to Sedona, I was still living in duality here. I was not unified, as I knew from my retrievals that I must be. I was at once both inside and outside of myself, at once intimate with this land and a stranger to it. With the rocks I felt whole and balanced, but in the town environs I felt separate and displaced. Perhaps because as a sacred site, Sedona was never meant to be inhabited but only visited for ceremony and prayer. My personal life was the perfect mirror for this incongruity. As an Aussie, I am quite outgoing, and while I had made many friends here, I still did not really feel comfortable in the community. Although my visa status allowed me to stay in the United States, my living status was still unstable. I had house sat for a friend, and when she returned, she recommended me as a house sitter to another person. Before long, I became known as one of Sedona's most reliable house sitters. This new "profession," along with occasional work as a naturopath, alleviated the burden on my pocketbook, but it also left me feeling unsettled and ungrounded. I was finally able to attain a measure of comfort and stability when I moved into a cabin near Oak Creek Canyon. A friend Helena, was the landlord, and when her tenant moved out, she asked me if I was interested in renting the place. She mentioned a rent that was hard to refuse, and when I went to look at the cabin I fell in love with it. It felt like home, and a sanctuary. Moreover, when I saw that the cabin was laid with emerald-green carpets, I felt that the earth had called me there. I happily moved in and over the next several months began to regain some measure of control over my itinerant life. Once settled, I focused my energies again on the earth retrievals. Over the next year I had a string of illuminating, if challenging, sessions with the rocks of Sedona.

One of my first pulls during this period was to Bell Rock, a solitary dome-shaped rock, considered a sentinel for newcomers at Village of Oak Creek. Bell Rock was, and perhaps still is, spiritually significant to the "New Agers," and it was a common question to ask, "Have you climbed Bell Rock yet?" as if climbing it were a necessary initiation into the mysteries of Sedona. The one-mile climb to the top certainly is a sort of initiation, as it is a test of one's endurance. But Bell Rock's reputation is based on more esoteric qualities. It is said that this sacred site is among the most powerful of electrical, positive vortexes in the area, and contains both a strong masculine energy and what is unabashedly called "extraterrestrial" energy, believed to be used by extra-terrestrials as an inter-dimensional portal or contact point. It is said that the rock sits at the juncture point of many intersecting "ley lines," or streams of geo-magnetic energy that run across the planet, and that extraterrestrials utilize the energy concentrated there as a boost to propel them in any direction on Earth, or even into other dimensions. Needless to say, I was intrigued to find out what Bell Rock would reveal to me.

It was another dry desert day when I chose to make my visit there. The climb was indeed difficult, and not made any easier by the scorching sun. After an hour of hard climbing and massive energy expenditure, I reached the top. Immediately my attention and energy were pulled toward an oblong rock, shaped like a sarcophagus. I went over and sat upon it to rest. A breeze cooled me down somewhat, and the breathtaking panorama of red-rock cathedrals contrasted against the brilliant blue sky, made me forget my aching muscles. Before long, I felt both rested and renewed. I was ready to tune in to Bell Rock. Perhaps what follows, was influenced by the tales I had heard about this rock. At the time, I chose not to judge what I felt and saw with my inner eyes, and I feel the same now as I recount this transmission.

As I sometimes did, I first spoke aloud to the spirit of place. "Humans want to get to know you. They see the awesome beauty of your form and stance." Then I let myself sink deep into my interior spaces, where I listened with an open heart. The answer began as a vision. In my mind's eye I saw several strange-looking beings. They had tall, slender bodies simply sheathed in nondescript garments, and although I could not discern their gender, they had a distinctly feminine quality to their shape and stance. They seemed inquisitive about me, although they did not attempt to interact with me. I felt they were connected to "reality" on a deep level, as if their beingness was at one with the Source of all being. I felt they possessed superior knowledge and insight, and that time was not real for them. Somehow they existed in past, present and future. With deep respect and humility, I began speaking to them with my inner voice. I did not plan the words as I wrote them down; they came of their own accord.

"I know you are in here, and you in this moment know I am out here, longing to get to know and understand you. You are powerful beings with a soft strength, and the knowledge you contain is boundless. You seem emotionless and compassionless in your ways; however, this is because you are simply in the beingness of momentary existence. You do not know of wars, marriage, birth, death, passion and fear, as we know them. You do not contain the need for feeling the human condition through emotion as we do, although you are inquisitive about the expression of feelings, as though they are a faint memory, a silent recall or an echo through time. It is now time to open the windows of time, unlock the doors of the dimensional passageways, and greet one another, work and teach one another in unison and safety. *Aho Mitakuye Oyasin*—To All My Relations."

I paused briefly. Then my inner speech spontaneously resumed, as I spoke once again for myself and on behalf of humanity. "Assist us in riding the spiral staircase of light and love home. Don't be afraid of us and shut us out of your deep connection to the creator. I see how your innocence is infused with wisdom, and I sense the accumulation of your evolution in form throughout the eons, throughout dimensions and interplanetary and stellar revolutions. You could be ourselves in our own future, who have become a refined and higher frequency of species, existing in the presence of creation without judgment or causality, who have learned to open the inter-dimensional doorways and ride into the void to access creational information and knowledge. Invite and assist us in following our way back to the creation source; assist and teach us in heightening our vibrations to meet you, to meet more of ourselves."

Even though I had managed to maintain a meditative focus, a part of me was aware that this transmission had come from my own inner core and yet had come from the rock spirit beings at the same time. Was I becoming one with the rock beings? At times I could not differentiate. Even though the information coming through seemed more abstract than usual, there was little I could do but accept this shift, go wherever it took me, and take to heart whatever it taught me.

It was several weeks before my next retrieval, which I undertook at the Palatki ruins, the largest Sinaguan (*sin* is Spanish for "without" and *agua* for "water") village in the Sedona region. It has been documented that the Sinaguan people inhabited the area from approximately 650 A.D. to 1300 A.D. The Palatki (a Hopi word meaning "red house") ruins were built around 1150 A.D. and were abandoned about one hundred and fifty years later for no known reason. The rock-walled sections around the ruins are peppered with pictographs and petroglyphs, some of which are documented to be nearly six thousand years old. As I wandered around the starkly beautiful site, I felt the pull of the ancient, and I was eager to begin a retrieval but I did not rush the process. I attuned to the olden landscape around me and felt most strongly pulled to a dwelling at the back of the complex that was built out of the cliff, with the cliff face as the back wall of the structure. The rock dwelling was small and had a low ceiling. In fact, it could not have been comfortable for anyone taller than about five feet. I remembered that Ariel Spilsbury had told me that the Anasazi Indians were thought to have been diminutive and petite. This ruin brought that reality home to me in a blatantly physical way. I am only slightly taller than five feet myself, so I felt right at home here. I entered the dwelling and sat at the juncture where the manmade adobe sidewall met the cliff-face back wall. I quickly sank deep down into myself, and then continued to journey down into the depths of the earth. The connection came easily and intensely. I silently asked the rocks to reveal to me any information helpful to humankind at this time.

I continued to sink deeper within the earth and rocks, into the blackness of darkness, where I sensed the spinning motion of a vortex, a swirling mass of energy growing out of nothingness. Here I felt the consciousness of no-thingness merging with the purity of thought, giving birth to the spark of creation. From this creational point, the transmission began.

> It is here that all creation was born, with the exception of no thing. It is here from the unlimitedness of no-thing that one reaches the limitlessness of all.
>
> Like a lens of a camera, spiraling and swirling out, opening to all possibilities, the eye of All That Is seeks out its own experience through the living of it. At the edge of reality as it is known, it has reached the suspended state of its search, and we are now returning home. The grand camera has taken its photo shoot of all that is and the lens is closing in; the greater eye has seen and lived through the experience of Allness and, yes, we are returning home.

The retrieval was short and more obscure than any other one, but as the secretary to the earth, I was not in a place to question it or its validity. I held strong in my process to trust in the information given, for if I had started to doubt my capabilities, I would also have had to call into doubt the call of the earth and the assignment given to me to unearth its wisdom. So, I let the retrievals be: not dissecting them as I had once done, but instead accepting them at face value. There was just something about this period of my life in Sedona that defied explanation, and I knew I had to simply go with the flow with this mysterious rhythm of being.

My next retrieval came at a place I came to call Keyhole Cave. I am not sure of its actual name. It is a fairly large cavern situated at the base of Thunder Mountain, which faces the township of Sedona. I gave it its name because the opening to the cave is shaped like a gigantic keyhole. Every time I drove along Highway 89, which parallels this formidable mountain, I would notice the dark opening of this cave and I vowed several times to visit it but never did. Then one day, a few weeks after my last retrieval, I began to fantasize about going into the earth physically. I felt an irresistible pull to go as deep into the Mother as I possibly could. Keyhole Cave was the perfect place to fulfill this inexplicable compulsion.

As I drove to the cave, my thoughts drifted with the tides of my memory back to the dream I had in Australia, during the time when Sedona was just a word to me. I remembered that in the dream, I had been in a cave and the rocks had talked. They had instructed me to place the fingers of one hand in some small cavities at the back of the cave wall. By doing so, my fingers were arranged in a particular configuration that became a code that allowed me access to the inter-dimensional doorway of the rock-spirit world. I had to keep the fingers of my other hand moving, wiggling around, to keep contact with the physical human world. As the dream memory came back, I joked with myself that I had invented a "rock technology," some sort of earth-based computer through whose touch pad one could access the information stored within the rocks. I could not be more of a secretary than that!

When I finally reached the cave, I couldn't wait to get inside. But I slowed myself down and first honored the spirit of the cave, asking it and the spirit of the land for permission to enter. Their response was unclear. A foggy sensation rose through me both physically and mentally, and then I heard a strong, inner "No." I was momentarily crestfallen. Was this retrieval that I felt so called to do, not going to happen after all? Why was I being denied the opportunity to enter deep into the earth when the call to do so was so strong? I asked the spirits another question. "May I sense their communication from outside the cave? I immediately felt the answer. "Yes." I walked a few yards to a flat spot among the rocks and boulders that were strewn around the cave's entrance and sat down. It felt right that I should be facing the keyhole opening to the cave. If I couldn't be in the cave, at least I could see into the world of the rock spirits.

The retrieval started with a feeling—a shift in perception really. As I stared into the dark opening of the cave, I felt witness to sheer perfection. As my gaze penetrated the darkened depths, I felt as if I were penetrating a shaft of truth that went deep into the bosom of the earth. I felt as if I were outside myself, pure beingness, waiting in a kind of suspended stillness for nothing, or "no-one-thing" and yet I felt the rhythm of everything. I felt what I can only describe as a coming home to awareness—of my being, of the Earth's being, of the soul of this cave. I knew in that instant that the stones have mastered unconditionality. They hold the beingness of the natural world without needing to be anything but what they are—which is both nothing and everything. At the same time, I saw that touching their energy was like looking into a mirror of my own being. And we all can do this. If we are awed by our lives, we will see and feel the rocks as awesome; if we are bored with our lives, we will see and feel the rocks as utterly boring. If we empty our minds, however, then we may receive their messages, which reflect back to us the course of our own lives. The stones somehow merge Spirit and Matter. They are poised within the polarities, and somehow beyond paradox. They are at once ignorant and inert and also wise and sentient. With this realization, I felt myself slip easily and effortlessly into the meditative space within. And there, the stones spoke to me.

The ancient Anasazi knew their wise relatives—the rocks. Here they anchored the spirits of their guides—the eagle, raven, hawk, coyote, owl, bear, elk, and mouse—and moved with them through the passages of birth and death and around the wheel of life. Here in the majestic stone libraries they stored ancient information from galactic realms that is waiting to be retrieved and released into the future. Here in the mountainous rocky canyons are the cradles of their birthing, their ancestral burials, their doorways into their dreamtime, and their mirrors of light to reflect unto them and remind them of who they really are. The truth is seen and witnessed here, as truth speaks, seeks, and reflects truth.

I sat in the silence following this transmission for a long time, just reveling in the energy of this sacred space. I was not required to crawl into the womb of the Mother after all. Just witnessing the opening to her birth canal, as I came to see this cave opening, had been enough. Still, the retrieval was another abstract, poetical transmission and I wasn't sure what to make of it. How was I to use this information? Would it make any impression on anyone else that read it, or heard it? As I drove home that day, I struggled more than usual with these questions. I felt that Sedona was testing me, or teasing me. All I could do to find answers, or at least some measure of comfort in my questioning, was continue to do my job as secretary to the stones. Still, I made a silent request to the spirit of Sedona to speak to me in more concrete terms in the future. I asked for a signpost that could lead me to a deeper connection with the earth, and I asked that the sign be concrete and undeniable.

That signal came some weeks later, while I was riding in a friend's car. Keith was a new friend. I had met him several months before at an Earth ceremony, drawn to him by the color of his shirt—emerald green! We had just returned from a late afternoon drive and had pulled over to the curb where my car was parked. It was then that I asked about the owl's wing that was dangling from the rearview mirror of his car. I asked if I could touch it; Keith nodded affirmatively. As I fingered the soft feathers, I told Keith of my own connection to the owl as a totem, and how once back in Australia I had entered into Owl's energy world and been initiated by a spirit owl. He listened without comment, and then he reached up and unhooked the owl wing from the mirror. "I've had this wing for two years," he said, "and I've been waiting for the right person to give it to." He handed me the wing and asked if I would like to take ownership of it. I said I would be honored. "It's yours," he declared. As I took the wing, I thought back to my request that Mother Earth and the spirit of Sedona send me a sign that led me to a deeper path of the earth. This was it, I was sure. Owl was my totem. I had been wandering as a secretary for the stones for nearly two years now, just as long as my friend had had this wing. Now it had been gifted to me—a testament to my journey and its rightness. That moment also forged a new bond in Keith's and my friendship, for from that time on we playfully referred to each other as "Owl Brother" and "Owl Sister."

The Native Americans, among other indigenous tribes regard the owl as the harbinger of death, and therefore it is a bird that is at once feared and revered. But I saw it as a totem of an alchemical process of rebirth—of the dying of an old part of the self and the birthing of a new part. I sat in silence with the wing and thought back to the twelve-foot owl that had once come during a momentary vision back in Australia. I remembered how it had enfolded its energy around my own and how it had communicated a message to me. What had it said? "I see you and honor your journey. And the time will come when you and I will come to know one another as one." I felt shivers up my spine. And then another memory surfaced, this time of a dream I had had only a few days before but had forgotten until now.

In the dream, I was walking into a rock cavern and down into the depths of the earth, where I knew that my personal sacred sanctuary was. The only light along this path was what I knew to be a sacred flame, which was eternally alight. I was wearing a flowing, emerald-green gown. When I got to my sanctuary, I knew that many people would come to seek my counsel, for I was an oracle. But I did not communicate audibly. Instead, I saw into a person's soul, with the penetrating visual acuity of an owl, and then illuminated what I saw there. They could then see what was in their innermost being and reclaim any parts of themselves that they had lost. It was like I was conducting silent soul retrievals on each person.

As I drove home that afternoon, with the owl wing on the seat next to me, I had a feeling that time was of the essence and that Owl was again awaiting my arrival into its domain. Suddenly, that did not seem like such a good thing. Owl is a tough taskmaster, and I felt the weight of the responsibility of working with Owl energy. Anxiety started to rise within me. As the sun sunk behind the red rocks, I felt the darkness fall upon my emotional state. I began to regret accepting this gift. I began to question whether I had the strength to carry "Owl Medicine," as the Native Americans call the sacred energy of an animal totem. I was pulled from my worry by a strange beam of opaque light that traversed the darkening sky. I pulled over to the edge of the road to see if I could determine the source of this light beam, but I could not figure it out. Oddly the beam of light began in the darkness and ended in the darkness. My feelings of worry and trepidation about working with the owl wing intensified. As I sat there in my car, in the dark, I suddenly heard the voice of Owl speak to me in my thoughts.

Amalia, I am an ambassador for the realm of truth. It is true that I hold the passage from death to birth, as does everything else that matters on this planet. For I sit in the darkness, in the decaying of life, as we know it; yet I see through eyes of light revealing the light of day of a new birth to come. If you focus on the fear, then so shall it be that you indeed feel and experience it. But if you focus on the love, then so shall you indeed experience love. It is your choice, my dear.

I started the car again and drove into the night toward home. Despite the positive tone of this message, I felt riddled with anxiety about reconnecting with this powerful medicine. As Owl had suggested in the transmission, I breathed into the love that lay hidden in the anxiety to try to dispel it, but I couldn't help but think of the owl as a messenger of death. I wondered what in me still needed to die, and if I could survive yet another "spiritual" death and find joy in a rebirth. By the time I got home I had regained my sense of inner calm, but that was soon shattered when I listened to a message on my answering machine. There had indeed been a death. A friend from Australia had left me the sad message that Michael Hutchence, the lead singer of INXS, had died. I sank down on a chair and bowed my head in sadness. Beautiful, glorious Michael had left us. Had passed over to the other side. I had often traveled with INXS as the band's massage therapist and health consultant. Now I, and no doubt thousands of other fans and friends of Michael, felt the loss of this radiant point of light. I lit a votive candle in honor of Michael, and I would keep it burning in vigil for seven days and nights. Later that night, I danced a prayer for his soul, that it would take easy flight back to Source. As I danced, I thought of the strange light beam I had seen while driving and I called out, "Choose the light, Michael! Choose the light!"

So began a two-year apprenticeship with Owl medicine. I began a course of "Owl dreaming," asking Owl to counsel me through dreams. I also delved into the mythology and native teachings about the relationship between Owl and Eagle, the other bird that seemed so connected with my life and with my call to the journey with the stones. I was inspired by the relationship between the two as I read about them and as I came to see their relationship and feel it myself. I knew that one day I would write about it. I attempted to start that writing process whilst sitting on the rocky expanse beside the flowing waters of Red Rock Crossing, with a view of the sacred site of Cathedral Rock. The auburn autumn leaves, the babbling creek and the flight of the raven set a magnificent stage for my undertaking. I was working on my laptop computer and began to write spontaneously, a sort of free-writing. I chuckled to myself as I remembered once joking with my ex-husband Marcus that one day I would sit with my laptop in the desert and be a secretary for the earth. My intent was focused now, not frivolous, and this is what I wrote.

"The eagle swiftly swoops up the wind, harnesses the radiant rays of the sun, and carries these rays like arrows upon its back. Its sight is as clear as day, for it has become one with the radiant sun. With eye-bright vision, its focus intensely deliberate, nothing is hidden from the eagle, and with the first sighting of its prey; the arrows of light are shot into its target. The eagle is a solar bird, flying high, close to the sun, gathering information from Great Spirit to then spread this magnificence over the land and its peoples. The gift it brings is the ability to see a situation from a long distance away; it sees through the eye of the sun, the eye of God, hence alighting any given situation with Great Spirit. Its wisdom is harnessed from the Temple of the Sun, holding ancient memories and carrying them into the future millennium. It is thus an ambassador from the ancient land of God, sheathed with filaments of fine gold threads, reminding us of our God place within. The inner masculine half, the king within each and every one of us, the part of us that knows what it wants, sets sight on it, aims and goes out and gets it. The part of us that penetrates the fields of our dreams. The part of us that sees very clearly what is going on around us. The part of us that shines in the glory of being alive!

"The owl, on the other hand, sits still in the shadows of the night, enfolding these shadows under its wings to decipher its silent message. Its vision illuminates the dark of night, and just as the moon reflects the light of the sun, the great owl's eyes capture the golden sun and reflect it within. The owl is a lunar bird, gathering illuminated wisdom from the eye of the Goddess herself to await the inner dreamer's wakefulness; it is when the dreamer awakens that this silent wisdom embarks upon the inner seer. It sits in the silence with Truth, knowing that the light of day has witnessed its journey, spiraling this light into the cauldron of the soul to brew, slowly into wisdom. The gift Owl brings to us is the patience to see what lurks in the shadows of our own beings, illuminating the dark corridors of our minds so that we can see who we are and where we are heading. Its wisdom is harnessed from the Temple of the Moon, which also holds ancient memories and carries them into the future millennium. The owl is the ambassador from the future age of the Goddess, draped with fine gossamer filaments of silver threads. The owl reminds us of our Goddess place within, the inner feminine half, the queen within each and every one of us, the part of us that feels what it desires and calls it forth from the land of silence, the land where everything already exists. Bringing it forth by invitation only and awaiting to receive it. Owl illuminates our field of dreams and gently alights us to our quiet knowing."

Owl and Eagle represent the union of opposites, the merging of dualities. Wasn't that what most of the retrievals were teaching? Duality is illusion, yet we cling to it as our deepest truth. Either-or. Good-bad. Right-wrong. Divine-Earthly. They were each necessary to the whole. Everything in the transmissions and in my own life "re-sounded" with the message of how necessary it is to give up this illusion and to unify opposites, to give up once and for all, the illusion of separateness. I knew that the heart, not the head, is the place where this merging takes place. But how difficult it is to live purely from one's heart!

Meanwhile, despite my challenges with the transmissions in Sedona, my home life had finally settled into a pleasant routine that allowed me the space and provided the perfect environment to grow and change. My fairytale cabin was nestled on land adjacent to the bank of Oak Creek Canyon, a sixteen-mile-wide gorge through which streams meandered and a waterfall fell in a glorious sheet down a sheer rock wall. From my back veranda I could look out on to the creek, which in the rainy season roared past the cabin and then wound its way into the red-rock canyon. The land was lush with white-skinned sycamore trees, the garden was filled with fairy energy, and graceful blue herons skimmed past along the creek, where the smooth, wet stones seemed Nature's most elegant sculptures. I could even see the brave face of Mt. Wilson in the distance. This surely was my little piece of heaven—my Garden of Eden, my own Emerald Green paradise. This was the perfect place to spend time peeling back the layers of myself and to situate myself in ceremony, seeking communion with Earth's nature and with my own sacred inner nature. It was also the perfect place to receive Alejandro, whom I had last seen nearly two years ago in Maui. I always knew I would see him again, and the time had come. Even though his visit was brief, we managed to enrich each other just as we had in the "good old days". We spent long nights catching up with each other, exchanged massages, laughed until our bellies nearly burst, and sat with reverence amid the red rock caverns. Ours was a sweet reunion. We had come full circle, and on saying our good-byes we felt whole and complete with each other.

During my time there, I was also graced with a "spirit sister," Ranjita Enocha Ryan. She had lived in the area for more than twenty years and was a spiritual steward of this canyon and its environment. She totally "got me" and what I was doing in my mission as secretary to the rocks, and I spent a lot of time with her. Magic abounded at Ranjita's house, which was located between what she called "Canyon Mama and Red Rock Papa", (configurations depicting the feminine and masculine principles of the land). She would often flatter me by saying that Canyon Mama called me over from the other side of the world to be with her. Ranjita's charm was especially revealed whenever anybody wanted or needed something, as she was always providing a cornucopia of whatever was desired. For instance, if I was a little hungry, she offered not just a piece of fruit, but also a large basket of all the fruits in season, or an openhanded display of her favorite goodies. Her generosity led her to create "Your Heart's Home" retreat center, which welcomed anyone who felt the need for sanctuary. She provided an amazing atmosphere where people could realign with their highest self and be nourished back to health and well-being. She truly taught me about selfless service.

Interesting things happened when I was with Ranjita or in her home. One day for example, when I was house-sitting for her, an iridescent blue-green hummingbird flew through an open window and crashed right on the "power spot" in the living room where Ranjita and I often held ceremony or performed sacred dance. The tiny bird lay there stunned. I carefully scooped it into my palm and tended to it for four hours, sending it loving energy, doing Reiki, praying over it, singing to it—determined to do whatever it took to restore it to flight.

During this energy work, I opened my own psyche to the little bird in an effort to understand what its crash into my life might mean. Its message was to watch out where I was going lest I crash myself. I delved into the Underworld with it, in a kind of spontaneous shamanic journey, and I visualized the tiny bird laying in the darkness of its own fear. I understood that I was somehow cowering in the dark with my own fear, too—a fear that the beauty of my life and environment could end at any time.

After hours of ministering to it, the bird was alive but was not in any condition to fly, so I finally made a little nest-bed for it. Over the next several hours I fed it water, milk, the Bach Flower "Rescue Remedy"—anything that I thought might restore its strength and help send it flying back out into the world where it belonged. At one point while I was tending it, I remembered that in the tarot of the Medicine Cards—written by David Carson, the hummingbird was noted as a totem for solving the riddle of contradiction and duality, and that its feathers could open the heart chakra. I whispered, "The heart is the porthole through which dualities are merged." Hummingbirds are considered gifts from the gods, sent to bring success in matters of the heart. This last association was so strong that in certain parts of the world, herbalists dry and powder the hearts of hummingbirds for use in love potions.

I had bonded with this tiny injured being, but I could sense it was close to death. In one last attempt to help it survive, I held the quivering bird close to my heart and infused my own heart energy into it. I even invoked the archetypal hummingbird spirit and then spoke and sung to it of its sweetness and its freedom flight and its importance to the flowers' reproductive cycle as it feeds on the flower's sweet nectar, truly the nectar of life. At one point I was even moved to tears. At another, I fell into the dreaming of the hummingbird spirit, closing my eyes to feel its spirit and feeling uplifted myself by its freedom song. I felt an amazing "at-one-ment" with this trembling spirit of Nature, and its energy was immense within me, allowing my spirit to feel set free to soar in an ecstatic flight that transported me to a soft surrender and then . . . I opened my eyes and looked at the bird and saw that its own spirit had taken flight. It had died in the palm of my hand, close to my heart. I did a sacred dance to honor the bird's Spirit journey to the next world and then I ceremonially buried it, under the sun-baked rocks.

It was with the spirit of Owl, Eagle, and now Hummingbird that I set out for my next retrieval—to West Fork. I had heard that the West Fork area provided one of the prettiest hikes, with its densely forested terrain of pines, firs, sycamores, maples, and oaks. Every fall, the maple leaves turn into a multihued palette of orange, maroons and golden yellows, which attracts tourists from all around. The forests here also contain Ponderosa pines that smell like vanilla beans. As I hiked into the forest, I passed by a picturesque but abandoned grove of apple, pear, and plum trees that surrounded the ruin of a lodge. I followed the trail into the forested canyon, where imposing red-rock cliffs surrounded the trees. I walked for at least an hour before I felt the energy pull of a large rock wall that rose upward not far from the trail. I went over and sat in front of it and let myself dissolve into my inner core, where still and silent I opened my heart to hear the Earth speak.

The breaking apart of two beings is the attempt of Spirit to bring harmony to a situation. The holding on, the stuck-ness, makes the boundary rigid, so movement is held hostage and life appeased. The more one holds on, the more one fears the letting go, then the greater the illusion of damage at breaking point.

Breakage. Break Age. Break the cycle; break the bread in celebration of the shared communion. When two parts stretch away from each other and break apart, the tearing in the middle is the area from which resolution is created—an open space that gives way to wholeness.

Holding on, harboring old hurts, and sweeping the dust under the carpets—until, the bubble of illusion bursts. At first, it is shocking that the pretty balloon is pricked to pierce the illusions only to be faced with a reality that seems empty, dark, unknown and scary. This popping of the bubble releases the holding, the harboring of fear in its many guises, opening the space for the new. It releases the substance of fear, so the tears are shed, the grief felt, the anxiety expended. This substance of fear was the very cause of the tear in the fabric: the container could not be filled any longer. We can learn to release the container and live in the open space, the unknown place where love is born. Freedom (free-dom), free dominion, (free dom-in-ion), freedom in, on and all around us.

The message revealed the infolding relationship between separation and union and how duality in Ultimate Truth does not exist; it is the mind that perceives it so and engages it thus. I thought of all the ramifications of this message. I considered how the mind only exists in the past or the future, in this or that. Mind does not seem to exist in the present moment, only pure awareness does. Even the physical anatomy of the brain itself has two sections, two hemispheres that *together* are responsible for the brain's holistic function: the feminine, intuitive side and the masculine, logical side. These two hemispheres are joined at the central point by the corpus callosum, the part that deciphers, translates, balances, and gives validity to both sides. Duality, valid and divine as everything else, is an integral aspect of the whole, so it would seem to make sense to say that it does exist in the world-of Apparent Truth if not the Ultimate Truth. But there is always a connection, a merging of the two into one. This greater aspect of the Truth, of the folding of one into the other, offers us an open invitation to experience a situation as it is, without the active engagement of the mind of judgment that separates this from that. This point of merger is the place of the watcher, the I Am presence in each of us, the God self that is all encompassing, that will draw us into the realm of unity and toward the freedom we seek.

I had my own daily point of merger in Sedona—Sugar Loaf Mountain. Whenever I needed to be reminded that I was more than my body, or my mind, or my spirit—that I was a merger of all three whose sum was greater than the parts—Sugar Loaf Mountain was there to remind me. Very often at night, I would visit Sugar Loaf Mountain, a rock mound shaped like a loaf of bread that was considered the heart rock of Sedona. It provided the easiest and closest access to the rocks from town and is known to contain the heart chakra energy of the region. It was here late at night, that I would ground my energy after being reeled into the complexities of humanness and the convolutions of relationships. It was my connecting point, a place where I could reset myself into balance and center myself in my heart before I went off to bed. Like many other power spots or vortices around Sedona, Sugar Loaf Mountain is replete with small deposits of quartz crystal, which is a magnifying and projecting stone that helps send messages out from the earth into the human realm. This place reminded me of how ubiquitous duality appears to be: for me the quartz crystal represents the crystallized light of the stars and yet here it was embedded within the red-rock earth. Here the white light of the crown chakra merged with the red base of the root chakra. Anyone who opened to this power spot could feel the energy of wholeness that radiated from it. Not long after my West Fork retrieval, I received this transmission from Sugar Loaf Mountain.

Deep, still deeper, sinking into the center of our being, we are one with existence, with all that is and ever will be. Open, open, to the experience—allow yourself to expand into the oneness. Let rise from the well of your existence the rich knowingness that arrives from silence and stillness. To surrender, to hand it over, opens the door of truth, and to empty your chalice and pour out its contents is to open to the receivership of love's divinity. As you pour out the dense matter of shadows, fears, and limitations, you invite in the spirit of love and more love. Through the dissolution of density and darkness, to the scintillation of light and Spirit, you become a pure vessel, a container of pure knowledge—the essence of All That Is. Now we may drink of the divine chalice and be filled with the nectar and the glory of life, and taste the life we seek.

For me, this was the feminine voice of the earth speaking. I had no sooner let this voice find a nest within me to settle than I heard a voice that entered into me as a masculine energy. This was not an Earth energy, it was more a voice from within myself, qualitatively different from what I heard from the stones. I let it speak nonetheless, and it taught me not about emptying the chalice of the self, but about wielding the sword of truth.

Blue neon light of laser beam, an invisible ray to the naked eye, only he who dares to be held in the light and revealed unto himself, has the power to draw the sword and carve the truth from illusion. Like Archangel Michael, who wields his swift sword and slices the veils of illusion to reveal the truth, which stands alone in the stillness of time and space.

The sword reflects the level of conduct you have reached. For held in the physical grip of fear, the sword kills and spills blood; but held in a spiritual plight, the sword reveals the truth by purifying the ethers around it. So hold the patronage of the sword and use it to cut out the pattern of your design, which is your true blueprint of life.

Sedona felt like that to me—both a chalice and a sword, both soft and hard, accepting and rejecting. No matter how many retrievals I did, no matter how many signals Spirit sent me that I was on the true path of my life, I still felt occasional "down" times, when my blue mood would stir the pangs of self-doubt. I was living a duality of self that I knew was an illusion but that I could not seem to overcome. How were the many aspects of my life—the retrievals, my sacred dance, my travels and explorations—all coming together to create a greater whole? I couldn't feel that wholeness for myself—or at least I could not maintain it. The landscape of Sedona was an ever-present reminder of my schism within. Even though Sedona was a small oasis in the desert, it was still desert country. It was clear that the plants and flowers had to struggle to survive the arid desert, sporadically revealing blooms that were dwarfed from lack of water. The sun's rays created a blanket of exasperating heat that was often hard to bear. There were times when I felt the harshness of desert life would dwarf me, too. At these times I felt alone and spiritually barren. My social and love lives at times felt fruitless, going nowhere fast. To top it all off, I was struggling financially, spending so much time out on the land in my "Earthwork" that I overlooked the work I needed to do for my own survival. Naturally, at these times, my doubts got the better of me and I would appeal to Spirit for more confirmation that I should be here, listening to the rocks. "Am I really implementing my true work? Is this a worthy mission? Am I doing a good enough job?" The questions came hard and fast.

In the midst of one of these down times, I set out for Faye Canyon, returning there to do some intense soul searching. I perched myself on top of an angled rock slab that overhung the ridge, then laid down and had myself a good cry. When I finally sat up again and scoped the landscape around me, a landscape I had come to love, I suddenly couldn't find my connection to it at all. The entire canyon looked like a stage set, an illusion created to fool me into thinking it was real. A wave of doubt flowed over me. Then despair. Surely I was forsaken and lost this time. I had been tricking myself in the worst way. Nothing mattered. As I struggled not to surrender to the black wave of despair, I called out to the universe, to Spirit, to whomever might be there and listening: "What am I doing here, sitting on a pile of rocks in this desert? My life is hard as rock. I have struggled to survive to make ends meet, but for what?" The tears came again and I collapsed like a rag doll back onto the stone slab. I was in no mood or condition for a retrieval, and yet I heard an inner voice that I could not control. Through my sobbing, I listened.

Sinking down into the soul of the land, deeper and deeper into the stillness of the silence. The shaman within us dies to the outer world and summons himself to the underworld, sinking deep into his own desolate terrain, curtailing his senses and redirecting and turning them inward. Little but his own breath is the connecting link to life. He sees, feels, tastes, smells and hears no more, as he has died to the life he knew. All the senses now evolve into one new sense, one of sensuality—sense-you-all-ity, (sensing the All There Is). A new landscape is birthed, one where the shaman walks between worlds. He honors this death within, giving rise to a new spark of life.

You do not need to physically die to return and become one with the earth. You need to be still and sink into the silence; here you truly birth yourselves from the earth. The New Earth is awaiting you; you are one with the soul of the earth. Earth is calling each of you home, within yourselves, within your souls.

I lay still in the silence after the message. My self-pity seemed an indulgence that I could not afford, but I had a hard time releasing it. The earth had again reminded me of the mission I had agreed to fulfill—a mission each of us must agree to recover our True Selves. In light of that mission, my tears seemed childish, but also necessary. They had replenished my parched longing for a fertile land within my own being. By the time I left the ledge that day, I felt partially renewed by a primordial power that lay in the deepest recess of my soul. I felt more invigorated and marshaled a new eagerness for my work. I felt blessed by the richness and fertility of my mission with the earth.

I threw myself with renewed vigor into my work with the stones and decided my next retrieval would be at the Shaman's Cave. This site seemed perfect in light of the message I had just received. Shaman's Cave is a large mushroom-shaped red rock, facing the wide expanse of the valley green. Hidden in a wall behind the rock is an opening—a large natural hole in the face of the rock wall, which leads into the cave—a shaman's doorway. Within the cave, pictographs depicted the ancient movements of time, which remained still while many sacred ceremonies and rites of passage unfolded. Mohave rattlesnakes that coil on the earth and cackling ravens that continually swoop overhead are said to be the guardians and caretakers of this mysterious site. I had no problems with either as I ceremonially entered the shaman's doorway into the rock underworld, eager to meet the spirits there. They were quick to meet me, and they provided a surprise. As they began the transmission, they spoke in poetry!

Out of the emptiness see what comes, out of the silence hear what is, and in the stillness feel what moves. The space of time is undivided, unfathomable. Through the eye of Matter we see the body of Spirit, and through the body of Spirit we feel the creation of Oneness.

Dancing feet stirring up the dust,
Inner visions undeterred by Earth's crust.
Moving wheels unlocking time,
We are indeed the creation's mime.

Traveling through doorways and windows within,
To embark upon new terrain we have not yet seen.
Twirling, dancing starlets as spectators from above
move their light through darkness to let in their love.

They see with eyes of starkness with no restraints upon their reign,
And let their wild horses within, fly with flowing manes.
They take these visions back to their thrones of sight,
To record their viewing on the great screens of light.

The fire is ablaze; mind is like a maze,
To find the way to stillness you must pass the craze.
Folding in the wings of foreign flight,
To set back home in the dark of the night,
The test is at rest, now time to nest.

Somehow this poem retrieval served to lift the last of the dark wave of self-doubt that had been hanging over me for so long. My inner rhythm for the work returned and a series of retrievals came quickly and profitably. I felt connected again to this ancient place. Sedona's red rock giants had stood watch over the land for more than three hundred and thirty million years. This land had been covered by ocean water four times, and the saltwater and wind had eroded the rocks, exposing the layers of sandstone and limestone that formed the colorful spires, arches, and rugged formations evident today. The rocks wore the ancient faces of stone kings and queens, of Aboriginals, and even of clowns; some had shape-shifted into birds, lizards, and elephants. They were the signposts of our modern culture, with names like Coffee Pot, Snoopy Rock, Chimney Rock, Lizard Head, Bell Rock, Sugar Loaf Mountain, and Cathedral Rock. I wanted to know them all.

With newfound vigor I headed out to Madonna Rocks to listen. This power spot is also the site of the Chapel of the Holy Cross, a spiritual citadel exhibiting a towering cross, rising two hundred feet from the ground. To the far left of the chapel are two pinnacles standing side by side, appropriately called Twin Nuns or by the locals as Madonna Rocks. I received the following transmission as I beheld the awesome panorama of buttes, valley and sky.

The momentous, the moment of us, of humanity, is now being caught in the web of time. In the center of the web, of the void, the records are stored and at the same time released and broadcast through the waves of light, like "emissionaries." At any moment we are invited to receive this information, tune into it, and ride the waves of the sweet chorus of life itself. There is much activity in the space around us, but just because you cannot see it does not mean it is not there. It is! You need only fine tune your awareness to the stillness where time is stopped and the other world of the invisible exists. The stone people are awaiting your arrival; you're awakening, at the meeting of the two worlds. They know that time is up and the alarm is about to go off-time to wake up from the dream. Time to see through the eyes of stillness and of timelessness. Time to see a new reality.

The new record is released. You are invited to listen, play, dance, and sing. Heaven is awaiting you right here and now. You have forgotten that you are the angels that have not fallen but are the ones who landed here to herald the New Dawn.

On the heels of that retrieval came one at Chimney Rock, which is one of the power spots I most love in Sedona. It got its name from the collection of three rock spires that tower upward like a chimney of the earth that reaches the sky. I was certain that this was the rock formation that had first appeared to me in my dream the day after I received the transmission of Sedona in my stone circle back in Australia, a dream that had started me on this quest. I often climbed the chimney as high as I could, sitting in a gap between two of the spires. I loved the energy I felt there, and now the energy was especially intense. As I tuned in, I heard the rocks offer their kind counsel.

There is a time bomb here. All of time explodes into the presence of now. It is gifted to you through the dark chimney of time. Through the heart of fire, you burn up the density of matter; through the ring of fire, you leap into the unknown; through the spirit of fire, you are cleansed, leaving you with the essentials of our yourselves—the crystallized essence of the divine.

Lack of clarity, is likened to a gray puff of smoke ascending a chimney, is the dark corridor of time, winding its way to merge with the clarity and purity of Spirit. Similarly, the gift of Spirit is given to you through the chimney, through the void, through the center of the spider's web, through the doorway, along the journey of the unknown, through the veiled darkness of the shadow realm. From there you descend from Spirit to the hearth of matter.

It is with the sinking into the unknown, into the stillness, into the depths of your being that you are gifted with the presence at the hearth of life, at the altar of your loving selves. At the bottom of the well lies the eternal spring, at the end of the rainbow lies the pot of gold and at the bottom of the chimney lies the gifts that Father Christmas leaves for you in your innocence, to be opened and revealed in truest presence.

I was receiving messages from the rocks more easily now; they were coming in strong and I was delighted once again to be "secretary for the earth." My next message came from the Birthing Cave. I had heard about this cave but had not until now visited it. This is a cave of great powerful feminine energy that was used by shamans, Native Americans for vision quests, and the 'birthing of newborns'. It had probably gotten its name from the formation itself, for as you enter the cave, the rock of the ceiling is split, look-ing like two thighs spread apart and open to the heavens. This site is regarded as a place of the sacred feminine, of the Goddess' Womb—of Earth Mother energy.

I sat in the cave in reverence, feeling protected and safe in the privacy of the Earth Mother's womb, her innermost sanctuary. When the stones spoke, it is not surprising that their message was about the dance of male and female.

Sexual energy is life-force energy. It is the marriage of Shakti and Shiva—the divine essence of the feminine merged with the grounded essence of the masculine. When the two realms meet and walk together into union, into love, the fires of life are kindled, the serpent's breath of fire is ignited, and alchemically the veils of illusion are lifted. Here, at this meeting place, at the hearth of the entrance of another world, surrender all of your resistances and constraints. Release the shackles of the mind; fear and struggle have no place here.

The energy harnessed through sailing the seas of love, reflects upon its surface, the intense illumination of light and heat emitted from the central core of love itself. This emission is transmitted from this core into the core of love within you; you are then transformed, healed and rejuvenated.

Through this passage, you can access the golden records of time. Through this passageway, you can rest into timelessness, nothingness, and everythingness—totality, as it is—where you come to know love. It is of the utmost importance to be rooted and grounded with the earth. Pandora's box kept shut on the basement level of your physical being needs to be opened and the fears, survival modems, competition, and anxieties released into the arms of your own selves. So that upon merging the Shakti/Shiva dance into union, the alchemy that occurs can transmute your physical and emotional love into divine love, the doorway to union with All That Is.

Love is the glue that sticks the universe together. Love is the newest and oldest drug that expands our consciousness, lifts us through our awareness into the grand kaleidoscope of existence.

After sitting for some days with this message of love and union, I decided to return to Rachel's Knoll, the site where my Sedona retrievals had begun. Somehow I felt that coming full circle was not only appropriate but also necessary to my continued work in Sedona. This time, as I quieted my mind, I peered into the realm of the rocks like a crystal ball to receive the message from the rocks. In my mind's eye, an old time piece—a gold stopwatch—appeared with a chain attached to it. Immediately following the appearance of the watch, I heard the words "At I'm Peace" arise out of nowhere. I knew this was a homonym—(A Time Piece) and smiled at the word play. Was Mother Earth and the rocks now using puns? I indeed felt deeply at peace as a short, abrupt message came forth from the rocks.

> Rocks are the gatekeepers for Earth Wisdom (Earth's Wise-Domain). They are majestic oceans of solidified waves of knowledge. Where there are rocks, there is preciousness in the form of earth jewels of either stored information or inter-dimensional doorways. You see here there is something to protect, as rocks are the guardians of Earth's gifts.

Unlike most other retrievals, I felt that with this one I could direct questions during the transmission. I asked, "What is in the earth that needs such grandness of protection?"

> Here in this ancient land are kept ancient timepieces to travel through the doorways into otherworldly realms. Where ancient Emerald Records are kept for safekeeping to be revealed at this time now when humanity may most benefit from Earth's messages. Here is where Earth's genetic codes and information records are kept, in Earth's laboratories, where new life-codes are created and birthed. Where creation performs its evolutionary work to steer and assist the consciousness of the ones who inhabit the earth. The rocks have acted to deter the masses' attention from Earth's long-kept secret. They know that people's consciousness will stop at nothing for the gain of their own enterprise and because of this, they act as guardians and gatekeepers to Earth's inner sanctuaries. Just like the sealing stones that cover caves

where the jewels are kept, where the chalice lies silently awaiting, or where Christ lay to be revealed into the resurrection of a new dawning era. The Resurrection awaits your remembrance to awaken from the dream, to awaken to the truth of your natural inheritance.

This transmission did not feel new. I had been told many times before how the rocks are guardians and gatekeepers of the truth of Earth Spirit. After this retrieval I knew it was time for me to visit Cathedral Rock, the grandest of all the power spots of Sedona.

Cathedral Rock majestically rises up out of the earth and undeniably stands on holy ground as an Earth minster. The rock is separated at its middle, creating a saddle where two huge spires stand back to back. It is Sedona's signature rock, where thousands of people have come to pray or simply sit in silent reverence. Artists and photographers from all over the world have tried to capture its grandeur. But how does one capture the ineffable? As a vortex, Cathedral Rock is a repository of energy. It is both an electric-masculine and a magnetic-feminine vortex. The legend attached to it tells of a man and woman who lived in the peaceful surrounding valley but who were anything but peaceful themselves. They argued incessantly, until the sound of their quarrelling created such a commotion, that they woke up the ancient serpent of the river's bend. The wise serpent silenced them by giving them a message, which conveyed something of the following: When two beings come together, they do so in deep respect and love for each other. They recognize and value their uniqueness, never competing or criticizing each other. They honor their dependence on each other and independence of each other. They understand that they walk their own path and seek their own way, yet share a common journey. The serpent carved the likeness of a man and woman standing back to back to illustrate their support for each other and yet independence of each other. It then declared, "Though you each look your own way, I set this stone in a high place of immense beauty and sacredness so you shall remember what I have said forever." It is said that the twin spires of Cathedral Rock are the frozen forms of this man and woman, standing back to back, facing opposite directions, as a testament to the resolution of this paradox.

I was inspired to story-tell this legend through dance at a location close to the site, and I invited my dear friend William Two Feather, an Apache medicine brother, to be my equal and opposite partner in grounding this Earth Spirit wisdom. My friend Rhiyana was inspired to film the dance for its use in her documentary of relationships, and came along with her camera crew. During our dance, William stomped the earth in command of his power of the masculine, while I fluidly and lovingly carved the air with my arms in the sure calmness of the feminine. We danced oblivious to anything but reverence for the rock and the spiritual message it symbolized. Our dance was a powerful prayer, and months later the video of it was on television. I had no idea then what an impact this dance would have on my journey. For now I was simply happy to be in full communion with the rocks, free from the inertia of my self-doubt and my own inner demons that had so plagued these first years in Sedona.

It was odd enough that I had not chosen to do a retrieval at Cathedral Rock before now. I had a tremendous respect for this site, as I do for all of Mother Earth. But there was something special about this site. I had often come here to sit, even to climb, but I had never made it very far up the rock, and certainly nowhere near the top, where the man and woman stood back to back. I understood that this was a site of initiation that I could only step up to when I was ready to enter the sacredness and union that lay at the center of my own heart. I still was not there.

In fact, it took me another nine months before I felt ready to make that ascent. During that time, I spent most of my time more formally studying as an Earth priestess under the dominion of the Fellowship of Isis in the Sacred Union Lyceum. They were nine months well spent, and at the end of that time, I felt ready to climb to the top of Cathedral Rock. It was not that I needed this training. The earth retrievals were enough. But they were so solitary. My psychological self needed connection to others, a community within which I could collaborate. My time in this Temple of Isis gave me what I needed emotionally to accept that I was ready to make the ascent to the sacred marriage of the stone beings at the top of Cathedral Rock. The pilgrimage I was about to make was momentous to me.

The day of my "initiation" on Cathedral Rock dawned gray and cloudy. Rain threatened. It was not a good omen for the climb. But I had made my decision to make it to the top and rain was not about to stop me. Slowly, yet surely I trekked up the winding trail with my head bowed down to the earth. Every footstep was offered as a living prayer. Occasionally I gazed upward toward the sacred couple to let them know that I was approaching. Halfway there, it began to drizzle and the wind kicked up, but I marched on undeterred.

Nearing the top, I noticed a large cave off to the right of the small trailhead. A single tree twisted itself out of the cave entrance, reaching for the light and the open space in which it could grow unobstructed. I immediately identified with that tree, feeling my own desire to grow unencumbered and free, to stretch toward the light without getting scalded by the harsh fatherly sun.

When I arrived at the very base of the rock spires that were the sacred couple, I shrieked with joy—there growing at their base amongst the dryness desert rocks, was a small mound of the brightest, most vibrant emerald-green moss I had ever seen. It sparkled like an emerald jewel at the red-rock juncture, right there between the masculine and feminine spirits of stone. I felt that my pilgrimage had led me here to the living proof of the sacred union of opposites. This was symbolic of the "Resolution of Dualities into the Integration of Oneness." I gave thanks to the sacred couple, to the stones, to the Earth Mother for giving me the privilege of serving them, for seeing and understanding this emerald-green message in moss.

I sat down at the feet of the monumental couple and pulled out some earth gifts that I keep in my medicine bag to make my offerings. I carefully laid out bee pollen, tobacco, corn, sage, and a container of water and placed them in an arc around the mossy growth. I sprinkled the bee pollen around the area in commemoration of the royal-golden path, a path on which we ourselves are pollinated into oneness with the Mother, the Queen at the center of the matrix. Then holding a pinch of the tobacco up towards the sky, I offered it as gift of respect to the native spirit of this land. Next, I sprinkled the corn as a symbol of the fertility and sustenance of the cyclic abundance of the land. I burnt some sage purifying myself and finally, I dribbled some water on the rocks and mossy growth, offering the land and the rocks its life-giving and renewing properties. I also had a drum that I had recently made with me, and I pounded on it and sang to the Ancient Ones until I was spent.

As I sat there after my celebration, I pondered how this site was for me a marriage on many levels; a journey inward to marry the sun and moon that reflected the light of my own inner masculine and feminine. A journey that led me to an altar within, where I can reconcile the opposites into the union that I was longing for. Soon I felt the call of the rocks as their secretary, and I reached into my medicine bag for a sheet of paper and a pen. I was ready to receive a transmission from Cathedral Rock. I sat in front of the mossy mound to here Earth's voice.

The Emerald Doorway is an open corridor, an invitational access to an inter-dimensional realm. Those who have long forgotten the illusory passages of guilt and fear, who have returned to their awaiting innocence in the name of love's presence, who have reached the top of their inner stairwell arrive at this doorway. They are now ready to enter, the initial test has been undertaken and the initiation is about to begin. The key to this doorway within is faith in the divine, the diving into the pool of the unknown with no telling of the outcome. This faith and trust is born from the knowingness of love, the source of life itself. Diving in with the risk of never being the same again. Diving into the fear, which has held you hostage to the known realms of limitation, the seeming safety net that has strangled your very will and breath for life. Initially diving into this pool seems like diving into a pool of death, feeling like asphyxiation, a clutching grasping quagmire to escape from. Yet it is the clutching and grasping that actually create this tunnel of darkness. This is the birth through the corridor of darkness, the initiation into the unknown realms of love that you have longed for and remember as your birthright. To have faith and leap into this pool, to let go and surrender, is to dive into the lightness of being, the porthole and gateway, the corridor to the realm of love, the heart of oneness. The Emerald Doorway awaits, and the freedom of the heart in the sacred Garden of Eden is within you.

The earth spirits had spoken of diving and leaping into the unknown, letting go and surrendering into the porthole, into the ocean of love. I wanted to know what to do once I had dived in, so I asked the earth spirits if they would elaborate.

Be grounded, be still, go within to the central core, everything spins around you but you are at rest in the silence. The energy this creates will propel you into the next dimension. Stay still within; everything else knows what to do. Movement passes through the stillness; it is like watching a movie—you are motionless, not thinking, just watching and feeling, detached yet involved. There is no concern to fix anything, to do anything but just to let it pass through you as it is already done, just like a movie—the movie is made and now just watch and enjoy it.

The stones had spoken in gentle response, telling me how to negotiate the passage but not where the passage would take me. I was soon to find out, and, of course, the destination was not any I could have predicted.

Chapter 10:

Dancing up a Storm.

I had been in Sedona for nearly three years now. Originally I had intended to stay only six months before returning to Australia, but Sedona was not going to let me go yet. She had not finished eroding away my rough places and reshaping me, as she does so slowly and patiently with the rocks. I had settled into a new life in Sedona, and I had become known as both a retriever of Earth Wisdom and, increasingly, as an Earth Spirit dancer. Something had shifted within me that day when I had danced in ceremony with William Two Feather. My dance had changed from a personal expression of the fusion of my own body, mind, and spirit into a public testament to Earth-based spirituality and awareness. I began to embody the earth wisdom transmitted to me from the retrievals in a new kind of dance that expressed the body's wisdom. My dances became a kind of retrieval in their own right: movements—body prayers—through which I could transmit the messages of the stones and Earth to the people watching or participating. By harnessing the life-giving energies of Nature and embodying the soul of the earth in the vital force of dance, I could inspire people to remember once again, their own sacred connection to the earth. It was not long after that dance ceremony with William that I began to offer what I can most aptly call "Earth Spirit Dance™."

I called my first dance workshop "The Emerald Doorway: Dancing the Dualities into Oneness," and during it, I coached people into using their bodies to express the archetypes of the sun and the moon as masculine and feminine principles. I also had them use movement to harmonize the energies of the upper and lower chakras—energy centers—of the body, which I explained as the counterparts to the energies of Heaven and Earth or Spirit and Matter. Through dance, I invited participants to weave these three upper and three lower energies into one more cohesive flow of energy that is eventually embraced and integrated in the heart chakra—the central energy center that is the Emerald Green doorway of the self. As they merged dualities into oneness, the dancers could better sense the expansive space of the grand "I Am" instead of only the partial aspects of themselves that they were so used to experiencing and expressing.

I also created another dance workshop called "Awake the Snake™," which helped people use movement to dig down into their interiors, like reaching deep into the dark interiors of the earth. In this dance, they delved into their shadow self and had the potential to awaken the kundalini energy, which Eastern traditions see as a primordial energy that is curled like a sleeping serpent at the base of the spine, or the root chakra. The area of the root chakra is the bedrock of the body-spirit connection, and this workshop with its wilder and more intense movement, helped people unleash their primeval selves just as a snake uncurls itself and rises to life, a living spiral of energy rising upward.

In both workshops, I actually took people out onto the land to dance, where they could make contact with the red earth, feel the wind or the heat of the sun on their bodies and immerse themselves in the energy of the natural elements. The dancers could participate in their own kind of Earth retrieval, connecting energy body to energy body with the land and extracting information that moved them, physically, emotionally and spiritually. They were dancing their spirit "out loud," and I could feel the joy they experienced and that Mother Earth experienced as her children moved in joy within her playground.

One person in particular became an advocate of my dance. I first met Lane Badger on Thanksgiving Day. I was wearing a wreath of autumn leaves upon my head, and that had caught her attention. She literally took me by the arm and led me away from the group we were with so that we could talk privately. From that day on, we became fast friends, and Lane was an enthusiastic promoter of my dance performances and workshops. For instance, of her own volition she designed an ad for me and placed it in her regional magazine, *Four Corners*.

Nothing much came of the ad until about six months later, when I received a phone call inviting me to serve as Mistress of Ceremonies for a gathering of five hundred women at the Summer Solstice Goddess Festival, which was to be held near the Jemez Mountains of New Mexico. The organizers gave me free rein to design a participatory dance ceremony that would be the feature of the festival. I accepted the invitation, although I was nervous about undertaking a dance on such a large scale. I had led plenty of small groups in sacred dance—but five hundred!

I was not sure what to do, and so, as I always did, I turned to the earth for advice and counsel. My answer came in the form of a memory of a dream I had had years before while at Hána, on the island of Maui. I had dreamt of two rings of women dancing, one group forming a circle that moved clockwise and the other forming a circle turning counterclockwise. As the two circles overlapped at the center, the dancers formed a Vesica Pisces (the elongated elliptical section that is formed when two circles overlap, which symbolizes union.) In my dream, I felt the dancers formed two cosmic "wheels" and with each step forward, the dancers ticked off the time on a cosmic clock. These dancers had been in step since the beginning of time. With each step the women also used their bodies to individually form what I understood to be mudras, or sacred body positions, that expressed Mayan glyphs. They stepped, held the pose, and with the next step, with the next "ticking" of the cosmic clock, they transitioned into a different glyph. When the wheels met and overlapped, or "clicked" at the midpoint of the Vesica Pisces, it was as if the combination of a cosmic code or lock had been revealed and the wheels stopped. I was aware that I was witnessing the wheels of creation stop for the first time ever and felt that somehow I was directly responsible for the glitch!

The next thing I saw in my dream, were the women breaking formation and casually stepping out of the circles and gathering in groups, like at coffee breaks, chatting and visiting. Meanwhile, I was off to the side, observing, and overcome with emotion. With tears streaming down my face, I pointed with one hand at the group of women and with the other hand I held my crotch, as if I were feeling the wound of my womanly parts. I cried out, almost in apology, "I can't! I'm sorry, I can't! I can't do it!" I wasn't sure what it was I couldn't do. The women had become quiet, and I was desperately looking from one woman to another, hoping to find compassion and understanding in their eyes. I felt as if I was looking into their souls, and each one was looking into my soul simultaneously. Every one of them began to tear up, a few stood there with tears spilling down their cheeks as well. It was clear I was receiving their compassion and understanding, for their eyes seemed to speak, "We know. We know."

At the time, I did not know what to make of this odd dream. I provisionally interpreted it to mean that I was in some stage of healing the divine feminine within me, perhaps even healing some damage in my female genetic lineage. But now, with the sudden rising of this dream to memory, I knew it additionally served as a premonition of the dance I would be leading with a huge gathering of women.

I decided to offer the "Dancing the Dualities into Oneness" program while adding the "Wheels of Time" dance to it, although conducting such a complex dance for such a large group was going to be a challenge. I prepared ahead of time, and arranged for the women to bring their special regalia—foot rattles, loose clothing, and black or white headbands—so that when it came time for each group to split into the two wheels, it would be easier. Those wearing the white headbands would form one circle, while those wearing the black bands formed the other. I wasn't sure if this new part of the dance would work, but in light of the power of my dream I was determined to try.

When I got to the dance site, I discovered that the five hundred women were all gay, bar just a few, and I had no idea how they would take to this dance experience. As I interacted with many of them on the day before the dance, I sensed that many were deeply wounded and in severe judgment about their own femininity. Many also were openly hostile toward men, and I wondered about the strident dualities of energy I was feeling here. There were moments when I felt literally that I was in "No Man's Land," and my own judgments toward these women began rising to the surface. This dance would be a challenge for me in terms of working through my own issues. But my most important concern was wondering if this dance could help some of these women break through their stuck energy so they could touch the wholeness that was beyond duality and judgment. I could do nothing else but trust Spirit and proceeded with my plan.

That afternoon, as I lay in my tent staring through the triangular, screened section at the top of the tent into the blue sky, I felt pangs of self-doubt. At one point, I closed my eyes and prayed silently that the dance would not only be accepted, but also that healing would take place in whatever way would most honor this gathering of women and their link to Mother Earth. Upon opening my eyes, an eagle streaked across the sky in the small space of the opening in my tent. I felt my prayer had been acknowledged and that everything would be in divine order. I spoke aloud to Mother Earth. "Earth, I am here to do the work, for even if only one person gets it, that will make a change. I am here, and I will herald my love and energy for you and these women with my utmost intent."

The next morning, I trekked out and into the area around the Jemez Mountains to visit the rocks and to retrieve their wisdom. The dance wouldn't be offered until late afternoon, so I had plenty of time to explore the area and attempt a retrieval. I often went out on the land before I offered a dance workshop. I liked to sit with the rocks to harness their energy and wisdom so that I could more clearly offer it over to the participants of the dance. On this day, I spontaneously intoned a message to the land, speaking quietly but audibly.

"Snake-serpent lying dormant in the belly of the earth, how long have you slept here? Since before time begot us? You carry the ancient codes of life on this planet. You guard the keys to the genetic time codes of life in the tinged spots that you wear around your neck like a strand of glistening beads. The light of these protective beads of wisdom blinds us and so we cannot really see you. We are in fear of the unknown, of the riddles of life you carry and hold in your bag of tricks. Teach us, Wise Snake. Dance into our lives, move through our bodies, and help us remember who we are." I sat quietly after speaking these words, and before long I heard a response rise in me, funneled up through my being from the depths of the earth.

You are blinded by the light of the pearls of wisdom I carry because you choose fear instead of love. Through fear, you are blinded by the light of knowledge and separate yourself from the source of love that you are. This paralyzes you, freezes you with fear. By choosing love, you are not blinded but illumined by the light of knowledge, which unifies you with the source of love that you are. This doesn't paralyze you. It frees you, not freezes you. It is time to awaken to your senses and feel your bodies, for the body never lies, just as the Earth Mother never lies. Use your senses, trust in your senses—your intuition—and move with your energy into freedom. Freedom of the Heart in the Sacred Garden, Mother Earth.

Fortified with this message, I spent the rest of the day enjoying the gorgeous scenery and meeting the women who would assist me during the ceremony. By late afternoon I was eager for the dance. I dressed in my regalia; an Emerald Green Lycra jumpsuit and a mask that I had made painted with the moon on the left side and the sun on the right and with emerald green colored feathers shooting from out the top. I introduced myself, explained how the dance would work, and then ceremoniously honored the goddesses throughout time: Isis, Aphrodite, Demeter, Persephone, Diana and Mother Mary and Mary Magdalena. I honored the four directions along with the Sun and the Moon and Heaven and Earth, and then I made an invocation to the Heart of All Matter and to the Spirit of Matter, to ignite our passion and help us feel our aliveness. I asked the women to breathe into their bodies, to breathe into their feelings, to bring their awareness to the present moment and to connect their vision to the earth. I then launched into the dance part of the of the ceremony by dancing a short solo "EarthSpirit Dance." My intention and energy was focused on merging the essence of ancient indigenous tribes with this group, with fusing all of us into the One Human Tribe. My dance was an offering to the women, to Earth, and to the ritual we were all about to perform.

When I completed my ceremonial dance, I signaled the women to start moving their bodies. As they caught the spirit, I stirred them to loosen up, to let go, to melt into their body and let it move them. As the ritual of "Dancing of the Dualities Into Oneness" began, I did not need to explain too much as most of the women knew to follow me, to watch and follow the movement of my own body. They did so, more skillfully and enthusiastically than I had dared hoped. During the first phase of the dance ritual, I directed them to move into the nature of their masculine self by dancing the qualities of the sun, which are radiating, penetrative, and willful. We danced the electro-energetic spirit of the earth, the planet Mars, and the zodiac sign of Leo. Then we danced into the lower chakras of the body along with their correlating colors: red at the root chakra, orange at the sacral, and yellow at the solar plexus to embody the fire of the sun and the grounded principle of masculine energy within us. The women were amazingly comfortable with this part of the ritual dance and they moved with confidence, power, and strength.

Next, we transitioned into the dance of the feminine qualities of the self. We danced the qualities of the moon, which are emanating and embracing. We danced the magnetic energy of the earth, the planet Venus, and the zodiac sign of Cancer. Then we moved through the colors of the upper chakras of the body: white at the crown, violet at the third eye, and blue at the throat. We embodied the element of water and the crystalline, silver energy of the moon. The women were now fully into the dance, swept into its undulating kinetics. This was more than a mass of moving bodies—it was an ocean of togetherness. And, although the women had shifted from the wildness of the masculine dance to the gentleness of the feminine dance, the group energy was still rising.

Finally, the integration began. The energy of the lower and upper chakras was to be merged at the heart chakra through the dance of union and wholeness. The dancers' energies moved like their bodies—as one giant organism—and it coalesced into the collective heart energy. The emerald bridge formed between the upper and lower chakras, between masculine and feminine, dissolving the dualities. I could feel and see the intense green energy swathing the crowd of dancers, and I felt overcome with gratitude for being here and part of this experience.

The best was yet to come—the wheels of dancers. I was going to embody my dream. Without effort, I was able to direct the women into two giant wheels, one of women wearing white headbands and one of black. We were completely bonded now, and we seemed to move as one mind. I had previously situated four tiki torches wound with emerald green ribbons around the dance area, where the wheels would come together, to represent a doorway the women would pass through. The white and the black now wheeled around and through each other, the white wheel moving clockwise, the black counterclockwise. They were merging light and darkness, overcoming separation and duality. At every fourth step, I directed the women to spin around in place while holding one hand at their heart and with the other held out toward the center of the wheel, to draw in the energy of that wheel. As the circles met in the center, creating the overlapping Vesica Pisces, a woman from each circle joined hands and danced through the flaming doorway in symbolic representation of the dissolution of opposites and the movement through the Emerald Doorway to wholeness. Finally, the dance ended, and there was an upwelling of elation as the women spontaneously cheered. They were roaring with joy at the tops of their lungs, and I leaped off stage and danced among them, moving through the Emerald Doorway with my arms held up high and my heart bursting with the joy of a mission for Mother Earth complete.

The rest of the evening was joyous and emotionally charged. Women were walking around as if they were on "Cloud Nine," or else they were huddled in groups expressing what they had felt during the dance ritual. Some were sobbing their eyes out! Something deep had been unleashed, hearts were opening, and healing was taking place. I tended to the women as best I could, both accepting their thanks and soothing their emotions. That evening and over the course of the next day, I was pulled aside by women who felt compelled to tell me of their healing experience and by others who pushed cards and gifts of thanks into my hands. I was invited back to lead the ceremony again the next year.

For weeks after the ceremony, I was in a space of deep gratitude. The dance ritual had been a healing not only for many of the women, but for me as well. I now understood the dream I had of the dancing wheels of women. I deciphered it as the prophetic pursuit to free the genetic time codes of all women who are bound by the wheel of fear and release them into their sense of awakened self. This solstice event gave me even more confidence that leading such dance ceremonies was part of my work for the earth. Only a few months after this event I performed on stage for an audience of more than twenty thousand, dancing for the trance-digenous music of *Lost At Last* at a Burning Man festival at Pyramid Lake, Nevada. The most significant and surprising aspect of the dance was not only the magnitude of the event, but the Emerald Green laser light show that pierced its iridescent light into the dark of the audience before me. I was literally offering Sedona's rock wisdom through an Earth dance for thousands of people amidst emerald green laser beams!

After a restful few weeks, with my heart wide open and receptive to the wisdom of the stones, I resumed my retrieval work. I headed northeast into the Painted Desert; a plateau region of multi-hued rocks of pale oranges, tawny browns, pinks and grays. In the silent suffusion of colors, I received the following transmission that was tied to the kundalini serpent energy that had been unleashed during the ceremony.

> *The serpent uncoiled after a long, winding sleep and awoke the spirits of the land. As it uncoiled and slithered out from the womb of the Earth Mother, it carried with it the tales of the Earth and spoke of it in the tongue of Wisdom and the Flame of Truth. This "painted desert" appears as if a serpent dragon has breathed its fiery breath to sear the surface of the land. It has baked still the trees, petrifying them with a gleam of wisdom and a glare of truth. It holds life in the stillness of a land with no time, in a place in space and in the bones of the old crones of our land's ancient ancestors. The serpent resides in the land as the keeper of wisdom and truth, and it resides within us as we, the keepers of the land, find our way on the ever-winding road to peace on Earth.*

Over the next year, I traveled a lot, especially between Sedona, Arizona, and Santa Fe, New Mexico, offering dance workshops and participating in special events with my dear friend Lane. I felt I was traveling along the ley lines—broad energy lines—that run along the earth between Sedona and Santa Fe. A border town, Gallup, New Mexico, radiated a particularly strong energy. Here the red rocks are simply spectacular, seeming more stark and desolate than those of Sedona. These rocks were calling out to be listened to. I felt they were a storehouse of stories just waiting to be revealed. What's more, the area of Gallup was an ancient crossroads for Native American tribes as they moved by horse or on foot. One day, as I was driving through, I decided it was time to stop and listen to the rocks there. As I drove, I opened my energy to the landscape and scanned the horizon with my eyes and my heart to intuit where I would stop. A few tall red-rock spires that stood alone in the desert called to me. They looked like tall maidens of the desert, guardian priestesses who had been solitary for a long time but were now calling me to keep them company. With only a little difficulty I was able to drive quite close, and I hiked the rest of the way. I sat at their feet and readied myself for a retrieval.

I was rather surprised by the feeling of the land around the spires. I felt the emptiness here, of desolation even. In Gallup, man had introduced to the landscape, massive creations of his own, mostly factories that spewed toxic poisons that destroy the life force of everything around, even leeching into the minerals—the vital substances that sustain the land and bring balance and harmony to it. This same feeling of deadness filled the empty desert space around me. There was not much remaining here except the dead bones of animals and the empty shells of rocks containing only the memory of time alone. I had to brace myself to continue. To find my power, I pressed my spine back into the base of one of the megalithic rock spires. At least something here reached with dignity high above the desolation. I took several long, deep breaths, imagining my body filling with Emerald light, and I exhaled in a slow, steady rhythm and imagined this healing light flowing out of me and back into the land and rocks. I was trying to recharge the earth, to re-code and reactivate the land, reviving its life energy. This exercise in reinvigorating the earth became my retrieval. Instead of the stones giving information and providing insight to me, I was instead ministering to them. I sat there doing my work for the earth for a long time before I felt restored to some measure of equilibrium.

I finally got up and began to hike back to my car. But after only a few steps I felt pulled to turn around and face this guardian priestess spire again. My work was not complete here after all. I let myself blend with the energy I felt coming from her, and in that quiet space of connection I spontaneously returned to my Emerald energy work. I envisioned a spiral of Emerald light shooting out from me and covering her. As I held my hands up high, sending the light out with gratitude and love, I felt an intense sisterly bond with this ancient lady who rose with such solitary hope into the sky. I felt her energy coming toward me, and I received it with gratitude as an activation of sorts for myself, rather like a soul retrieval—a memory recall of my ancient self. I received a subtle communication from this Ancient One as she acknowledged the ministering energy work I had just done on behalf of the land. She was honoring this new twist to my work, letting me know that my work was expanding. I was not only to retrieve wisdom from the rocks but to also give back by bolstering diminishing Earth energies when I came upon them. I thought of the Native American concept of the Beauty Way, which is an understanding of connection between all beings and the harmony that comes when all beings live in balance. The Beauty Way for me would be both to receive from the earth and to actively give back, not only to the people of the earth but to the earth itself. This was my redefined work.

Finally, I turned once again to leave and I had not taken ten steps before I saw, there before me on the red desert floor, ten owl feathers. I was taken aback. Owl, my totem ally, undeniably confirmed the information I had just received from the priestess spire. I carefully gathered the feathers, giving thanks for this signal and receiving them as a gift from Earth's spirit for the energy work we had just exchanged. Much later, I gave these feathers to a friend of mine, Donna Kay, who is a gifted craftswoman and who curiously enough, is known as White Owl. She worked the feathers into a white buckskin outfit that she made for me for my public dances. Whenever I wear it, I am dancing not only for myself and the people who come to the dance, but for the spirit of owl, for the priestess spire, and most of all, for the earth and rock spirits.

My next pilgrimages were to two sacred Native American sites, Chaco Canyon and Canyon de Chelle (pronounced Canyon da Shay.) These are two of the most profound canyon ruins of the Four Corners region as they were the major centers of Anasazi civilizations. I went first to Chaco. I had been forewarned that Chaco Canyon felt "eerie," and that many people felt the presence of the Ancient Ones there. This didn't surprise me, for the Anasazi were a thriving culture until they mysteriously disappeared. Anthropologists offer differing explanations for their sudden mass exodus from their exquisite rock dwellings, but no one really knows what happened or why. As I descended, in a stance of reverence, into the canyon toward the most famous grouping of ruins, I felt the mystery of this place myself. The multistoried rock houses nestled close to the red canyon walls are a marvel to behold. You can't help but wonder how they were made, what kind of culture thrived here, how these people bonded so intimately to the land, not only because they lived within the rocks themselves but because the earth had so obviously mothered them there. And then it had all ended. In the dry and lifeless surroundings, I felt the void of a displaced mystery that hung in timeless suspension and pondered the possibility that if the human race continues to denounce its relationship with Mother Earth, then perhaps it too may disappear from the face of the earth. All I could do was trust that through the retrievals, the rocks and the Earth Spirit itself would provide insight.

I opened my heart to the stone ruins in which I was wandering and felt called to a nondescript space between the rock house edifices. I sensed that the towering rocks looming over the ruin complex oversaw every movement I made. I bowed to the rock beings, then sank down onto the earth and pressed my forehead against the rock face and entered that place of silence within. I felt energy spiraling within me, and I felt myself be pulled down into an energy vortex. Then I heard the rocks speak.

> The journey into the unknown is the sacred spiral of life. Grandfather Eagle rides the natural thermals of the sacred wind, spiraling high into the great sky. Great Spirit's breath is the moving pathway of the sacred spiral, down which we descend into the plane of matter. It is the paternal breath that holds the pattern of the great design, impregnating Spirit into the maternal, the Matter of all things. Patera Sky and Matera Earth, the grand parents, the grandmasters, holding the edges of the grand loom for the weavings of their creation as they come into being. From the central point of this sacred spiral, which is the void, the place of no-thingness, evolves the conscious movement of creation, which fills space, seeks and expands the knowingness of its source, of itself. Moving and dancing into the light where sacred dreams and visions abide. Great Spirit calls, and it is that call that winds us in, to once again re-turn through this spiral path to the sacred source of Love.

As I always did, I sat in the silence for a few minutes after the retrieval. Then, as I was rising to leave, I looked up and was astonished to see, carved high on the rock wall above me, a large spiral. I was astonished, for it was such an immediate and undeniable confirmation of all that I had just retrieved. I was sure that, like the owl feathers that had been placed in my path by the spire priestess, Chaco Canyon was now reaffirming in the physical world the information I had just retrieved from the rock-spirit world. In the Native American tradition, the spiral is a symbol of "the journey," either the unfolding journey to a physical place or toward the realm of Spirit. Through the retrievals, I felt I was taking both kinds of journeys at once.

As I hiked out of the ruin, the wind picked up. It blew through my hair as if it wanted to whisper something in my ear. At first I thought I was imagining things. But soon I was confident that the wind spirits had something to say. So I stopped and stood in the softness of the breeze to allow the wind wisdom to reveal its message to me.

The wind, too, knows of the sacred spiral as it weaves and moves its way through space. Its consciousness pierces into the unknown, seeking knowledge as it slinks upon and around the ancient ruin walls that had once housed the people of its land. The Ancient Ones who moved in the cycles of the ancient pathways of the sun and the moon, the wind and the clouds, the stars and the sky. They listened to the message of the wind, the spirit of the stones, the call of their Earth mother, their visions and dreams. They knew, too, of the sacred spiral path back home to their ancestors and of their Creator. The wind holds memories of passing moods, passing encounters, and passing dreams. It's like the tongue of Great Spirit that licks and tastes the memories and history of the land and its peoples, assimilating them into its own inner journey, through its spiral pathway as a carrier of knowledge and information. The sacred wind is not only the courier of information, but seems to purify us and cleanse our lands. It is Great Spirit's breath that cleanses our soul and clears the passage for our journey home.

I thanked the spirit of the land, smudged myself with the smoke of burning sage, and offered some bee-pollen to the rock beings. I set up camp, and after a long sleep and a breakfast of scrambled eggs and toast, I drove northwest, back into Arizona to visit Canyon de Chelle.

It is notable how each ancient site contains its own embodiment of the Spirit of Place and how it holds in its own way, a revelation of wisdom. Canyon de Chelle combined a magnificent vastness with a desolate sparseness that made me think of the eagle riding the wind in an expansive sky, that overlooks the vistas of the parched desert and the hard canyons below. It was at once "more than" and "less than." Perhaps all ruins are a paradox, embodying a seemingly empty presence but pulsing with the aura of the life that once thrived there. One such ruin is the famous White House, a cluster of ancient stone buildings tucked at the base of a five-hundred-foot sheer rock wall. Access was not permitted to the actual site, so I scouted the area for a more tangible connection with the rocks themselves. I was drawn into an old desolate orchard, and while walking through the dry thicket; I noticed a large cave in a nearby cliff wall. As I approached its entrance I asked if I might enter so that I could glean its wisdom to offer it back to the people. Once I had intuited an affirmative response, I entered the cave. I merged with the unique energies of Canyon de Chelle and listened to the rocks talk. Their message hummed with the qualities of the energy that Canyon de Chelle was imparting to me:

Time has passed; long ago is now. Seasons move like the clouds above; crows hark and loom the airways heralding the memories of our ancestors. Do not forget who you are and where you have come from. Your heart lies deeply in the core of the earth. Your experience in life is like eating an apple: enjoy the flesh of the fruits of life and gain nourishment from the absorption of your experience. Eat slowly; chew well, for there is no hurry. If you hurry, you are left with indigestion. Take your time to listen to the earth, ingest her fruits and the wisdom of life slowly, for like an apple, you eventually will reach the core, the heart of the matter, where the seeds of the memory of whom you are lies.

The memory of being is about being one with the earth, one with the sky, one with the space of time, one with who you once were in the ancestral arc of life and one who you are in the future to come. The seeds of knowledge lie in the core of your heart and deep within the bosom of the earth. Hear Earth's heart beat; listen to the wisdom she offers through your own heart.

You are one with the earth,
You are one with the earth.

After the retrieval, I stood at the mouth of the cave and energetically waved an emerald green spiral into its darkness. I touched my lips to the outer rock wall and breathed my gratitude into it.

On my way back through the orchard, something caught my eye—a crouched form that became visible only at the farthest reaches of my peripheral vision. As I focused more intently, I saw it was an old, hunched woman who I took to be about ninety years old. Her face was lined and her eyes pierced into me like the rays of an intense sun. I did not approach. I simply nodded my head in respect and projected the wisdom of the cave to her, hoping that I had not encroached upon her privacy. Without a word and without taking her eyes off mine, she slowly walked over to me and pulled from her large apron pocket a fresh, rosy apple! I gratefully and silently accepted her gift, and thought of it also as a gift from the cave for awakening its senses. I ate the apple slowly and mindfully, core and all, just as the earth had instructed.

As I continued to wander the ruins of Canyon de Chelle, I did what the rock spirits had always directed: open myself to them slowly, with awareness and patience to see where I needed to conduct a retrieval. Now I was drawn out into the distance, to Spider Rock. Spider Rock is a famous monolithic spire that sits at the bottom of a valley nearby, and rises with an awesome dignity of eight hundred feet high. Although it's a narrow and spindly-looking spire, it holds immense significance for the natives of the area. Spider Woman is a major figure in Native American lore, a primordial Mother who weaves the stories of "The People." Even though I didn't hike down into the valley to get close to the spire itself, I was able to tune into the energy of the rock from where I was at the cliff's edge. I felt a strong resonance with this landmark and I opened myself to its feminine qualities, its motherly beckoning. What first struck me was the "voice" of the narrative, which was different from the other retrievals. I thought the perspective was coming from a Native American's point of view, for I heard someone talking about how Spider Woman taught "us." I soon realized, however, that the "us" was the collective—humanity in general. It was like we were remembering ourselves through the energy of Spider Woman.

Spider woman taught us how to weave, to be creative and industrious with the threads of life. She showed us how to take our hopes and dreams and move them in and out of time, to weave them through the fabric of the life of our existence. Our hopes and dreams must be woven in and integrated into our life in order to hold in creation the design we desire. If these threads of our hopes and dreams are not anchored and woven into our existence, they become loose threads of desire that are forever longing to be connected and integrated into the total design, the tapestry of life.

Spider Woman also teaches us of sacred geometric lines that can be interfaced onto the stars of our night sky. These constellations are like our thought patterns, which act as templates that are stamped and suspended in the unlimited sky-field of our consciousness. The sacred design is created from the linear dimensions joining one star to the next or one thought to the next, creating constellations of thought patterns, which influence and govern our actions. Thus, the language of thought becomes the concrete language of the physical that allows us to write our lives and live our stories.

Spider Woman also teaches us to discern whom we do and do not allow to be woven into the sacred fabric—of our web of dreams. Many are afraid of Spider Woman, as she sits and waits in the center of her web in the void of her creation. This is the place where we are most afraid, as it is the unknown place, the place of no-thingness, the place from where all of creational existence emerges. It is the place where once we enter, we no longer exist as separate entities but merge with and emerge from the true design that we create.

I was impressed with the scope of this retrieval. It seemed to bring together all the other retrievals. They had each provided a piece of the story of what it means to be human and walk in harmony with the earth. But this transmission seemed by far to be the most holistic, encompassing, and far-reaching. I felt that I was at a place of initiation, having completed one level of my Earthwork and was now spiraling up a notch. The inclusion of dance into my work, and the impulse to activate the land with the Emerald Ray had been escalations of my service to the earth. But now I felt another major shift coming. I couldn't put into words what I was feeling, and I couldn't really say why I was feeling it. I just knew that something had shifted within me and with my relationship to the earth. I felt a "coming out of myself." Perhaps there was a new way I would make this work more public. Spider Woman's message was for the collective, but it had been unusual in that we seemed to be talking to ourselves through her. I sensed that there was a definite reason for this strange narrative shift—and that it had to do with me weaving all the threads of my work together in a more public way. As always, all I could do was wait patiently for Spirit to show me the way.

Spirit hinted at the shift that was coming on the first day of the new millennium. I had been invited to give a ceremonial dance for the Sedona 2000 Conference, and I had asked my dear friend John Dumas to assist me. He is a highly gifted musician whom I often called upon to play didgeridoo while I danced. The theme of this particular dance ceremony was "transition"—to mark the completion of the old paradigm and the bringing in and the grounding of the new. It was a transmission of the new Earth Spirit energies that would usher us through the doorway of Oneness. The dance itself isn't important to this story, although it is necessary to say that I undertook it with great reverence and focused intention. What was important was that through it, I met Rabbi Gershon Winkler. A few weeks after the ceremony, I received a phone message from Rabbi Winkler, who had witnessed my dance and now gushed with praise. He was, he explained, "astounded" by the dance. He said he had never seen anything quite like it and that it was so powerful and pure that he could hardly look at me directly during the dance. I thought that was the end of it, but he called again a few days later. He stated flatly, "Amalia, whatever it takes,

I want you to come here and do whatever you do. Come and perform your magic at my retreat center." He went on to explain his counseling and spiritual work, and that he leads retreats every couple of months to bring people together for more intense experiences of Self and Spirit. He was very adamant in his invitation. "I want you to be part of it," he declared. "I don't care what it costs. All logistics will be taken care of and you will be paid whatever you require."

I did participate in his next retreat, which was themed "Lighting the Story Fires Within," and I shared the dance spirit I had gleaned from Earth's myth with the participants. It was a wonderfully fulfilling and nurturing experience on my part and theirs, but best of all, I began what I was sure was a life-long friendship with Gershon, as I call him. Rabbi Gershon is a man of wisdom, if a bit unconventional. He is a "shamanic rabbi," interested in the mystical and metaphysical, and has written numerous books on Jewish mysticism. He also has a quirky sense of humor and is somewhat of the "sacred fool." I can honestly say that he is one of the most extraordinary persons I had ever met. He also provides constant insightful counsel. One day for example, while talking with him on the phone, I "spilled the beans" so to speak and told him all about the personal inner challenges I was experiencing along my spiritual journey, and he imparted some wise advice. He said, "Amalia, focus on your hatching, not on your egg shell breaking." I was taken aback by that insight as I thought back to the weird and wild "vision" or "dream" or whatever it was that I had had back in Hawai'i about the dragon being hatched from the giant egg. He seemed to speak to my very soul. And his advice was very pragmatic, for I knew that on a more mundane level he was telling me to focus on the goodness of what was coming into my life and not to worry about all the rest.

The dance at the retreat was a complete success. Rabbi Gershon's and my intent had been for me to embody the teaching in movement, into a kinesthetic teaching, and I had been able to do that. In fact, the Rabbi was so impressed that he told me I was going to return to lead a dance segment at his next annual retreat. He seemed adamant, and I did not protest. I recognized him not only as a new and dear friend, but as a spiritual mentor as well.

While leading the dance section at Rabbi Gershon's that first time, I also discovered that the rocks in the area shared his sense of humor. I suppose the truth could be that the rocks could take on the personality of a person who spends so much time in close proximity to them. In any case, when I did a retrieval in the area, I received the following whimsical poem from the old white, craggy rocks.

The time has begun,
We have been spun.
To thread into the new,
We are so few.

Look into the now,
Don't ask how.
Be still like the rocks,
It will knock off your socks.

So stay attuned to the quiet within,
Where all that remembers has no sin.
To dance and move with the wind in time,
While shaping our soul into the existence of rhyme.

To know who we are in becoming our star,
Without having to go too close or too far.
To return home to the light within,
Where all is reflected to our heart's akin.

The next year, after I lead the dance for Rabbi Gershon's group, I went back out amongst the rocks and again received another poem from the rocks.

Ancient calling in the whispering winds,
Ushering you forward to stay within.

Come inside to that place you've not been,
For here lies your wisdom and sight of a queen.

Moonlight steeps into the dark of the night,
The memory of love rekindles the flight.
Spread your wings and carve through the sky,
Take a deep breath and release your fear through a sigh.

Hold your vision too soon,
You'll be there by noon,
Where the sun rides the sky,
You'll be feeling high.

So return in to the silence where all is revealed,
And next thing you know, you'll be completely healed.

That year, on my return journey to Sedona, I visited some ancient Anasazi ruins called Wupatki and Honanki, which are both several hours north of Sedona. These two sacred sites are suffused with an aura of a deep and forgotten history that longs to reveal itself, to re-awaken in modern man a respect for the integrity of the old ways. While there, I met a young friend Bucky Wilcox, whom I had planned to meet at the ruins. Together we roamed the sites and bathed ourselves in their ancient energies. Bucky, wise-for-his-age and a fellow Earth worker knew these ruins fairly well, and served as my guide as well as my spiritual companion. He took me to several out-of-the-way sites that I would most probably not have discovered on my own. We also took long, lazy hikes through the area. What most caught my eye during these sojourns, were the ancient rocks that were strewn across the desert floor like bones in an ancient burial ground. One rock in particular had caught my attention. It was a broad slab of rock, relatively innocuous looking, but with a commanding energy that pulled me toward it. I felt the rock was waiting for something. Could it be me? Was it me? I walked over to it and asked its permission to touch it. When I received an affirmative answer, I laid my hands upon it and looked across the horizon toward the sacred San Francisco Peaks, that were clearly seen between an open space of the rocky canyon and whose distant tops were shining from the snow that capped them. I felt the power of these mountains, which are held sacred by the Hopis and other Native Americans in the area as a demarcation boundary to their "homeland" and as the "spirit place" of the departed souls of their ancestors. These peaks are also home to the Kachina, the Hopi "Spirit Beings," which inhabit animal spirits, ancestral spirits and nature spirits that descend from the mountains at certain times of the year to perform ceremonies with "The People." I felt a clear and strong "ley line" of energy running from the San Francisco Peaks and my "sensing platform" stone. I closed my eyes and prepared myself for a retrieval. The transmission came in the form of another poem:

In the far distance the cry in the sky,
Of the ancient people's voices whispering why?
The many prayers and visions foretold,
In the mountain peaks do they sacredly hold.

White-capped peaks, sun bleached beaks,
Reflecting the stories that to the rocks have reached.
A place of holding, the place of still,
To bring into matter a heartfelt fill.

This lone flat rock in the valley below,
Does its work doing nothing to remember "the know."

In the early afternoon, as Bucky and I trekked into the remoter parts of the desert, we came across a sight that astonished us. There on the face of a large vertical rock was the carving of an eagle and a snake. It was obviously an ancient carving, with timeworn edges, although it was clearly visible in the rock face. The eagle was in flight, heading down toward the earth while the snake, curiously, appeared with a protruding belly, as if it were pregnant, and it was ascending toward the sky. We marveled at the carving and wondered what it meant, as these symbols were usually depicted the other way around—the eagle towards the sky and the snake toward the ground. In the Native American tradition, the eagle is the most revered of the winged ones because it is said that it can fly closest to the sun, to the All-Seeing Eye of the heavens. As such, it carries the prayers of the People to Great Spirit. The snake is the animal that lies lowest and closest to the ground, and so it has a most intimate relationship with the wisdom of Mother Earth. It listens to her counsel and, as a wisdom keeper, delivers her precious messages to the People. I deciphered this image as a depiction of balancing the polarities, of bringing the dualities into union of bridging Earth to the Heavens and descending Spirit into Matter. Bucky contributed to the puzzle by saying that the eagle represented North America and the snake, South America, and the overall image symbolized the passage of the tribes to and from each nation.

I felt especially moved by this carving, for I too, was learning to move easily and well over Mother Earth, and to soar in Spirit to the realms above. Like the eagle and the snake, I had developed my own unique way of moving in the world, as my dance illustrated and celebrated. Dance was becoming a more important part of my Earthwork, and it was taking me public in a way I had never imagined. Through movement I was inspiring others to get in touch with their own spiritual sense through the physicality of the body. My dance ceremonies were rituals that linked people to the Earth Mother and the Emerald Wisdom, and to their own innate inner wisdom. Through such a freeing and re-awakening of our body and soul we slip the bounds of self-limiting beliefs, reconnect with our Earth Mother, and move closer to union with the Heart of Oneness in all things. That day in the desert, and on many other days before and since, I acknowledged the call I had followed and I gave thanks for the stones for nurturing me along the path of my destiny.

Chapter 11:

Call back to Hawai'i.

Bridging the dualities and dropping into the heart where oneness lies, is clearly the path of my destiny. Bringing consciousness into the unconscious, light into darkness, and love into fear and to restore balance and harmony, by embracing the entirety of self. The red rocks had surely cleared and prepared the path toward my destiny, but I still could not seem to reconcile the duality between the feeling of inner richness and the external reflection of lack in my life.

On the one hand, I was abundant with love for myself, my friends, and for the earth. I was given the keys to several different homes from beloved friends who wanted me to feel at home in theirs. I was well known for my dance inaugurations and workshops, and I was flush with the excitement of continuing to experience the world anew. On the other hand, my external circumstances were challenging. Even though my car was reliable, its shoddy appearance with the occasional dents here and there did not reflect the abundant self I felt within. My financial state was uncertain; the proceeds from the sale of the land and business in Australia were coming to an end, and I just could not seem to get on top of things. I was working as a massage therapist four days a week at a prestigious resort and seeing personal clients in my off hours. I was giving dance performances and workshops, managing a social life, and writing this book, a labor of love that often kept me up until three in the morning. I knew the principles of manifestation. For example, "Whatever I focus on, expands" and "The universe will give me whatever it is that I want," but abundance, especially in material form, was not finding its way to me—or perhaps I was not letting it in! I felt like a wondrous flower trying to bloom in the harsh elements of the desert. Fancy metaphor aside, I was just plain fed up!

Questions flourished. How could I bridge this duality? How could I create the lifestyle I wanted and deserved? Hadn't I given up everything I knew to fulfill the mission I was given? Shouldn't I be well compensated for all my dedicated work? I searched for answers, but found few. I remained in what I perceived as a void of lack, and I was willing to try to move the energy toward the upswing in any way I could.

My friend Rhiyana suggested I join her in creating a "Treasure Map." She explained that this was an embodiment of desires, actually representing the things and circumstances I wanted to manifest in my life. The idea is that by repeatedly viewing and focusing on the things you want to create in your life, you are affirming them into your psyche and therefore magnetizing them into your material world. To make our Treasure Maps, we would cut pictures and words from magazines and paste them on a large poster board.

Actually, I had twice before created a Treasure Map, many years ago back in Australia. I had been astounded at how my desires had manifested, for example, a free sailing expedition in the Greek Islands, a trip to Egypt, and even the exact Elna sewing machine with the same colored buttons! So, I knew this technique worked and worked well, and I happily agreed to make another now.

I eagerly pasted onto the board, pictures of the things I wanted to manifest or create in my life: a gorgeous adobe home in Sedona, a life of comfort and adventure, which I represented with a picture of a lady who had just debarked from an airplane and was walking down a red carpet surrounded by waiters who were at her command. I pasted in various other pictures, including a woman having a massage on the beach, of dance events at sacred places around the world, of a woman radiating good health and happiness, and so on. I even added a picture of a BMW car that I had always dreamed of owning. I also pasted in some text phrases and random words, such as "Contributors," "LUCKY" (in large orange capital letters), "Helping you get the things you need and want," and "Elevate your lifestyle." This was, after all, an opportunity not only to focus on all the things that I desired, but also to push myself to be a bit audacious—to dream big.

Even though I pasted in a picture of my dream car—a BMW—on my Treasure Map, I decided to take "luck" into my own hands and make a gesture to the universe that I was serious about changing my circumstances. So, I applied for a bank loan to buy a secondhand BMW or another car that would reflect my new level of abundance. Even though it seemed that I was putting myself under further financial pressure, I knew that going for what I wanted felt better than to complain about not having it. I launched into an intensive search for a great used car, but every lead I followed fell through for one reason or another. Even when I thought I had finally found the car I really wanted, I was strongly advised against the purchase by my mechanic. I was overcome by frustration and felt completely unplugged from the source of creative possibilities. I had to go deeper within myself to find the answer to living with grace and ease. Although I knew all the answers lay deep inside, in the silence between my thoughts, I had allowed worry to get the better of me.

I decided to do what I do best, and that was to dance my way into abundance. I planned a date with the rocks to dance my prayers into reality. I dressed in my white buckskin outfit, which was gorgeously detailed with with my spirit owl feathers and white dove feathers from Sedona; I painted my face with a paste I made of red desert powder and water, making streaks across my brow and arcs across my cheeks. I took my portable CD player, drove to Cathedral Rock, and climbed to the first platform, where I would hold my dance ceremony.

To begin my dance, I pulled out two large white feathers from my medicine bag, holding one in each hand with the intention of dancing my flight's path to Great Spirit. I grounded my energy by planting my feet like taproots into the earth and took a couple of deep breaths with a sigh on each exhale. I then pointed one long white feather toward the horizon and moved it in an arc slowly from east to west, then from the great above to the great below, and then in a clockwise circle in honor of the wheel of life. With intense focus, I spoke my intention aloud to the spirits of the stones: "I have come here to do the Earth Work. I have heeded your call, left my country, my home and family and done all I can to carry through my part of the deal. I was commissioned by you, and want to be compensated fairly for all the hard work I have done. Now pay me." I was angry. Then I moved slowly and deliberately with the feathers as my guides and called out all the things I wanted. "Bring me a car that truly reflects the abundance I deserve. Bring me a beautiful place to live. I want to be supported in my finances so that I can finish my book with ease and grace." Then, with might and force, I summoned the pent-up frustration that I harbored deep in my body and soul and used it as fuel to propel my prayer up to the sky and also plunge it deep into the earth. I danced, wielding my power like a swordsman. I danced to the beat of drums that thundered from the boom box. I danced until I felt I had torn the fabric of existence apart, so that loud and clear, Spirit could hear me.

The next day, I visited my girlfriend Salena and told her about my feelings of lack and of the prayer dance I had undertaken to change my circumstances. Salena is a gorgeous Italian gypsy-artist-musician-healer with an inherent gift for reading the tarot cards. She offered to do an "on the spot" mini-card reading for me to determine why I was having such difficulty, especially in manifesting a decent car. After the cards were shuffled and chosen, she began the reading by blurting out, "Oh my God, *mio Dio!* I can't believe I am the one telling you this, but you are going to leave Sedona, I can't believe it. I am your best friend and I don't want you to leave, but the cards say that you are going away to replenish your energy and that it is important that you do this for yourself." The rest of the reading was interesting, but it was difficult for me to get past the idea that I might be leaving Arizona. Interestingly, I had already been scheduled to see another friend, Claudia, back at my house later that afternoon. Claudia is also an accomplished card reader and healer. I decided to withhold my opinions until I had that second reading and was inquisitive about whether it would correlate with Salena's information.

As I drove back to my house for my meeting with Claudia, I thought about why I was even interested in the tarot cards. Why was I entrusting my destiny to such readings? After all, wasn't I the one teaching people to go straight to the source—to Creator God and the wisdom within-for information and answers? I was confused and tired by the time I got home and Claudia arrived. As we sat on the carpeted floor and she placed the cards before me, I felt apprehensive. I decided to stop resisting and relinquished my struggle, I trusted that Spirit would provide the guidance I sought. Not far into the reading, Claudia's words caught me off guard. She explained that she saw me going away to the Hawaiian Islands for quite a while to rejuvenate my energy and source of creativity. She explained, just as Salena had, that this trip was important to my completing my mission with the stones and the earth. She then pointed to a card that illustrated an Emperor sitting on his throne, and made a prediction: "An older distinguished gentleman with silver hair, holding a considerable amount of wisdom, power, and wealth will assist you and support you in ways that you have not even conceived of. You must accept his help, as it is of great importance that you learn to receive. He will show you how you can live your life in ease and grace. This is a karmic payoff, and you must accept his help in order to complete the karma between you. Your wheel of fortune is at hand; it is time for your abundance now."

I questioned Claudia about the nature of the relationship that might form between this mysterious silver-haired gentleman and myself, and she assured me that everything was all right. "This will be on your terms, Amalia. Don't worry about anything. It will be great for you and for him, too. He has equally a lot to gain from you too, mostly spiritually."

Was this the clear response I had demanded from the rock spirits? Or was this already in the cards, so to speak? I had no clue what to think about these messages about a move and what sounded like a mentor or patron. All I knew was that something released in me after that reading. The tension and worry that had been accumulating over the past few months cascaded out of me like water in a waterfall, leaving only a gentle pool of comfort. How quickly my outlook changed!

After Claudia left, I sat on the couch and thought back over my life during the past five years in the land of the red rocks. During that time, I had on several occasions packed my bags to leave Sedona, but it had never let me go. "You just aren't ready," I would hear the stones declare. Sedona had cleansed me and cultivated within me the capacity to realize my full potential. Now, like a mother bird, perhaps Sedona was about to push me out of her nest. I inwardly agreed to go, and almost instantly I made a decision that I would take action. I would visit Hawai'i again, just for a few weeks, to take a peek into my destiny. If the spirit of the earth wanted me in Hawai'i, I would make the first move and see if the stones or Mother Earth then took the lead and showed me where I needed to be and what I needed to do.

The day after the tarot readings, I quickly made arrangements for someone to take over my clients at the spa, made reservations for my flight and arranged a car rental. I planned to visit three of the islands, beginning with the Big Island of Hawai'i, and then going on to Maui and Kaua'i. When my dear friend Lane Badger got wind of my plans, she offered me a five-day stay at the Dragonfly Ranch, a bed and breakfast located on the Big Island's Kona coast. I graciously accepted her generous offer, and the reservations were quickly made. Everything was flowing easily and gracefully, which I took as a sign that I was on the right track.

A few days later, I hiked up the Chimney Rock trail to the wide rock platform that overlooks the ominous shadows of both Thunder Mountain and Chimney Rock to speak to the stones. I lit my sage stick and smudged myself, then offered the smudge smoke up to Great Spirit as a prayer. I pinched a little pollen and tobacco from my medicine bag, pressed the tobacco in a crevice in the rock and flung the pollen into the wind before me. I stood tall with my arms wide apart and asked the wind to cleanse my body while it rushed over me. I felt the towering shadow of the stones loom over and enfold me in its dark and quiet dim space. I felt the certainty that, yes, it was time for me to leave Sedona. I cleared my mind and quieted my thoughts, connected my heart energy with the stones, and asked the spirit of the stones to support me in this new path. I waited for a response and soon received their wordless but no less clear answer through a sudden feeling of lightness in my heart and a profound sense of rejuvenating energy running through me. I also appealed to the spirit of Hawai'i by visualizing the swaying palm trees and clear blue ocean. I made a formal request aloud to the spirit of the Islands: "I have been directed to visit you to replenish my being, and I request that one of the islands make a bid for me, if it is meant that I stay with you awhile. But please make it clear and make it simple. Thank you. I look forward to meeting with you once again." I ended my ceremony, and before leaving, I bowed to Chimney Rock, blowing a sacred kiss to this of most sacred spaces.

My flight brought me to the Big Island of Hawai'i in the evening. I picked up my rental car and drove south of Kailua airport for fifty minutes to Honaunau, where the Dragonfly Ranch is located. Despite the late hour of my arrival, the owner, Barbara, who lived on the premises, made every effort to make me feel welcome and at home. Even though I was alone, she showed me to the Honeymoon Suite, the most prized and private suite at the complex. As I unpacked my belongings and then sank into an outdoor bath that was lined with black lava rock, I looked up at the night sky, bright with stars, and felt that my desire for a luxurious lifestyle was, at this moment at least, being wondrously fulfilled. I submerged myself deeper into the hot water, consciously releasing any "struggle energies" I might be carrying in my body. I wanted to begin my stay in Hawai'i with a fresh, enthusiastic, and graceful start.

As I emerged naked from the bath, I decided to dance my thanks for this auspicious start to my visit. Dripping wet, I moved under the moonlight sky, using my body to say hello to the spirit of the land and ask its blessing on my arrival here. Addressing the spirit of the land is like visiting somebody's home—it is wise not to barge into, but to announce your presence by first letting them know of your arrival, then asking permission to enter and awaiting a reply. I went to bed that night with comfort that Hawai'i welcomed my arrival and slept as peaceful as a newborn babe.

The next morning Barbara offered me fresh fruit from the garden and some flower essence remedies to ease my transition onto the island. She walked me through the organic gardens and up to a magnificent labyrinth that was constructed on a platform high over the tropical jungle, which overlooked the wide expanse of the ocean. Later that day, she took me to Honaunau Bay to an incredible snorkeling area that the locals call "Two Step." Between the excellent *Lomilomi* (Hawaiian massage) that Barbara gave me, an authentic hula class that she arranged for me to attend, and a helicopter ride to see the island from a bird's-eye view, I was having a marvelous time on the Big Island. Needless to say, Barbara Anne *Kenonilani* Moore (*Kenonilani* means "heavenly noni", the noni being a Hawaiian fruit that contains a wide range of healing properties) and I became fast friends.

One sunny morning a few days later, I was dancing under the outdoor shower amongst the lush greenery of the Honeymoon Suite when Barbara happened by and saw me. When I finished my shower-dance, she rushed over and proclaimed, "I want to dance like that and I want the whole world to see your dance!" Then she began to reel off ideas about how she could accomplish that. Two possibilities came to her mind—a dance workshop that I could lead at the labyrinth on the premises and a dance I could perform that very night at a dinner party hosted by a close friend of hers. I was appreciative of Barbara's enthusiasm and can-do attitude, but I explained that my dance was not entertainment. It was a ceremony, a medicine transmission for Mother Earth and her people. Barbara assured me that my dance at her friend's party could be done in a way that was sacred, and I reluctantly agreed to go. I was not entirely sure about this idea, but how could I turn down this wonderful new friend who rendered me so much assistance, shown me such kindness, and took such a genuine interest in my work? This dance would be a way for me to give something back to her and her friends.

That evening, I dressed up in my soft buckskin outfit, placed my *chachayotes*, (seedpod rattles) around my ankles, and wore the jade vine lei and headpiece that Barbara and I had strung in the sun that afternoon. Barbara drove us to her friend's house, and as we pulled into the driveway I was taken aback by the magnificent entryway. The driveway was lined with thick-canopied trees that formed a magical tunnel that was bejewled with strings of lit-up fairy lights. I felt like Alice entering Wonderland. Barbara turned to me with a smile on her face, "Oh, by the way," she said casually, "you are going to fall in love with this man."

"What?" I exclaimed more in surprise than question.

"You will fall in love with him, and he will fall in love with you."

"Why are you saying this, and mentioning it just before I give my dance?" I questioned her. "I like to be empty before giving a ceremonial dance, and now you're telling me this?"

She didn't seem to hear my rejection of her prediction, and simply repeated herself. "Oh yes, you will. And he'll just love you."

"But how do you know this?"

"I know this," she declared, "because I know who you are and I know who he is."

I was aware of my resistance to her opinion. "Okay," I replied, giving in to my curiosity and deciding to play along in this odd conversation. "Tell me his name, and I'll be able to tell you whether I will love him or not."

"Lucky Bennett."

"No, that's not a name I resonate with. I will not fall in love with him," I retorted.

But Barbara dismissed me and continued insisting that she knew better.

"Okay," I replied, "tell me what he looks like."

"He's an older man, with silver hair and beard, and the clearest sparkling blue eyes you have ever seen."

As a defensive mechanism, I suppose, I became sarcastic. "Sounds like Father Christmas to me. Not my type. I have a "Geronimo complex," I informed her. "I like the dark, long-haired type."

Barbara did not reply as we finally pulled around and parked toward the front of the house. It was an architectural dream. To get to the front door, we had to cross a small bridge that arched over a koi pond. The pond was beautifully landscaped and lighted, so we could see the large orange, silver, and golden koi fish swimming below us. The scent of tropical flowers, which grew in profusion all around us, was perfume on the night breeze. I felt as if I had entered a magical kingdom, and my apprehension rose. I was in the midst of natural beauty and manmade luxury, and all my "intentions" of the past few months came flooding back to me. I could not help feel that I was walking into a dream far grander than any I had intended energetically.

The house was as gorgeous and sumptuously decorated, and the dinner party was in full swing. Guests were clustered in groups here and there talking and laughing—and drinking and smoking. I tugged on Barbara's arm and pulled her aside discretely to tell her that I was not going ahead with the dance because the guests seemed intoxicated, and the room smoky, and I did not feel that this was an environment I could work in. She appealed for me to do the dance and sat me down by the pool and asked, "Amalia, what is it that you need? Tell me and I will make sure that whatever you need is arranged." I thought about it for a moment, and answered, "The only way that I will dance, is if everyone put down their drinks, stub out their cigarettes, and go outside under the stars and form a circle within which I will dance." Barbara nodded in understanding and then left me standing off to the side as she went about organizing everything. Everyone seemed to comply quickly and without complaint, and before long we were out under the night sky on the stone patio by the waterfall pool, with tiki torches casting flickering shadows around us.

Barbara briefly introduced me to the guests and then quickly popped the CD of sacred music I had brought into the music system, which was wired to speakers out of doors. As I focused on creating a sacred space for my dance, I noticed that Barbara had placed a chair in the circumference of the circle among all the standing guests, and our host, the mysterious silver-haired man with the unusual name of Lucky, took this seat of honor.

As the music filled the area, I slowly and reverently entered the circle carrying in my left hand a large abalone shell filled with smoking sage and in my right hand, two long white feathers. I moved in step with the drumbeat of the music and as I made my way around the circle, I looked deeply into each person's eyes and with the white feathers smudged him or her with the healing sage smoke. When the rhythm of the music intensified, I set the abalone shell down at Lucky's feet and danced with a feather in each hand. In the light of the torches, Lucky's blue eyes sparkled like twinkling stars and his energy seemed open to receive my dance for the sacred offering that it was. I turned and moved into the center of the circle, and began the dance. At first I focused my dance on Lucky as I emitted healing energy toward him, then I danced for all, with sacred abandon. As I finally wound down the dance, I slowly and ceremoniously bowed to Lucky, and then moved out of the circle. The circle of guests was quiet; entranced I think, but as I walked toward the house, where I would change into my eveningwear, I heard them erupt into applause.

Later, when Lucky and I had a quiet moment to speak alone, the depth of his centeredness struck me. He exuded a quality of calmness and benevolence along with a commanding presence, generating the energy of a loving king who contentedly but assuredly ruled his kingdom. In a nutshell, he was decidedly different from most of the men I knew. Most of the men I had worked with or been in relationship with had not "had it together," but Lucky seemed sure of himself both inwardly and outwardly. I was intrigued by his composure and confident manner. Even though he was not "my type," he was certainly a type that I wanted to get to know and explore. At one point in our conversation, he leaned over and whispered in my ear, "By the way, did I tell you how deeply touched I was by your dance, and how beautiful it was?" I thanked him. As we spoke throughout the evening, his inner maturity sparked my interest, and I began to feel open to the possibilities that could grow between us.

During the drive back to Dragonfly Ranch, Barbara bluntly declared that she had witnessed "the electricity" that was happening between Lucky and myself. I admitted to feeling drawn to Lucky, but I flatly declared that he was not my type. Barbara just smiled and said nothing more on the subject.

During my last five days on the island, in between my explorations of the island, I had opportunities to see and spend time with Lucky. By the time I left for Maui, we had formed a close friendship. And, to be truthful, there was a part of me that had fallen in love with him, although it was more a sacred bonding than a romantic attachment.

My trip to Maui distracted me from Lucky. Since I had once lived there, I was quickly immersed in a sea of people and parties as I contacted old friends and made plenty of new ones. My time there passed quickly, and even though Maui was gracious, I could not feel the untouched sacredness of the land of which I need to take root. Soon I was headed to my next destination, Kaua'i. I had never visited this island, and although I appreciated its dramatic landscapes and the lush greenness of its primordial mountains, I was energetically and emotionally distanced from this land. I simply wasn't feeling the flow of my inner sense. Everything else seemed to flow with difficulty, too. Accommodations were difficult to find and I never felt that I settled in there. In fact, within the first two hours of my arrival, Kaua'i took my blood when I stepped barefoot over a river rock, slipped, and cut my toe. It was clear to me that neither Maui nor Kaua'i were making a "bid" for me, as I had asked in prayer before my travels here. Without a doubt, it was the Big Island of Hawai'i that had chosen me. So, for the last week of my trip, I headed back to the Big Island.

I saw Lucky again, and I visited the volcano Goddess, Pele, to consult her on the matter of my relocation to this island. The island was often referred to as "The Rock" because it was the newest island to have been formed from past volcanic eruptions and so a lot of the land was still uncovered by greenery. Because of this, it was not the prettiest of the Hawaiian islands, for much of it resembled barren moonscape rather than the lush tropical expanses of the other, older islands. But it was the island where indigenous roots seemed to go deepest and be most alive. It was the least untouched by modernization and overbuilding. For the type of work I desired to do—I *needed* to do—this island was the best. It promised the most fertile ground in which to nurture the seeds of my creativity into fruition.

In my pilgrimage to Kilauea volcano, where Pele lives, I hoped to receive the blessing of this ancient land. I took with me gifts of bananas, tobacco, and a lei, and made my way to *"Hale ma'uma'u"* (*hale* meaning "house," and *ma'uma'u* referring to a type of fern), which lies at the summit of Kilauea. I sat on the edge of the nearly lifeless crater, which looked like a giant thumb had pressed itself into the earth. The sulfuric mists left trails in the wind, and the misty air was filled with profound quietness.

I spoke to Pele softly, and made my offerings by tossing the white-flowered lei, bananas, and a large pinch of tobacco into the crater. In the stillness, I received an answer through a stirring in my heart, through a certainty that rose within me as a feeling that Pele approved of my finishing my Earthmission here on the island. I bowed at her in reverence and with gratitude, drawing my hands into a prayer position and bending down to touch them to the earth.

Then I decided to do a full-scale retrieval. I was not sure what I would retrieve, as the lava around me was barren and sulfuric smoke wafted up from its crevices. There was no evident sign of life in this area of the crater, and yet I was sure that Pele's life force was strong. I wanted to find out what the stones had to say. Not long after I entered the meditational space of the retrieval, I received what I can only describe as a compassionate wrath.

Look what you have done with your outrageous anger and wrath. Mis-contained passion of war and fear has led to despair and death. You are still fuming and will not let go of your pain and anguish. You have been turned to molten rock and have a hardened heart that weeps fiery, bloody tears that call out to the justice of the gods to return you to love. Your toxic, gaseous fumes are choking the life around you, nauseating the very life principle that you despise. You have left no sign of love or life, and yet deep down in the caverns of your core you ache in deep pain and long for the very things you have destroyed. You left us with your sour sulfuric breath Pele, any wonder we fear anger, how can we take responsibility and vent our anger if you our goddess have destroyed the safety of letting it go?

Perhaps you are reminding us of what will happen to us if we do exude and explode our wrath as you have done. Did you take all the unleashed and misguided anger from the earth and her peoples to release it for us all and to let it be known to us of the dangers in playing with fire as our own mothers did also warn us against?

There is a deep beauty in you Pele, one that many are intrigued about. You have left a silence, one that is of emptiness and a voidance of movement of life, yet with the tenacity to bear the fruits of your reign.

Deep down I feel you stir, the longing for creation to express itself slithers like flowing red serpents with hissing forked tongues, lashing with the desire for the taste of life as it could be.

Pele, I pray for you that you may rest in peace and that you lay down your weapons and be raised upon the altar of love. The calling of love does beckon you to be gentled by the grace of love. You Pele, who have known darkness, don't be afraid to dissolve into the light of love. Don't be afraid.

You are alive Pele, your stirring passion draws many near to you, we feel your presence under and in the earth where you reside, we cannot see you other than your hissing hot steam that seeps out of the cracks in the earth that you yourself created. As we draw near, we feel our own inner stirrings of the desire to create. We sometimes see your red molten lavic body and when we lay our sight in awe of your beauty and power we are staved of breath.

You are a goddess, a deemer and redeemer, a creator and destroyer. You are the unknown and we are intrigued by your presence. You seem to destroy and yet from your devasta-tion, born is life anew. At your outskirts, new and lush life drapes your body with royal canopies of emerald tropical forests that is dazzling to the sight. Birds, butterflies, dragon-flies and insects of all kinds are happy to be your royal subjects. The minerals you have strewn across the barren floor have become the plush carpet of which teeming life exists.

The transmission came to a sudden halt and the questions came flooding in. Was that a retrieval? It seemed more like my commentary to Pele than a retrieval from the stones. Who and what was expressing itself, was it the stones or myself that was speaking? It had not felt like me, but if it had actually been me, who was I to have the audacity to speak to Pele, the Volcano Goddess, like that? Pele is described as passionate, volatile, and capricious. Would she reject my brazen thoughts and admonish me by denying me access to the island now? This was the question that most pressed on me. I had come here to honor Pele, and now I wondered if I had offended her.

I cleared my thoughts with a long exhale and sat in the silence seeking an answer. I realized that the witness in me had not only been addressing Pele, but had been addressing that part in me and in all of us that had felt the repercussions of our own anger and wrath. As a goddess, Pele provided the perfect mirror for us, the grand template for us to see ourselves in the greater unfolding design. I, like most of us, could relate to the cry of love that lies under the belly of anguish, pain, and fear.

I did not receive any more wisdom from the stones or from Pele that day, and so I left feeling uncertain about my commitment to move to the Big Island of Hawai'i. Instead, insight and advice came from other sources, especially from Lucky.

The day before I left the island to return to Sedona, Lucky sat me down and made a declaration that he felt that I was part of his family now. He had abundant means, and he did not want me to struggle anymore with the financial lack that I seemed to be caught up in. He opened my left hand and gently placed on my palm a small silver signet embossed with the image of an angel with outstretched wings. He spoke as he pressed the silver medallion in my hand, inviting me back to the Big Island to be near him and to finish my book without any worries. He said he would buy me a car and provide a house for me to live in so that I could fulfill my mission to the earth without being stressed about my physical needs. He asked for nothing in return.

While I was fascinated by his proposition, and overcome with his generosity, I also was very guarded in my feelings. How could he ask nothing of me in return for such generosity? I thanked him for his offer but spoke up about my reservations. I could not go along with his plan if I thought that I would be required to go against my best instincts and inner desires in any way. Although I truly loved Lucky's being, I was not "in love" with him. I told him that I had already mastered "obligation" in my marriage of fifteen years to Marcus, and that I was through with being beholden to anyone in that way. I tried to judiciously cover every possibility that I could think of, to expose every "loophole" that might in anyway jeopardize my personal independence and sense of values.

Lucky listened patiently and allayed all my concerns. His was a magnanimous offer, and he unconditionally agreed to support me in any way that I needed so that I could go ahead and do the things I do best—to dance and write my book and mostly just be myself. He expected nothing in return, except that I fulfill my potential.

I was left stunned by his words. Everything I had prayed for, that I had worked energetically to manifest, was happening. It was at this very point that I realized that the mysterious silver-haired man from Claudia's tarot reading had materialized—with the unlikely but perfect name of Lucky. I wanted to tell Lucky that the hand of Spirit seemed to be moving in all this, but somehow I just couldn't. Perhaps it was because I could hardly believe it myself. The Big Island had made a "bid" for me in a grandiose way that I could never have imagined. Lucky was offering to make my

Treasure Map a reality. I could hear Claudia's words about how I must accept his offer and what it all meant as if she were sitting next to me and repeating them: "Your wheel of fortune is at hand; it is your time for abundance now." I also remembered her explanation that, "He has equally a lot to gain from you too, mostly spiritually."

Finally, I was able to speak again. Although I said only a few words, they came from the depths of my soul: "Thank you, Lucky. I accept."

I returned back to Sedona to say goodbye to my beloved friends and rock spirits and packed up my belongings. As I was rolling up my Treasure Map, something in the corner caught my eye, and I shrieked to my friend Lane, who was helping me pack: "Lane, look there in the corner!" In large orange letters, the word "LUCKY" was pasted. We both stood there, our mouths agape. I had no idea when I had chosen that word to add to my map that it would be a person's name. I searched over the map for other words and phrases I had pasted on it. Suddenly, a narrative unfolded: "Lucky," "Contributors," "Helping you get the things you want and need" and "Elevate your lifestyle!" The words spelled out the result of my journey to the Big Island. "They don't call it a Treasure Map for nothing," I joked. Even though this play of events felt farfetched, I could not help but admit that the Treasure Map had been a powerful tool of manifestation for me. I could now appreciate more fully, that as individual expressions of God, each of us have unlimited creative abilities to create the reality we want, and that our will is ultimately not separate from the will of God.

It was only days after this insight that Lucky called and asked me to pick out a car for myself. In my mind, I ran the list of cars that I liked and desired. But I also realized that I was thinking along the lines of "what is reasonable to ask for." I was still somewhat in my old patterns, proving again how hard it is for us to truly live our creative, God-like potentials. I finally told Lucky that I wished to have an Isuzu Rodeo. His response was not what I expected. It was as if he had seen into my depths to reveal how I was still holding myself back. "Come on, you can do better than that!" he said.

I realized he was right. But I couldn't think straight, so I told him I would call him back. The next day I called him with my decision—I wanted a Ford Lexus. Lucky still was not buying into my scarcity thinking. "That is highly unacceptable," he declared. "I was thinking more along the lines of a BMW." My heart leapt. I immediately wondered if I had ever made mention of my dream of owning a BMW. And why hadn't I just asked for it myself, since that was my dream car? I was not about to test the universe any more. "A BMW it is!" I agreed. I was blooming in joy.

On the day before my flight to Hawai'i, I climbed up Bear Mountain for one last meeting with the rock beings. The late afternoon sun had left a mysterious haze draped in the air, tinting the rocks with a pinkish tinge. I lay down at the top of the mountain, in a spot that was lyrically dotted with spiny cacti and relaxed my spine into the rock that supported me. I inwardly declared my heartfelt love and gratitude to the earth and then the words "A Class Journey" surfaced. I remembered the dream that I had back in Australia when the moon had spoken to me. She had suggested that the name of my book ought to be called "A Class Journey." I realized now, that my life's journey is indeed like a class, and the book I was studying from, involved me as the prime character, the author of the book, and the reader as well. Sedona had taught me the grandest lessons of my life. I was soon outside of time and in the Dreamtime of the earth and the spirit of my being began a communion with the spirit of the stones, communicating with the silent language I had come to know from the rock spirits.

I lay there with my eyes closed, drifting in a sea of relaxation, until I felt the urge to open my eyes. When I did, I saw a bee hovering only one inch from the middle of my forehead. I had not previously heard its buzzing, but the sound of its wings now seemed to be singing me a sacred song. I felt the bee was pollinating me with a blessing from the Queen of Mother Nature's Hive. Directly behind the bee, the golden-orange orb of the setting sun shone like an ancient Egyptian medallion. I was overcome with feelings of appreciation and gratitude. Tears welled up and spilled down my cheeks as I felt my heart infused with love for the magnificence and beauty around me and inside of me. I thought of the pollen song of the Navajo, which I had sung during my travels in Mexico. I wiped the tears from my eyes and the afternoon sky quickened into clearer view and there, above me, between the bee at my forehead and the golden sun, a solitary eagle was riding the thermals. A bee, an eagle, and the medallion sun—I knew they were all there together to bid me farewell and it is in this beauty that I live with the earth.

I lay unmoving until my earth-spirit messengers had gone and the sun had set. I so loved the red rocks of Sedona and was going to miss them terribly, but Spirit had answered my prayers and I was following its lead. It had been barely more than three weeks since Salena and Claudia had read the tarot cards and revealed my new path. Spirit not only moved in mysterious ways, but very quickly, too!

Chapter 12:

The Flowering.

I left Sedona and flew to Hawai'i, where my new life awaited me. Lucky picked me up from the Kona airport, drove me to his house, and set me up in the guest room. It was agreed that I would stay there until I found a studio apartment—which materialized in two weeks. It was perfect for me—spacious and open, with access to a pool and hot tub, and it was just around the corner from Lucky's house and property. My BMW was on order, being outfitted and accessorized to my specifications. It was due to arrive from Germany in a few months. In the meantime, Lucky offered me the use of one of his cars, a black convertible. My transition was going well, to say the least, and between spending time with Lucky and exploring the island, I was settling in easily. But I was also feeling a deep need to get back to work with the rocks and earth energies of Hawai'i.

I had attempted retrievals with the lava rocks on several occasions, but I was always mystified by their nature. I could not feel the earth energy on this island as strongly as I had on the mainland. The energy here felt diluted, perhaps because of the breezy winds and abundant water surrounding the island itself. The mainland felt more solid and deeply rooted to the ground of the earth but the energy of this island felt more ethereal, like a bridge that is suspended between Earth and Heaven.

Interestingly, I learned that from an esoteric perspective, the islands of Hawai'i correlate with Earth's heart chakra. The heart chakra is seen as the bridge between the lower and upper chakras of the body, with the lower ones associated with the earth realm and the upper chakras with the spiritual realms. I could resonate with that, for to me, Hawai'i felt like the portal between the two worlds of the fixed and the unfixed and of the material and the spiritual. As such, it was the perfect place to merge the dualities within the self and arrive at a place of union and centeredness. (Perhaps this is why Hawai'i is a popular destination for weddings and honeymoons.) I suspected that I had arrived at the perfect place, the Garden of Eden, to merge the dualities within myself, to unify the "Adam and Eve" within myself in a sacred partnership— into Oneness.

I set out to visit Pele again, but this time I decided to go at night so that I could see her at work in the glowing darkness. I took with me offerings of sage and plumeria flowers, my portable CD player to provide music to dance to, water and a strong flashlight. When I finally arrived at the end of the long and winding road to the coast, many others were gathered there. We all looked up at the lava streaming down the mountainside, mesmerized by what looked like Pele's fiery red hair cascading over the shoulders of her great earthen body. I parked my car and walked carefully over the lava field toward the nearby coastline to take a closer look at the flowing lava. I took a few more steps and then stopped, transfixed once again. A massive neon-orange river of liquid fire poured out of the mouth of the land and into the sea at nearly fifty miles an hour!

I sat down on a rock pulling a silk scarf over my nose and mouth to protect myself from the sulfuric fumes while I witnessed this timeless phenomenon of primal beauty. Sometime during my solitary sitting I heard an ancient voice arise from within me and speak: "Primordial innocence—An ancient cry of a new dawn." I felt this was a declaration from Pele and quickly grabbed a pen and paper to note her words. Then I felt the pen being led across the paper in a kind of automatic writing:

Walking on the black lava rock, I feel the danger of a footing unsure in the dark of the night. One careless step on this lava rock could either lacerate my feet or burn them to a crisp. The skin of the earth itself is burnt; it has not been spared for the life that it holds. In anticipation of seeing Pele's fiery glow, my vision has become focused and my blood runs quicker into the heart of awaiting.

I see it; I see the fiery orange glow of red trails oozing down the side of the volcano like roads mapping out the path of creation. Streaming down and over the edge of the lava cliff-walls into the ocean, where the waves engulf the molten magma's devouring appetite. The earth inferno is phenomenal, like a live theatre that is staged by the elements of life that engage its play. I see an eternal battle between the elements, for as the molten lava flows into the ocean, laying down the law of the land; the ocean waters muster up a large wave, crashing up against the land to wash away the afterbirth. The cold blue ocean extinguishes the fire, as the molten red-hot blood of Pele moves relentlessly forward. The fiery goddess with her lashing tongue and the water goddess with her waving arms—the two meet here at the edge of creation to battle it out. A war that has stood through time is seen right here at the cradle of the earth.

Here at the meeting place of the elements, where Pele's fiery rivulets pour into the waters of the ocean, emerges a crackling sound and eerie orange-gray smoldering plumes of smoke that are raised by the breath of Spirit, heralding the aftermath of both a hot and cold war. And here at this meeting place, a new formation of land mass gradually creeps into *the bed of the ocean. Witnessing the two opposing elements of earth and air, and of fire and water, offers a dance of creation beyond imagination.*

I did not analyze what I wrote, although I noted the theme of the coming together of opposites, the union of duality, and the cataclysmic nature of such a joining of polarities. I accepted that message as both personal and universal, knowing that deeper understanding would unfold in time. After a long silent pause I packed up my belongings and moved on.

The warm air blew softly against my cheek as I carefully made my way back across the old lava field to my car. I thought of the little I knew of Hawaiian legends. For instance, that this island is known as the Land of Fire and Ice, for Pele's greatest rival is Poli'ahu, Goddess of the snow-capped mountains, who lives on the mountain of Mauna Kea (meaning "white mountain.") I could not help but think of the differing images of this island, and it occurred to me that where one goddess starts a fire, the other one puts it out, and their battle continues ever onward. I was hoping this was not a message about my own still warring inner aspects. I hoped that my move here to the Big Island was the culmination of my work of achieving inner harmony.

As I drove, however, I could not stop thinking of the island's polarities. Another comparison that pressed itself upon me was of the "underworld" activity of the volcano and the "aboveworld" activity of the dolphins and whales. Where the volcano is solidly anchored to the earth, with its eruption flowing down into the ocean, the dolphins and whales rise up from below the waters to burst forth their joy. The volcano is rooted to the bowels of the earth, laying down its foundation in an austere manner. The dolphins and whales, in contrast, float in Earth's amniotic fluid to transmit joy and freedom. The volcano reminds us to ground our energy and to release the pent-up emotional fire within us—the jealousy, rage, anger, fear and other dark emotions that we bury so far down. Through such a release, we free our creative impulses and can more truly lay down the foundation of who we are. The volcano represents the lower chakras of the body through the elements of earth and fire and the colors of red, orange, and yellow. The dolphins and whales of the sea, represent the upper chakras of the body, the elements of water, air, and spirit and the colors blue, indigo and white. They remind us to flow with the currents and ride the waves of joy in life, and to remember to play, using the group "pod mind" to feel the oneness of our species. They teach us to remember to breathe the life force up through the crown of our heads, releasing our dreams in a fountain of creative imagining and, thus, of creatively living our dreams.

As I drove back from Pele's domain that night, these and other ideas that I had formulated over the years came flooding into me. If we look at Earth as our greater body, we can correlate its different features to aspects of the human body. The rocks are the structure—the bones of the earth—where a large proportion of the DNA, of Earth's genetic information and wisdom is stored. The trees are the lungs of the earth, taking in carbon dioxide and breathing out life-giving oxygen. The rivers and ocean, the body fluids of the earth, and the electromagnetic currents and Ley Lines of the earth, its nervous system.

The seven Hawaiian Islands have even been correlated by Pila Chiles, in his book, "The Secrets and Mysteries of Hawai'i" to the seven chakras of the human body. The Big Island, the newest and youngest of the islands is the first chakra, where the red molten lava is spewed forth to lay down the foundations of the earth element itself. It holds the energy of survival through of creation and destruction, for at any moment the wrath of Pele, the volcano goddess, may erupt to make new land or to obliterate it.

The next island up the chain of islands is Maui, which correlates to the color orange of the second chakra, the sacral center of pleasure, sexuality, and creativity. Maui is known as the "party island," where the melting pot of pleasure, openness, and beauty nourishes sensuality. It holds the water element in the way that life flows freely there, unencumbered from finding its own way.

Lana'i comes next. This island is known for its productive pineapple plantations, which glow yellow-golden under the sun and so correlate to the solar plexus chakra. Then comes Moloka'i, the green island in the middle of the chain, serving as the heart link, the bridge, between the upper and lower chakras. On Moloka'i, modern life seems to have been left behind so that people can enjoy the simplicity of beingness. O'ahu, the next island in the chain, correlates to the throat chakra, vibrating as the place of business, commerce, and communication between so many segments of society. Then there is Kaua'i, which is the third-eye chakra, for with its astounding beauty and spiritual energy, it is the visionary aspect of Hawai'i. Finally, there is Ni'ihau, the seventh and oldest island, which correlates to the crown chakra. Ni'ihau is the "untouchable" island of purity, where access is strictly limited to native Hawaiians or to those invited in as guests of those who live there.

I thought of this as I drove, not paying much attention to anything in particular—until I spotted a large flat rock along the rocky coastline. This commanding stone drew me towards it, and I knew I had to stop and dance upon it. I quickly pulled over and walked over to the stone, with my portable CD player. Then there, under the dark sky with the waves crashing behind me, I danced for Pele, thanking her for all her creative endeavors. I danced my heart for Pele, imitating the swirl and the gushing power of the lava, moving, as it does like the fiery flicking tongue of a hungry serpent. I danced for the union of duality, for the healing of the split within myself and each of us. It was a glorious dance—a sincere prayer of thanks to Pele, to whom I had begun to form an alliance, and one of humility toward the Big Island, with whom I was still struggling to communicate. I made a commitment to return to Pele the next day.

The next morning I went out bright and early to the calderas of Kilauea to collect more indigenous wisdom from the lava rocks. I found a flat expanse of lava rock to sit on, and tuned in. The connection came quickly.

The energy of the land is new and young, it is unsettled. It is like that of young adolescent who is discovering himself, new to the whole wide world. It is recently developed and has yet to put roots down or settle itself into the silence and stillness within.

Everything here expresses itself like the flowing movement of a Hula dance, unfolding the story of the land and its creation. The volcano is stirring, and when you sit still enough you can feel Pele's turbulence: her blood is boiling, moving and seeking a foundation to rest upon. The lava rock is light and lifeless, as the fires of creation have burnt the hell out of it. It does not have much to say, as it is new in the world and therefore does not have too much knowledge to impart—or perhaps it does not even know how to speak it yet. It is unlike the red rocks of Sedona, which share a deep stream of knowledge, like the lineage of elders who speak with the tongue of profound wisdom and humor.

The Big Island of Hawai'i is like the oceans' surface, with much movement—sometimes it is slight and sometimes moving with all its might. There is the activity of fishes swimming all about, while dolphins and whales breathe out their spout. Even the flowers here explode with the movement of unfolding.

I sat in the silence that comes after a retrieval, both delighted that the message had come so quickly but still uncertain as to the nature of my connection to the spirits of this land. The retrievals here in Hawai'i were so unlike the ones in Sedona. They were more like inner commentaries than actual retrievals. I could not go deep enough into the soul of the rocks to listen to their wisdom and the silence within. Only noisiness and busyness seem to prevail here. The lava rocks did not seem to contain the ancient wisdom that Sedona's rocks held, instead, in their infancy they are still seeking to find their own footing in the world. Their energy feels turbulent and in constant motion, like a small school of fish in an eating frenzy. This frenetic energy was suffused with another energy, one that had a light and porous quality to it. In contrast, the stones of Sedona were heavy with wisdom, transmitting eternal silence and stillness like that of an ancient elder sitting firmly and solidly at the center of his circle. The Sedona rocks were wisdom banks, pure conduits to the soul information of the earth. The lava rocks, on the other hand, seemed to be restless, in a search for their own existence. This made sense to me, since Sedona's rocks are said to be on the order of 330 million years old, whereas those of the Big Island are dated to only about 500,000 years ago.

The bottom line was that I just could not relate to these rocks, as well I could to the older rocks of Sedona. Even though the metallic nature of the lava rock causes them to emit a high frequency of electromagnetic and healing energy, their porous makeup did not seem to retain much of the density of information and wisdom that the more solid and ancient rocks of the Southwest did. This might have also been the result of the low silica content of the lava rocks, since silica is elemental to crystals that can be programmed and can retain information. Perhaps the answer really was rooted in a personal preference. Perhaps I simply felt a deeper affinity and soul connection to the red-rock spirits of Sedona, and therefore I could more effortlessly tap into their lineage of indigenous and ancestral wisdom. Still, despite my clear connection to the rocks in Sedona, I knew that the Big Island was the perfect place for me to complete my Earth project and to make manifest a new and more whole self.

The Big Island became a force of nature in my life, as did Lucky, who continued to assist in my inner transformation— and outer transformation as well. Lucky Bennett has an eye for aesthetics, and he did everything in his power to get me to truly believe that I was a woman full of beauty and able to express the glory of myself. Whatever self-doubts I had about myself, Lucky soon exposed and helped me heal. He supported my creative potential as a writer and as a dance facilitator. When my custom-made BMW sports utility van arrived at the dock from Honolulu, he celebrated my good fortune, as if I, and not he, were responsible for it. The car truly was the stuff of dreams. I had chosen an exterior color of deep Emerald Green—for obvious reasons—with a cream-colored interior. I was so delighted with this dream car that I honored it with a special name: *Bella-Menehune-Wanjina*. The initial letter of each word spells out the make of the car (BMW) and each word has a special meaning: *Bella*, which means "beautiful" in Italian; *Menehune*, which are a legendary race of small people of Hawai'i, similar in nature to pixies; and *Wanjina*, the Australian Aboriginal Creator God. I called her Bella for short, and she is one of the most significantly beautiful gifts I have ever received.

As I settled into life in Hawai'i, Lucky, like a lighthouse, continued to shine a loving light over my life. He has an insatiable joy and is spontaneous in his zest for life. Lucky would counsel others and me; "There is nothing in the world that is worth taking you off your joy. The universe will give you exactly what you want and focus on. Abundance is always available, all you have to do is keep your valve open to receive it." He would go on to explain that like a faucet in a house, in order to get the water you want, the tap must be turned on, and the valve must be open. Lucky's valves were wide open all right! I have never seen him disappointed or despondent. His example helped me live what I had always believed but could never seem to consistently practice.

Lucky is among the most respected and well known of architects of Hawai'i, and his creativity is a large part of why he is so successful. His house designs are a stylish fusion of the modern with the ancient Hawaiian, and always brimming with both aesthetic beauty and common-sense functionality. He moved to me a new level of confidence, especially in believing I could be successful at whatever it was that I attempted.

The shadow of "less than" that had for so long kept the brightest light from my life, began to fade away. Everywhere, I began to see not only possibilities but also opportunities. My life began to take on a new flow and I was now more at ease in my financial and physical life. The change arose from my more intently honoring myself as a creative designer of my life. But Lucky was the mirror through which I was able to see and accept that teaching. My life now was a stark contrast to my earlier life, especially to my childhood, when I had learned to stilt my self-expression to please others and had bought into the limitations others told me existed in the world. Lucky returned me to the throne of my exalted self. He was living proof in my life that I was not separate from the universes within and outside of me. I saw how I am a fractal of all of creation, reflecting itself in the hall of mirrors.

As I grew into a deeper connection with my real Self, my spiritual relationship with the 'āina, (the land) of Big Island deepened as well. Over the next few years, I continued to explore its multifaceted and primordial nature—from the cascading waterfalls of Waipi'o Valley, which pour into giant stone bowls; to the underground steam caves, which give off the hot air of Pele's searing breath; to the warm mineral-water ponds where I and others bathed to heal body and soul. I learned to read the body of the Island like a different kind of Treasure Map. I scouted out the green volcanic lakes; visited places like Hilo, which is the rainiest place in the United States; and explored Mauna Kea, which is the tallest mountain on Earth when measured from the ocean floor, and its sister mountain, Mauna Loa, which is the largest single mountain mass on Earth. Everywhere I went, the unique temperament of ancient Hawai'i was evident in its dramatic landscapes and its culture. The Big Island of Hawai'i was like an incubator in which I grew into my fullness. Even the name "Hawai'i" itself reverberated with meaning for my journey. *Hā* means "breath," *Wai* means "water" and the letter i refers to "area." Hawai'i is a place that is made of the elements of breath and water, the two essential properties of life. These highly concentrated forces of natural elements contributes to the island's *Mana,'* its high charge of Spirit Force and Divine Power.

Breath as a spiritual connector to all things, is a vital and integral part of the ancient Hawaiian culture and even today, some native Hawaiians still greet each other the ancient way, by touching foreheads and exchanging the essence of each other's life and spirit force (their *mana*) by breathing in one another's breath. When I saw this type of greeting and embrace for the first time, I felt I had witnessed a bridging of the self and other, and of the past and present, for through such a greeting each person allows the other's ancestors to enter into the body of present time. The Hawaiians to this day call white people *Haole,* meaning "without breath" with *Ha* meaning "breath" and *'Ole* meaning "without." This name might have an historical context arising from when the natives first saw white explorers, who greeted each other with a handshake. But it probably goes much deeper than that, invoking, as do most ancient native practices and words, an understanding of the spiritual nature of life.

So, despite my initial difficulty connecting with the lava rocks of Hawai'i, I never gave up attempting retrievals. They had become part of who I am, how I live in the world, and how I connect with Nature. Like a lifeline to the land of Hawai'i, Pele became my guide into the deeper recesses of Earth-Spirit culture. One day, for example, I took the hours' long drive through the lava fields to revisit her in her magical cauldron on Kilauea volcano. I went in the late afternoon so I could again see Pele alight in the dark of night. A myriad of tourists had also gathered there, and I joined them in a walk across the lava fields to pay homage to this primeval goddess. I sat close to the neon-orange spew that oozed over the black rocks, and watched Pele as she worked to lay down the law of the land. The other people around me did not settle down, but their activity did not distract me from reaching deep within myself to that place of stilled silence from which I connect with the Earth Voice. Pele's message came through lyrically, as a descriptive poem.

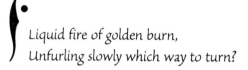

Liquid fire of golden burn,
Unfurling slowly which way to turn?

The heat amasses and escapes into the breeze,
For here indeed, you will not surely freeze.

Sometimes timid, sometimes stark,
Pele is the Madame that is most seen in the dark.

Oozing slowly, she moves into the grooves,
Be careful, for she might burn your hooves.

She crackles and pops as she gives off her flame,
As the membranous womb gives birth to her fame.

Such a rare beauty all come to see,
At how wondrous a goddess she has come to be.

This poem is suggestive of a new contemporary nursery rhyme, which seems to personify Pele perfectly. As the creatrix—a matrix of creation—she plays her tricks and spellbinds you at the center of her crafty web. She makes the riddle of creation easy to decipher, for by observing Pele's dance, you can see that by releasing the pent-up energy from the core of your being, this powerful energy can be utilized for laying down the foundation of your creation, no matter what you choose it to be. She teaches us to let loose our energy, to allow the steam of our own being to rise up. She encourages us to allow our energy and intention to coalesce into the vision that we seek.

After the retrieval poem, I wandered away from the crowd and found a secluded spot in full view of the strands of Pele's red-lava hair. I put on headphones and danced to my favorite music. I let loose all the energy that had been pent-up in the pit of my stomach, following Pele's example, so that I could further lay down and ground my creative ideas into form.

The next day, I returned to Kilauea volcano, and this time I hiked into the center of one of its larger calderas. As I stepped carefully over the rough, clinkery lava rock, I noticed it glisten in the midday sun. I crouched down to take a closer look and saw that out of this seeming black lifeless rock shone the opalescent colors of a rainbow. How befitting this was, as I had recently read a Hawaiian legend that described the original Hawaiians, as the Children of the Rainbow, and that the rainbow was their source of spiritual power. Right here anchored in Pele's dark and desolate cauldron, lays the light and hope of the rainbow, a link between this world and the other, of Matter and Spirit. I decided to sit here and listen to the *pohaku*, (the rocks).

Earth's Na'au—the power center, just below the navel—is churning, for there has been a long-awaited time to come and it is near. A new goddess will be birthed by all on this planet and she will step in time and stand beside the god within.

The garden of a new Eden that has eternally been,
Is re-opening its gates, for this we have already seen.

Through the heart of our own beingness we shall go,
Into the heart of the earth we will doth know.

There we will be sown like a seed growing in time,
To burst our aliveness within the universe's rhyme.

With our roots in the earth planted mighty and sure,
Will our trunk and treetops be sprightly and pure.

From all the messages I retrieved at Kilauea, it was clear that Pele was a mistress of manifestation. This is a sacred site that is a cradle of birth, especially of the delivery of innocence. Despite this being a site of seeming destruction and of fire and rage, it is also one where a beautiful creation is born from the ashes of the old.

I was especially attracted to another sacred site—Púuhonua O Honaunau, which is the home of the *Ali'i* (ancient royals).

Commonly known as "The Place of Refuge," it is a sanctuary where defeated warriors and noncombatants could come to remain in safety until the battle was over. In addition, those who violated the *kapu*—the sacred laws-often tried to escape to this sanctuary, for if they managed to get within its confines, their lives would be spared. When a kapu was broken, the penalty was always death, as a broken kapu could bring the wrath of the gods down on the people in the form of volcanic eruptions, earthquakes, tidal waves, or famine. To protect themselves from these catastrophes, the warriors pursued the kapu breaker until he or she was caught and put to death. But if the kapu breaker managed to elude the pursuers and make it to the sanctuary, they were spared because no blood could be shed there. In fact, the *Kahuna* (priest) would perform a ceremony of absolution for the offender, who would then be released.

To this day, the remains of a massive stone wall—ten feet high and seventeen feet thick—still stands at the site. It was this wall that separated the royal grounds from the *pu'uhonua* (the place of refuge). Outside of the wall is an oblong rock, approximately twenty feet long. This is the Stone of Keoua, (the high chief of Kona) and equally known as the Stone of Kane. Kane means "man" or "creator of the universe." In the Hawaiian tradition, man and Creator God are given the same title, acknowledging that man has little or no separation to the God force. There were many Kane stones that stood upright throughout Hawai'i. They signify power, strength, and the energy of creation, but when the kapu (the sacred laws) system ended in 1819, one year before the missionaries arrived, the stones were said to lay themselves down. Perhaps when we all stand tall within ourselves and remember who we are as sacred gods and goddesses, then these magnificent stones might raise themselves once again.

One day while visiting this sacred site, I sat down and scooted as close as I could to the Kane stone. I touched my forehead to its sun-warmed brim. The heat of the stone seemed to melt the constructs of my thoughts, allowing a clear passage for my inner sight. I wrote down what I saw, felt, and heard on a piece of paper that I had slipped out of my medicine bag.

The shifting and shaping of worlds lies still in the absolute-ness of itself, as the momentary gift of ever-presence, unfolds in the sea-scaped vision of time. The sacred breath of the wind, along with the ocean's surge has shaped an ancient being that lays itself to rest in time. The light of day and of night is ushered into the recesses of its own being to "resonate" and "emanate" the power of the gods. It rests upon the fire-baked earth and lays its bones as a prayer for peace, reminding us all to stand tall and remember who we are.

I bowed in prayer position and thanked the Kane stone for its message. Then I crouched down closer to the surrounding rocks and heard them speak to me: "Amalia, it is time for you to grow up." What did that mean? Was I being too childlike in my approach to life? Was I too naïve in the Garden of Eden? I surrendered my mind and heart into the earth and laid my bones down as a prayer for peace, and I felt and saw what the rocks were asking me to do. I realized that ever since I had left Australia, I had been delving entirely into the underworld of the earth. My commitment to "grounding" myself with the earth had kept me in the seed and rooting stages of my development. As a human seed, I was now asked to grow tall and remember who I am—a being of both the earth and of the heavens. I had been in the womb of Mother Earth for too long, and the stones were now asking me to allow myself to germinate, to push through the soil of consciousness and to give birth to the flower that I am. To scintillate myself toward the light of the Father Sun, unfurl my flower petals, and let them bathe in the sunlight and ripen the fruit of my seed; and then to let them spread throughout the world with the breadth of the spirit wind.

As I envisioned "growing up" into my life, I felt moved even deeper into my body, and I sensed the movement of a type of Hula dance, a storytelling dance to the spirit of the land, rise within me. I rose slowly from my crouching position like a growing seed pushing up from the soil. My arms unfurling, like leaves of a plant, and stretching slowly toward the glorious sun. On the full stretch upwards, I then flung my hands wide open to spread the seeds of my wisdom throughout the world. At just that moment, out into the Pacific Ocean that bordered this sacred site, a whale breached the surface of the waters in a magnificent arc and let loose a wild spray of water from its blowhole. I was at once thrilled and humbled, and I bowed prayerfully toward the whale. The whale is said to be representative of the ancient record-keepers, and I knew in the fullness of my being that I was to spread the word about the stone's, wisdom, and that my mission as secretary was morphing into a new role, that as speaker and storyteller to a wider audience. It was time for the stones to spread the seeds wider, and I agreed to be their conduit.

The next day I went to another of my power spots, which is locally known as "The End of the World," most likely named because it is an ancient Hawaiian burial ground for the warriors who had died in the war. From this place, it is believed their souls would flow out to sea and thus be blessed by the ocean and carried back to their ancestors. I sat on the rock ledge that jutted the sea, put pen to paper, and was inspired to compose a new EarthSpirit Dance workshop, which I called "The Seed of Manifestation." How better could I sow the seed of Earth's wisdom than through dance? To help people bring this knowledge into consciousness through the body of matter itself. To assist others to offer their prayers to the heavens, while also grounding themselves through the earth. Dance was the perfect way to allow them to embody the full flowering of self, and to seed their desires into the universe.

Suddenly, I remembered the dream-vision I had in Australia, when the eagle had zoomed in on me and had flown around and under the empty chair that stood before me. That empty chair had always puzzled me. Now I understood it's meaning: that I was not only a player upon the stage of this life but also a viewer of my own life's play. I was the director of my life but I could also sit back and be the witness to the unfolding adventure of my life. I am the doer and the non-doer. I can have my cake and eat it too. I can be in the Garden of Eden and eat from the Tree of Knowledge. I can be the fruit of my own harvest and be the harvester that enjoys my own fruit. I am the created and the creator, and part of my mission as secretary to the stones was to assist others to do the same.

Suddenly, as at no other time in my life, dualities disappeared, or, more accurately, they coalesced into union. I felt whole in a way I never had experienced before. Everything about my mission seemed clear to me, and I knew, with a certainty that had once been lacking, that I truly was ready to walk into my future as both a powerful creator and as a faithful observer. Hawai'i had made its bid for me, and in that bidding, the island had helped me find myself and clarify my mission. At this site called the "End of the World" I suddenly knew that my mission and my journey—as adventurer, as dancer, as secretary to the stones—had no real end, for every ending seeds the birth of the next moment.

Chapter 13:

Earth Spirit Wisdom.

Over the ensuing years, Lucky and I maintained our close relationship, which while a relationship of the heart, was not a romantic one. His heart was opened in that way by Anita Emerson. During their marriage ceremony, I lovingly performed a wedding blessing dance for them. Lucky and Anita are a remarkable couple; he, with his silver hair and those truest of blue eyes and she, with her black hair and the clearest of green eyes, formed a sacred union that I was looking forward to experiencing in my own life.

Until the time such a relationship came for me however, my primary focus would be to complete my Earth assignment, which would mean returning back home to Australia. I felt the call to return the sacred stones I had from Australia back to their rightful place, and I also felt the tug to visit my family, whom I had not seen for nearly eight years. In completing this circle, I felt I would be bringing one grand cycle to a close and beginning another.

Revisiting my past was indeed momentous. I was a different person, one I was not sure my family and friends would recognize—or understand. The transition was abrupt, as I left Hawai'i, which I felt was a place I inhabited like a living prayer—swimming with the playful dolphins and thriving within a garden paradise—and re-entered my mother's "Big Fat Greek Wedding" house, which was located next to a roaring eight-lane freeway. The dualities stretched the fabric of my being, and my inner task became the challenge of putting into practice the most important lesson I had learned from the stones: to remain centered in the stillness while allowing everything else to swirl around me.

As soon as the plane's wheels touched the runway at Melbourne's airport, my eyes welled with tears. I had adopted Earth as my spiritual midwife and mother for many years now, and I wondered how it would be to reunite with my own blood mother. When she first saw me, my mother's face was overwritten with disbelief at seeing her "long-lost daughter" again. Had I not held her up and coaxed her to relax and breathe, she would have fainted on the spot! Things got easier from there. In fact, it was a blast from the past to be with my beloved family and long-held friends. What made the most impact on me however, was my solo journey into the Aboriginal heart of Australia—to Uluṟu and Kata Tjuṯa, to return the two sacred stones I had taken with me so long ago when I had left Australia not knowing what the call to faraway lands meant or what awaited me in my life's journey.

I first flew into Yulara, which sits like a small marina in a desert of ocean. I booked into a hotel lodge, and then rented a small car. As soon as I entered my room, I picked up the phone and called Bob Randall, (a highly respected elder and acclaimed Aboriginal songwriter), whom my friend Judy kindly recommended. Bob was happy to meet with me at the coffee shop and, during the course of our conversation, invited me to his home to have supper with his wife, Hazel, and family. I spent three evenings with them, and learned about the land and its native peoples, for whom I gained a deep appreciation.

I then continued on to Uluṟu, which means "slippery rock", or: "great pebble" to the Aṉangu-the Aboriginal people of the area. Uluṟu is Australia's most famous natural landmark and the largest rock monolith in the world. I took a glorious five-hour walk around the brooding red colossus, and asked the spirit of the rock where it wanted its stone returned. I gravitated to Mutu Julu, a dried-up waterhole where the ancient dreamtime serpent is said to reside. As I walked, I felt the call of a trio of standing stones, who as a group laid claim on the stone that I sought to return. I made a simple ceremony, thanked Uluṟu for welcoming me into its sacred fold, and lodged the stone securely in a small crack—back to its rightful place.

I then asked if I would be welcome to undertake a retrieval, to honor the wisdom of this heartland. I felt the sacred stone give its consent. Soon I heard it speak, explaining its mission to me, speaking of itself in the third-person voice.

> Like an ancient anchor, lying motionless on the desert floor, Uluṟu secures the unfolding layers of creation through the stories of the dreamtime. It is an anchor of Spirit that silently listens to the whispers of the wind and cries of the ancestors. Like a solidified wave, its curvaceous shell remains a cavity of stone-silence for the ancestral spirits to dwell within, to incubate and to rest in the cauldron of creation.
>
> With its mighty command, this pregnant belly of stone radiates its power along the song-lines, broadcasting its silent song and humming us into being.

I awoke early the next morning to beat the fierce sunlight hours and drove 35 kilometers west of Uluṟu, to Kata Tjuṯa to return the second stone. This rock landmass offers a dramatic series of 36 dome-like rock formations, some standing at tall as 1,701 feet. Its name means "many heads" in the local Aboriginal language because of the many small stones that form the giants of stone. This is a sacred site for men, unlike Uluru, which also includes sites for women's ceremony. However, the spirits of the land allowed me to enter, although I felt them watching my every step during my five-hour hike through the Valley of the Winds. Bob's assurance that it was okay for a woman to walk the site did not allay my wariness. I was on guard.

The eerie feeling of the area reminded me of Chaco Canyon; empty and alone and yet filled with a sea of faces. A lone black crow seemed to be my guide, leading me to a ridge where it landed and sat looking at me with a watchful eye. I sat on the ridge, letting the strong wind that swept over the rocks clear away my thoughts. I then closed my eyes and bowed my head in humility as I returned the second stone.

I had had a good visit, reconnecting with my family and completing my mission of returning the stones. As I returned back to Melbourne to prepare for my flight back to Hawai'i however, I received some startling, but delightful, news. Marcus, my former husband, who had relocated to another part of the country a year ago, would be in town! I had to admit I felt a bit nervous; I had not seen Marcus for eight years. What was more; I was invited to have dinner with him, his wife Virginia, and his lovely mother. My nerves calmed almost immediately upon seeing him. We had a wonderful dinner, full of reminiscing and laughter, and we parted once again feeling the goodness of our connection and comfortably complete with all that had passed between us over the years.

I now felt complete and could return to Hawai'i in peace, in one piece whole and sound, with the strength of my fullness and with a hard-won insight into the dissolution of dualities. The earth's stone-wisdom had given me countless discourses on the resolution of duality, and my life to this point seemed woven from threads of opposites that were stretched over a grand loom and carefully worked into a cohesive tapestry of wholeness and wellness. A great cycle had indeed completed itself.

I had done my "Earthwork" as I had promised to do so long ago in Australia. Not only had I retrieved the wisdom of the earth, but I had dissolved the hard rock wall that enclosed my heart and also mined the gems of wisdom that lay in my inner depths. As secretary to the stones, I had garnered the benefits of their communications, and of the communication of Earth, and had reshaped my own inner culture. I had also begun to shape the inner cultures of others, especially through ceremony and sacred dance events. The stones had shared their wisdom, and it was time for me to recapitulate the lessons of my long journey. Only by reviewing the central points could I truly honor the breadth of the teachings.

Resolution of Dualities

Duality as in "dual-reality" crafts a trickster game plan of existence, as life can be ruled by perceptions based on judgment and separation or can be crafted from the ideals of acceptance and union. Duality can obscure the inner lens from which we see through illusion. Duality—this or that, me or you, male or female, inner or outer, real or imagined—codifies opposites. These polar opposites act as bookends that hold our body of experiential knowledge rigidly in place, preventing us from easily opening the volumes of intuitive and energetic knowledge that lie waiting within.

Most of us construct our reality upon dualities, and fail to see beyond the either-or of our world to acknowledge that deep within, the energy of the opposing poles is actually a force that keeps the space-time continuum of our universe—and of our individual lives—

intact and whole. Rowena Pattee Kryder writes in *Sacred Ground to Sacred Space,* "Dualities are opposite polarities of the same energetic force which occurs at the same pace to keep the universal energy in balance." One polarity is as valid and divine as the other, for each plays a role in forming the whole. Each has its perfect place in the grand design. How can we know day if we do not know night? How can we know expansion if we do not know contraction? How can we savor life if we have no cognizance of death?

Credit must be given to the illusive mastery of duality and its misleading change of face. A coin has two thin sides, but spin it on its edge and it appears as a fully dimensional, flickering sphere of light. Our lives are like that. They need the energy of synthesis to move them beyond flat either-or choices. This shift from a two-dimensional to a spherical reality, drives the evolution of the self. It moves us from being separate from our Source to being one with the Divine. We move from the veneer of surfaces to true dimensionality.

Think of the ocean. We focus mostly on its surface: the light shimmering and reflecting off it, the motion of the waves undulating across it, the wakes of boats moving over it. We can be mesmerized by this surface motion and mistakenly believe that this is all there is to the ocean. But the ocean runs deep, with forceful currents and abundant life beneath its surface. This is a reality we cannot know unless we risk diving in. Likewise, we cannot know the infinite possibilities of the Self unless we risk descending into our interiors, the inner ocean of being from which oneness arises.

In truth, there is no need for us to *actively* merge dualities, for one half of the polarity cannot exist without its polar opposite. They are already joined, married in their difference, in step as sacred counterparts. The wisdom of the stones is not about active discernment but about centered contemplation. What the earth is now asking of us is to witness and feel these dualities from the point of pure awareness, where totality is all there is. We are being asked not to judge one aspect of a polarity as better than the other, but to learn to intuit the space that joins them, to witness their play not from the mind but from the heart. For from the heart—the throne of the chamber of Self, we experience harmony and balance. There is only being here—the union of Self and Other. There is only one time here, the present, and the now. Only from the center of the heart can we know ourselves in all our aspects and love what we had once judged to be unlovable.

Integration and Oneness

Perhaps the most evident duality on our planet at this time is still that of the Masculine and Feminine. The ebb and flow of the "relationship dance," the battle of the sexes, has been ongoing, and to what end? At no time in history have we been so free to make unions and dissolve them. Separation and divorce are the norm, not the exception. We simply cannot seem to find "our other half." We try and try, but we keep failing. Why? Because our "other half" is within us, and we must "mate" with it before we can truly be ready to join in union with another.

The stones counsel us that before we seek a relationship with someone else, we need to establish a "real-lationship" with ourselves, with our inner male and female aspects also known as the anima and animus in Jungian psychology. This represents the union of the conscious and unconscious parts of ourselves, a merging of our light being with our shadow self. We must touch the energy of our secret fears and our hidden desires in order to illuminate who we really are. We must plug ourselves into the holistic power source within us to be enlightened about what it means to be a full and authentic human being. To learn to first love ourselves before we can selflessly love someone else.

When we consciously seek out all aspects of ourselves—from our potential to be grand, to our capacity for darkness—and learn not to judge ourselves, then we are on the path to freedom. That freedom starts within, at the center of our being, from which there is no place else to go and nothing else to do except be right here and right now with the Self.

Earth Wisdom

As our planetary power point, Earth provides us not only with the physical resources we need to survive, but also the emotional and spiritual energy needed to evolve. The electrical current that runs through our root (sciatic) nerves, which begin at the base of the spine and end at the soles of our feet, connects us with the magnetic current of the earth, creating a wave of electromagnetic energy between the two. The most basic function of walking barefoot on the land therefore enables us to become the grounding rod from which we can plug into Earth's grid to access its power and information. On an energetic level, we connect our DNA (our genetic information, both physically and spiritually) with Earth's DNA, to create a feedback circuit. The ancients felt this earth connection intimately; they lived according to Earth's rhythms, could read Nature's most subtle signs and dialogued regularly with the spirit world. We are only just now rediscovering this primal wisdom.

"Earthspeak" is not a lost language, and we can retrieve our memory of it by quieting our thoughts and going within. By deciphering the messages of the earth and honoring the revealed wisdom, we can expand our consciousness and we can heal ourselves body, mind, and spirit, and thus contribute to our planetary evolution.

Growing the Seed of the Self

The Creator planted within the hearts of man and woman, the memory of their divine-seed-essence. By returning to the center of our own hearts, we can, one by one, each at our own pace, sow the seeds of love from which we are created. As human seeds that are planted in the soil of consciousness, we must tend to this soil carefully and drink from the well of Source Being in order to speed our growth, to blossom and to reap a much richer harvest.

Like a seedling that is well cared for, as we grow stronger and stronger, we breach the darkness to pierce the light. The more centered and connected we are with the earth, the more easily we can withstand and respond to the oncoming challenges of life. Eventually, we will flower into our truest selves. Nothing in life matters more than that we reach our full potential. For, as each of us achieves fuller growth, we seed the next phase of evolution for the planet and for the cosmos.

Stone Spirit Wisdom

Rocks are the living repositories of Earth wisdom. They are the very backbone of the earth that reflects the moral fiber of its being, carrying the DNA not only of the geological composition of the planet, but of its spiritual resonance as well. They are genetic libraries, which contain the Akashic records of Earth's birth, growth, and being. They are Earth's soul recorders, encoding within their structure, the ancient mysteries and wisdom of Earth-Space-Continuum. They call us to move between the worlds, between the ages, between the paradigms, and they connect the Great Above with the Great Below. They are gateways to other times and places, linking the ancient past with the future through the here and now, and anchoring the knowledge and light of the stars all the way down into the core of the earth.

In their solidity and stillness, they remind us to ground ourselves with the earth. The rocks and stones of the earth serve as doorways through which we can descend to the heart, to the spirit of Nature—and into the nature of What Is. They are survivors throughout time that have withstood repeated cataclysms throughout the ages. They are anchors of energy that are grounded in Being. With nowhere to go or nothing to do, they are sages and ancient seers, reminding us to "be" with the presence of Nature. Through their very mode of being, they become catalysts for our own evolution.

Diving into the Void

Rocks invite us into the primordial and prehistoric cauldron of creation. By voyaging into their interiors, where they hold the messages that are beyond time and space, they lead us through our own fears to a place of stillness, where in our aloneness we shift into all-one-ness. The void—a black-hole, is at the core of all things. If you truly let go and surrender into the center of the self, into this void, you will travel through the "Gates of Hell" to the other side of being that is termed "Heaven."

Taking this dive into the innerworld of the self and of the earth can be a healing journey. In this still center of the self, you can begin to feel your feelings as they are, without judgment. You can learn to experience yourself in all your many nuances and manifestations, without having to collapse into being only one way. The void within may at first appear to be dark, but really, it is a place of clear-seeing-light. As the Hindu saying goes, "From the cesspool grows the lotus." So, this void is not a place to be afraid of, for it is the place of our origin, the space from which we arose into being, the initial point of pulsation into beingness. All movement and creation is born there, and from there we make the return back home to Source Being.

Sitting in Stillness

At the epicenter of the spinning void is absolute stillness. The rocks invite us to sit at the still point of our own being, but doing so does not mean you sit without moving; it means, instead, that stillness remains within you, while all else moves around you!

It is this centeredness that links you to the ground of being. The earth shares the spirit of its wisdom with us at all times, all we have to do is stop, be still, and listen to the silent voice of the EarthSpeak.

The well-known term "silence is golden" applies to what one finds in the center of the self, for there, the darkness lifts to reveal the light of the self and the universe. As a navigating force, silence leads you down the fractal path of "reality" into the essence of all things, where pure spirit dwells. It is at the meeting-point of all dualities, between the flux-filled play of opposites that you will find yourself grounded and centered. For, as we sit around the circle and suppose, Truth sits silently at the center and knows!

The Garden of Eden

The Garden of Eden is not some place that has receded into the dim recesses of history. It is the fertile ground of self. It is the paradise to our true nature. Through listening to, and observing Nature and through our loving interaction with the wisdom of the stones, we can once again inhabit this inner garden. Earth has beckoned us with her silent call, but most are deafened by the loudness of our own thoughts, to hear her messages. Being out in Nature, quieting our thoughts, and going into the stillness within, intensifies our ability to once again hear her wisdom and the secrets of our inner knowing. To access Earth's wisdom is to access the pure and untainted connection with the Self. As a living sanctuary for renewal and creation, Earth is a transmitter of the "Dreamtime" that exists between the worlds of matter and energy, between the intellect and the intuition.

Despite our neglect and despoilment of the earth, she remains our loving mother. She is always in energetic balance. The quantum shift into the "Oneness Code" has already been anchored by the earth. This "Oneness" template now transmits its energy to us so that we can decipher it and use its energy to further our own conscious and quantum evolution. Through Earth wisdom, we can turn the Grand Wheel of Life and help restore and regenerate ourselves, growing toward ever finer modes of being. Remember, we are seed selves, always moving toward a grander flowering.

We each contain the Adam and the Eve within ourselves, for they are the twin seeds of the fleshy fruit of humanness. Adam and Eve were once in union in the Garden of Eden, and that union was never broken—it was forgotten. The stones and Mother Earth herself help us remember that we are beyond duality. In the Garden of Eden we find our true innocence, and from the purity of that innocence we are reborn.

The Emerald Realm

The emerald, a stone of power, is encoded with the blueprint for oneness—for the union that is embraced in the heart. Emeralds are said to contain energy that can strengthen the heart and enhance physical, emotional, and mental equilibrium. The Greeks associated this stone with the Goddess of Love—Aphrodite, and it is believed that by wearing an emerald you can attract love into your life. As the central color found in the spectrum of light, green stands at the center of the rainbow, bridging the opposing bands of the violet ray and the red ray. At the hub of our own bodies, too, the heart chakra lies in the green spectrum of energy, a wheel of green light that transmutes the energy-information coming upward from the lower chakras of the red range and streaming downward from the upper chakras of the violet range.

Metaphorically, the emerald that sits at the throne of our own hearts, sits too at the throne of Earth's heart, for we are one with the earth. When our emerald heart opens to receive the wisdom of the earth, it also acts as a star-gate to our divinity, opening us to our cosmic connections. It is said in ancient wisdom traditions that we came from the stars, and one day we shall return there. The Emerald energy is the connecting link between the Great Above and the Great Below, between Heaven and Earth, between the Feminine and Masculine and between the Moon and Sun. Like the philosopher's stone that transmutes lead into gold, the emerald energy transmutes the pain and separation of humanity into ecstasy and union with the universe.

The Emerald Ray

The Emerald Ray is now being anchored into the earth, because humanity is fast becoming ready for the conscious integration into its physical body with its spiritual nature. Our next quantum leap of evolution necessitates this harmonizing of Self and Spirit—this is our new Earth code and our new code of Being. Earth as a living spiritual being has already made the shift, already manifested the divine union of its masculine and feminine aspects. It has grounded and seeded this matrix for us to embody. The doors to the sacred Emerald Garden are open and we are invited in.

The Emerald Records

The Emerald Records, physically laid down as the Emerald Tablets, are regarded as the oldest mystical writings recorded on Earth. They are said to be more than 36,000 years old and were inscribed by the "Thrice Born One,"—known as Thoth, Hermes and The Lord of Wisdom.

The material of these tablets is made from an unknown emerald green colored substance, supposedly created through alchemical transmutation, and is imperishable and resistant to all elements and substances on Earth. They are engraved with characters that are said to respond to attuned thought waves, which release the associated mental vibration in the mind of the reader.

I believe the Emerald Records originated from a different dimensional space-time continuum—from the star system Sirius, and were seeded on planet Earth by the Lord of Wisdom-Thoth-Hermes. They are representative of Earth's Akashic Records, which contain universal wisdom and the origin-lineage of the earth, recording its past, present and future. As templates of the Oneness Code, they contain the covenant of Earth Wisdom—the information that will assist in humanity's evolution from separation to union. Each of us can access this universal wisdom from within the deepest recesses of our earth-body-being; it is in our DNA as it is in Earth's DNA, and it is most easily accessed through the doorway of silence and through our entry into the Garden of Eden—of Nature. As John the Apostle wrote: "The laws may be carved in stone but the law is alive and in our hearts." Like an effervescent tablet that is dropped in a glass of water, an Emerald Tablet is a medicine for healing the earth and ourselves, of dissolving separation into oneness.

The Emerald Crystal City
The Emerald Crystal City is an inter-dimensional space of immense magnitude that contains majestic shafts of emerald-crystal rods of light that emit the union code out into the multiverse. From its core matrix, it broadcasts the emission of Heart-Wisdom and is the placenta that provides spiritual nourishment and genetic wisdom to planet Earth. This light of wisdom is like an umbilical cord that is the soul cord of Earth. It penetrates to the core, to the heart, of the earth itself, and so it is connected to the heart of every living thing on this planet. When enough of humanity's heart is instilled with the code and light of love, the earth will evolve into the *Emerauld*, the "Jewel of the Universe."

EARTH WISDOM DIRECTIVES:

Earth has given us specific directives that can help us unlock the secret of ourselves and facilitate our living as authentic beings. It shows us the way of self-mastery, and the road of return to the

Garden of Eden that lies both within ourselves and at the hearth of Nature. Earth invites us to allow the light of wisdom to unlock the codes of the self that inform every cell of our body and to bask in the life force that infuses every breath we take. We are asked to go within, to sit in the silence that is the "well stream" of wisdom, and to listen to the messages that flow there. Nature is the transmitter and we are the receivers. While I have detailed my own retrievals in this book, and I urge you to conduct your own; there are many ways to enter into communion with Earth Mother, and also the cosmic energies. Below you will find several sections that lead you through practices and ceremonies for forging your own personal connection with these energies.

Establishing an Earth Connection

Ground Yourself

We spend so much time in "our heads," letting our thoughts direct our way. We need to learn to ground ourselves, to center not only our physical beings but our mental and emotional beings as well. To do this, connect to the earth through your feet, standing with your feet shoulder width apart to allow your root chakra (located at the perineum, between the anus and sex organs) to open to Earth's energy. Your stance should be steady and strong, without being willful. Make an energetic connection with the earth, and feel the connection as clearly as you can. By making such a connection, whether you are alone outside with bare feet or standing in line at the grocery in high heels, you can steady yourself and become more sure-footed in your life.

If you want to make this connection even more visceral, you can imagine a thin, red laser beam of light streaming out of your root chakra and into the earth. When you feel the connection is well established, then begin to move your hips to spell out your name on the earth with this red-light laser beam. As your hips rotate, you will also be stimulating the kundalini serpentine energy that lays dormant at the base of your spine, which represents your personal power. By inscribing your signature into the ground, you are making a more personal connection with Earth.

As you practice grounding, and actually begin to feel more grounded in your life, cultivate your observer self and pay attention to the way you carry your body. Is your base secure, spine held straight and head held high? Can you walk as grounded as a rock and yet as graceful and light as a feather? Practice until you can. By walking with power, you will be centered in your body but open through your crown chakra, which is your major point of connection with the cosmic energies.

Learn to Earth Breathe

The earth is a grand recycling plant that takes dead matter and turns it into new life. For instance, dead leaves decompose into rich soil and also plants photosynthesize the carbon dioxide we exhale and release oxygen for us to inhale. But the earth can transmute our emotional waste into renewable energy as well, so that we can fuel our own growth and revitalization. By releasing what no longer serves us, the energy released can be recycled into something that will serve us.

To release negative energy: Stand with your feet shoulder-width apart and ground yourself. Then bring your attention to your breath. With every exhale, release any sighs, screams, tears or any emotions that are holding you back or tiring you out or otherwise not serving you, by letting them travel down your body and out of your feet into the earth. The earth lovingly and unconditionally takes it in and transmutes it for the greater good, like the dead leaves it recycles. No harm is done to the earth when you release your emotions with intent for conscious awareness. By releasing the stale emotional energy within yourself, you have freed up the space for new and healthier energy to empower you.

To invite in positive energy: Remaining in the grounded stance, as you inhale, breathe in Earth energy, allowing it to rise up your body and into your heart, filling your heart with the knowledge, wisdom, and stillness of the earth. Continue this exhale and inhale cycle for a few minutes, releasing old emotional energy and then pulling in healing Earth energy.

Use Earth Toning

To connect with the body, soul, and spirit of the earth, gently place your open mouth on the earth, upon a rock or tree trunk. On each exhale, allow the sound of your heart energy to flow through you and into the body of Earth by making a slow, drawn out tone. Don't worry about what sound you make; just let it come from your heart. Allow the sound to infuse itself into the earth, rock, tree, and offer your love to that natural object and accept back its healing peace.

PERFORM AN EARTH WISDOM CEREMONY:

A ceremony can be created for any reason: healing, manifestation, attraction, prayer, communication with the spirits of the land, and to offer gratitude and thanks. The most important criterion for any ceremony is your intention of goodwill. It is also of benefit but not imperative to know what the spirits of the land prefer as offerings, for example, sage, tobacco, pollen or corn are traditional offerings in the United States. In Hawai'i, however, flowers, Ti leaves, and bananas are common; and in Meso-America and South America, copal, feathers, and shells. In ceremony, however, anything that is imbued with your sacred intention is an appropriate offering. Before actualizing your ceremony with the earth, it is important to:

   1. Ground and clear your energy. Scan the area where you will perform your ceremony to locate the spot that you are energetically attracted to. Trust that you will be guided to the spot that is most harmonious with your intention for the ceremony. Then plant your feet like roots into the earth using the grounded stance described earlier in this chapter, and clear your mental and emotional energy by taking three deep breaths and letting go on the exhale with a sigh. Then clear your energy body and ceremonial space by "smudging" with sage leaves or bundle. To do this, light the sage and then carefully blow out the flame, so the herb smolders. Then gently, wave the sage around your body and ceremonial space, or fan it with a feather, allowing the smoke to waft through the air. If you don't have any sage, then sprinkle water over the area and then shake a little water over your body with your hands or without water, wave your hands around your body from your head to toes and back up again to clear your energy field. You can be creative, and find other ways of cleansing, but do make sure that you use some method to purify the space and your body, mind, and spirit.

2. Introduce yourself and your intention to the spirit of place. To establish a connection with the energies of the land, speak out your name or otherwise declare yourself. As you do, begin to feel your energy connecting to the spirit of place. Then speak (out loud or silently from within) your intention and kind of ceremony you will conduct. Remember the intention of goodwill is the main criterion, and trust that however you choose to perform your ceremony will be the perfect way for you.

3. Honor the land and spirit energies. Honor the Four Directions beginning with East, followed by South, West and North. Then honor Mother Earth and Father Sky and the Self that sits at the central point in the Grand Wheel of Life. Again, depending on which country or region you are in, it is customary, but not imperative, to pay homage to the deity or governing energy of the land in that area (if you know it). For example, in Hawai'i you may honor *Pele*, the Volcano Goddess. In the United States you might honor *Tankashila*, or *Great Spirit*; in Australia, *Wanjina*; and in Mexico, *Quetzalcoatl*.

4. Ask for protection and guidance. Ask from your heart that only those energies with your highest good in mind attend your ceremony. Address whatever spirit or deity you feel is a protective spirit for you, perhaps Archangel Michael, Christ, Quan Yin or the White Light. If you have spirit guides or totem animals, elemental spirits or helping angels, call them into your sacred circle as well.

5. Make an offering to the earth. Pay your respects and gratitude to the earth by making an offering of either a small handful of corn, a pinch of bee pollen or tobacco, water for the desert, flowers, feathers, sage, fruit, crystals or "special" stones, shells or whatever you feel is a special offering. Give it in respect and reverence from the depths of your heart and soul; this will create an open flow of energy between you and the spirit of the land and an atmosphere of respect and trust.

6. Perform your ceremony. As you begin your actual ceremony, remember to maintain a stance of reverence and love. If you are asking for something, ask not from your head but from your heart. You can either sit or stand or move your body with the rhythm of your prayer. Be sincere and pray with the purity of intent. Likewise, listen and be attentive for any messages and answers. Be aware of the sun, wind, trees, birds and insects around you. The answer may come in any form and from anywhere. Realize, too, that the answer to your prayer may not be immediate; it may come later, through a synchronicity or a dream.

7. Close the ceremony. Before closing your ceremony, it is important to express gratitude to the land and thank the guides and protectors you called upon, and ask them to return back from where they came. Give back to the land in gratitude for the ceremony by making a final offering of tobacco, water, pollen, corn, sage, copal, flowers, fruit, or even blowing a kiss. Cleanse your energy field by either smudging yourself with burning sage or by other means and also cleanse the immediate area to seal the energy to keep it pure and untainted. Ground your energy by bringing all of your focused attention back into your body. Inhale the spirit force of the ceremony into your body and then exhale this energy into the place of Spirit to do its work. Bow to the earth or do whatever feels like a completing motion to bid farewell to your ceremonial space. Give love and light, preferably Emerald Green light, sending it straight to the core of the earth for healing. After you leave the ceremony site, it is important to keep open and connected with the energy of the ceremony. Just because it has formally ended, that does not mean it still isn't working and weaving its magic in your life. Every ceremony you perform adds to the living bank of sacredness, reminding you to take each footstep in blessedness upon this Earth sanctuary.

UNDERTAKING YOUR OWN ROCK RETRIEVALS:

Earth communicates with us through all of its living expressions. Many people tune into the elemental realm to communicate with plants and trees, while others find a particular affinity with stones and rocks and still others with water. Divining through Nature is a simple and pure path to self-discovery where we can access the wisdom sanctuaries found in our own inner landscapes and thus connect to all of humanity, to the earth, and to the universe. We need to open our hearts, silence our thoughts, listen with intent, feel with receptivity, and tune into the frequency of the earth to begin this journey of discovery and to be touched with the grace of knowledge. Be present with the presence of Nature, with the being of Earth, let it speak to you and feel the magic it holds. The "Dreamtime," the place between worlds, of this reality and the "other" is available not only to the Shamans and Aboriginals of the world, but accessible to us all, if we stop and listen.

It is important for you to understand that in rock retrievals, what you are accessing is the "Spirit of the Stones." The rocks are conduits for the sacred spirit of Earth's soul; they are an expression and reflection of its eternal force. Instilled by their surrounding forces and historical bearing, they are also depositories for the Spirit of Place, holding the keys to the Mansions of Earth. Rocks carry both the physical and spiritual DNA of the earth, and encode the wisdom teachings that are now being released, when humanity most needs and is ready to comprehend this knowledge. Follow the steps below to perform your own stone-wisdom retrieval.

Decoding Earth Technology

1. Scan the rocks using your inner senses. To choose the rocks you will retrieve from, use your eyes as a tracking device, but look as much with your spiritual eyes as with your physical eyes. Scan the area to feel which of the rocks magnetize you or calls your attention. Trust your inner knowing, and understand that your first "gut" instinct or hunch is the one to follow. By allowing yourself to be pulled by a stone's energetic field, you are already establishing a link with it. As you near the stone, talk to it silently, letting it know you feel the call and are approaching it. Wait for a response. You will sense this response, and only when you have the stone's permission should you actually work with it. Even though it is respectable to ask permission, on the whole, rocks welcome the opportunity to connect with us, as they not only assist us in our evolution toward wholeness but also evolve through us as well.

2. Perform a ceremony. Make a small ceremonial offering to the land and the rock spirits, as outlined above. See the "Perform an Earth Wisdom Ceremony" section.

3. Ground yourself and connect physically to the stone. Get a clear sense of and connection to your body by taking a few deep breaths and exhaling with a sigh. Cleanse your body, mind, and spirit with smoke from a sage stick or other means.

Make a physical connection with the rocks by placing your hands, your forehead, or both one after the other on the rock face. You can also sit with your back against the rock if it is large enough. Feel the physical and psychic connecting points between you and the rock, and be alert to perceptions of heat or coolness, pulsations, electromagnetic currents, or other physical sensations that might arise.

4. **Open your awareness and retrieve the message.** When you are ready to actually begin the retrieval, sit comfortably and close your eyes. Allow your everyday thoughts to drift away as you quiet your mind. Tune in to the elemental stimuli, the wafting breeze, the warmth of the sun, the birds song, the rustling leaves, the feel of the earth beneath you. Open your awareness and conect with the presence of Nature, and allow it to usher you more deeply into the place of inner silence, into the zero-point of stillness, into the deepest part of your being. Be like a pebble that slowly and gently sinks down to the bottom of a well. When you are at the still point, you will feel as if there is nowhere else for you to go, that a great emptiness embraces you, but also fills you with a sacred presence. Sit with that presence.

Then intend that the connection between you and the stone be made manifest through the stone's communication to you. Once you have tuned into the realm of Stone Spirit, you have entered the place of the seer, the inner shaman, who sees and feels beyond the obvious and travels the spaces between the worlds. Allow the insights and messages to come without judgement or comment.

5. **Decipher and record the message.** Sometimes a retrieval message is crystal clear, but at other times the message may require some decoding. Try not to use your intellectual or rational faculties. Instead, be open and observe, allowing any associations to unfold, be they images, words, or sounds. Gently open your eyes and make notes if it will not disrupt your energy too much. Record the message even if it does not make sense to you.

It might later. It is important that you trust in the inner wisdom that unifies you and the earth into one mind or being. As a practicing secretary of the earth, it is your responsibility to record whatever is revealed through the stone you have just retrieved from.

6. Give thanks. Before you break the connection with the stone, give thanks in whatever way feels most comfortable for you and appropriate at that moment. You might simply talk to the stone, (silently or audibly,) but you might also feel inclined to dance, sing, tone or earth-breathe. Before you leave the site, remember to send out an Emerald Green spiral of light into the cosmos and into core of the earth, and give the Earth Mother your thanks as well.

SACRED DANCE:

As I have revealed in my personal story, part of my own way of honoring and connecting to the earth is through sacred dance. I have found that, in addition to breath work, dance is one of the most powerful means of inviting Spirit into Matter and of integrating body, mind, and spirit. Dancing with and for the earth is a wondrous and magical experience that will open up a new dimension of communication between you and Earth as a conscious being. To dance in the elements of Nature and dance the elements of Nature in you is as natural and ancient as the turning of night and day and of the cycles of the sun and moon. Dance also ignites the spark of life and vitality in our bodies, which reawakens the passion of our "body being." It releases stuck energies within the body-mind mechanism, so that we are freed from the past, more open to the grace of the present, and become vessels willing to contain the grandest possibilities of our future. Dance is not only expressive, and revitalizing and sacred, it is also healing. It heals the wounds of our separation from our environment; it helps us reclaim with joy, the fullness of our bodies; it heightens our sense of self-acceptance and increases our capacity to give and accept love. Below, I have detailed ways that you can express your own sacred nature and your connection to the "All That Is" through dancing in the out-of-doors and in harmony with Nature and Mother Earth.

EarthSpirit Dance

Most of the steps listed below have been explained elsewhere in this chapter. As with any other ceremony, a dance ceremony follows certain steps.

1. Ground and clear your energy so that you have clarity of mind and heart. It is of vital importance before dancing with the earth to be aware of your state of mind and be clear about your intention, for how do you know where you are going if you don't know where you are?

2. Prepare for your dance by wearing ceremonial regalia such as a headband, ankle rattles, face paint and the like. You might also hold ceremonial items in your hands, such as feathers, shakers or flowers. When you undertake your first dance, you might not feel comfortable adorning yourself, but preparing yourself in this way is no different from dressing up for a wedding or other important ceremony. Do what feels right for you. You can either use the sounds of Nature, or choose the rhythm of music that reflects the type of dance you plan to do: fast and frenetic for releasing and manifesting, or slow and flowing for healing and allowing, whatever suits your mood and intention.

3. Call in the elemental forces by feeling the wind through your hair, or the sun and moonlight on your skin. Connect with might of the trees, or with the strength of stones and boulders or the babbling brook. Establish a bond with Nature now, and you will find it much easier to connect deeply with the earth spirits during your dance ceremony.

4. Dance with the power of your spirit, and the spirit of the earth, stars, trees, flowers, and of all the other nature elementals that are nearby. Allow the energies of Nature to inhabit your body, and breathe this energy into you while you move with the flow of living awareness. Allow your body and spirit, not your mind, to set the cadence of the dance and to direct its flow as it changes throughout the ceremony. You might want to start slowly at first so that you can stretch the awareness of ease and grace into your body. You can mimic the movements of Nature: crashing waves, fluttering butterflies, tickling winds, and swaying trees. Or, trace nature's shapes with your body: the slope of a mountain, the turn of a riverbank, the curvature of a flower petal or the shadows of the stones.

While your dance will be joyful, it might also feel "darkened" as you begin to release energy constrictions from your body. You might find feelings of anger, guilt, shame, and such spontaneously arising. This is your body's way of releasing what no longer serves you. Allow yourself to feel these emotions without judgment and also allow them to flow out of your body, where the earth and sky can transmute them. Open yourself to feeling the pain of life and also to receiving the bliss of life.

Dance from your belly so that your core energy can flow through your entire body. Dance as grounded and solid as a rock and yet as light and free as a feather. Allow your hands and arms to move on their own and your feet to move however they want to move, perhaps tiptoeing on the earth or perhaps stomping on it. And breathe! Allow your breath to flow without restriction. Sigh, laugh, cry—wherever your body leads you, follow. Give thanks that you are being lead to the Heart of the Matter.

5. When you feel the dance is nearing its end, take a bow, bending deeply to honor the earth and forming your hands into a prayer position to symbolize the two hands of creation coming together and the bringing of dualities into union.

Dancing Your Dream Awake

In order to make our dreams come true, we need to wake up! Awaken the sleeping spirits of the land, the kundalini serpent energy at the base of our spine and the dormant seed of desire at the center of our hearts. By doing so, we open ourselves not only to receive that which we desire but also to flow more effortlessly in our life's calling. The universe gives you exactly what you ask for, but you must be clear about what you want. In the ceremony I call "Dancing Your Dream Awake," you marshal the Cosmic and Earth energies on your behalf. You do so with fervor, and even fierceness, through the movement of your body. The more you honor the earth and connect with her essential nature, the more the earth will manifest for you. Through dance, you are asking for what you want in a very physical way, which in turn generates the physicality of your asking. The ceremony has particular steps, outlined below, but always begin with the grounding and clearing procedures described earlier in the chapter.

1. Plant the seed of your heart's desire, of what you want to germinate in your life, by grounding your intention. This allows the seed to take root. Through the awareness of your legs, drop your intention like a seed into the ground, actually moving the energy through the soles of your feet and into the earth.

2. Harness the life force energy, calling forth your primordial self, your core energy. Summon through your body movements the energies of Nature that surround you. Breathe these energies through your entire body. Connect with the spirit of the land and the soul of the earth, tapping into the earth as a power source and drawing its energy up through yourself to provide the nourishment you need to seed your desire.

3. Dance your prayer into your body, speaking your desire through your body movements to Mother Earth and the Cosmos. Make your dance expressive of whatever it is you are asking and

dance it as a story. Use your imagination and trust that your "body-mind-heart" will speak clearly. Stomp your feet on the ground to let the earth and the universe know you are serious in your request to them. Wield your arms like swords that carve through the illusion of your own limitations. Feel the burning desire propel you through your dance, and allow your consciousness to merge with the nature energies so that you can also reap the benefits of their healing presence. Weave the polarities of Spirit and Matter, of Energy and Form—into Unity. Dance in prayer, knowing that your desires will be manifest in the best way Mother Earth sees fit and dance as if your prayer were already answered.

4. Allow the crowning to take place, which is the rise of energy moving up your body and out through the crown of your head in a fountain of joy. Perceive the energy jetting up from the top of your head and out to the cosmos, like a spray of palm leaves shooting out of its trunk, moving the energies between Earth and Heaven to fulfill your desire.

5. Give thanks by bowing to the cosmic forces in gratitude, in the certainty that the Law of Attraction is now working on your behalf. Through the physical expression of your desire in sacred dance ceremony, you are moving the energies of the universe to manifest your desire and ground it in matter. Finally, offer you're thanks to Mother Earth by propelling an Emerald-Green ray of light into the heart of the earth for healing.

THE ENTHRONMENT

Our self-mastery lays in our ability to embody the spirit force of our Higher Selves, of our God-Being. Our bodies are anchors for the light of creation, and the more we consciously infuse this spirit and light into our bodies, the more we consciously raise the vibration of our planet and speed our personal and collective evolution. By doing so we take our rightful seat on the majestic Throne of our God-Self.

After all these years, I have only now come to realize the significance of the empty seat that stood before me in my dream that long-ago night back in Australia when I first summoned Great Spirit to make my mission clear. I received the call to Sedona without even knowing what that word meant and followed Great Spirit's call, accepting the challenge of my journey. I understand now that the eagle that flew beneath that empty chair in my dream was really me, soaring toward my destiny. My throne had always been there, but I did not know enough about merging duality into oneness or love myself enough to see it, never mind to sit upon it. Perhaps for eons it had stood empty and waiting, silently bearing witness to my slow personal evolution.

Through being a secretary to the stones, by going within to the still point and merging with the stone-spirit energies, I have had my eyes and my heart opened. I have finally accepted the throne as mine. I now sit upon it in the humble awareness that my journey has been perfect—for me. Your journey is bound to be quite different from mine, but never doubt that your throne awaits you. Connecting to the stones can assist you in making your journey toward self-mastery, and so I urge you to undertake your own retrievals. There is no one more connected to us than wise Mother Earth. She is the womb from which we spring and to which we will return, and she cares for us as we live our lives between the sacred transition points of physical birth and death.

I leave you with "The Seed of Creation," which is not a retrieval but a final summing up that I was inspired to write one evening while reminiscing about all the adventures and trials of my Earth Odyssey and of my journey from duality to Oneness.

"The Seed of Creation"

A seed of thought, of the desire to create, was dropped to the earth like a teardrop from the heavens above; it was a seed of light, a seed of love that was offered to us by the Maker-Creator. This seed was of oneness, of wholeness, of union, of the spark of love itself. As it fell through the ethers, moving closer and closer to this third-dimensional plane, it experienced itself as more and more physical, more and more dense, until eventually it impacted the earth and cracked in two. It cracked into the likeness of God and Goddess, experiencing its separation into man and woman, revealing the myriad fractions of duality—of light and dark, love and fear, of this and that. Like seeds dropping into the soil of consciousness, Mother Earth, fertilized and nourished them, as she does, for it is Her nature to do so. She is an eternal source of love, providing a safe and pleasurable Garden of Eden for these seeds of love to grow, and flower in union with All That Is.

About the Author

Amalia Camateros is a ceremonialist and EarthSpirit wisdom guide who inspires us to reconnect with the Earth as a sacred temple of Living Spirit.

She is a Naturopathic Doctor and Counselor, who has worked in the field of health and consciousness for over 24 years. Her background includes yoga and meditation, creative dance, intuitive bodywork, rebirthing and beekeeping.

Throughout her extensive travels to ancient Earth sites and indigenous cultures, Amalia has explored the essential "spirit of place," from which her *EarthSpirit Dance*™ emerged. Utilizing the medium of dance for self-actualization, Amalia gleans information from the Earth and anchors it as body wisdom for the self, the planet and beyond.

She has garnered a notable reputation as a ceremonial dancer for the inauguration of special events and conferences and for her ability as a powerful facilitator of her *EarthSpirit Dance* workshops.

ABOUT THE AUTHOR ■ continued on next page

A service of her mastery is to integrate the Spirit Self into the body and to awaken the full potential of divinity.

Amalia is Australian-born and currently lives in Sedona, Arizona. She is available for radio interviews, speaking engagements, workshops and conferences throughout the USA.

"Amalia is a powerful shamanic dancer skilled in the way of the sacred weave, spinning our life force energies through the web of our being, across the thresholds of our body, mind and spirit, and beyond the psychic obstacles that often blind us from the gift of being."

Rabbi Gershon Winkler, author of Magic of the Ordinary: Recovering the Shamanic in Judaism and Kabbalah 365 and Daily Fruit from the Tree of Life.

**To purchase books,
and for more information about working with Amalia,
please contact 1-808-895-1984,
visit her website at www.earthspiritwisdom.com or
email her directly at info@earthspiritwisdom.com**

Stone Speak Magic

The front cover photo stunningly depicts the
messages of the Spirit of the Stones and of the Earth.

Can you see the two megalithic rocks that form faces in profile, that are nose
to nose on either side of the EarthSpirit Woman? The face on the left holds
the feminine force that sits quietly in the shadow realm.
Her eye is closed in reverence to the deep within.
She represents the lunar force, of the power of going deep inside.

The face on the right side, is wide eyed to the light of day. He holds the
masculine, solar force and projects his power outwardly.
With his mouth close to my ear, he whispers in the tongue of silent wisdom.

The emerald spiral symbolizing the Earth, sits between the dual forces of
Creation-of both the light and dark and of the feminine and masculine.
Along with the Earth, EarthSpirit Woman represents the heart of
human-ity, that is the portal through which
dualities can be merged.

CPSIA information can be obtained
at www.ICGtesting.com
Printed in the USA
FFOW03n1632110318
45539629-46299FF